1057

Republican Foreign Policy, 1921-1933

REPUBLICAN FOREIGN POLICY, 1921–1933

by L. Ethan Ellis

RUTGERS UNIVERSITY PRESS

New Brunswick   New Jersey

Preface

The search for new truth dates back at least to St. Paul,
who found the Athenians of 53 A.D. (according to the venerable chronology of the King James Version, Acts 17:21)
spending their time "in nothing else, but either to tell, or to
hear some new thing." Readers and, more especially, writers
of history are well aware of the perennial necessity to "revise"
older approaches. Candidates for the doctoral union card,
established scholars moved to resift materials used by their
professional forebears, and publishers seeking to exploit an
expanding market are, for not precisely identical reasons,
alike avid for a new angle.

It may not be amiss, however, to enter a mild demurrer
to this feverish hunt for innovation and to suggest the use-
fulness of attempting to view a period as its own inhabitants
saw and experienced it. This plea for a moratorium on re-
visionism is no mere stultifying demand for a return to history
in the Rankean sense of *Wie es eigentlich gewesen ist*. Set
against the compulsive search for novelty, it poses an impressive problem of historiographical bifocalism: Should history
be viewed through the stronger lens of hindsight, or through a
contemporary refractor perhaps less sharply focused but more

v

accurately delineating the contemporary scene? No one, of course, can perfectly perform this feat of visual gymnastics. The figure is introduced only to point to the advantages of trying to see historical events as they appeared to those who participated in them, beset as they were by urgent problems and day-to-day pressures, as well as to a later generation with 20–20 retrospective vision.

The author has tried to examine his chosen period in the light of the preceding remarks. To many of a later generation American foreign policy during these years seems barren of accomplishment; its practitioners appear less than impressive, if not stupid, imperceptive, and willfully blind to forces leading inevitably to catastrophe. In the light of their own day, however, these were men who had learned a hard lesson in World War I and who served a postwar generation which promptly placed domestic prosperity ahead of outside interests or obligations. The disappearance of prosperity into depression furnished them no cause to look outward; survival, here as elsewhere, provided an all-absorbing task. They were men, too, who spoke and acted for a nation only newly rich and lately powerful, which prior to 1914 had viewed the great world with a complacent indifference. They spoke and acted, too, for a public not broadly conscious of, or largely concerned with, matters beyond the immediate landscape They were keenly, almost pathologically, aware that their people were their masters and that no policy they might espouse could long endure unless it conformed to the fairly narrow norms of public opinion.

These conditioning factors, then, conduced to conservatism rather than experimentalism, and contributed to a number of policies which, although seeming to a later day to savor of isolationism or stagnation, were, from the contemporary popular and governmental standpoint, not entirely illogical. A recently concluded war and the subsequent bitter struggle with self-seeking associates over the ensuing peace settlement, for example, hardly pointed toward intimate relations with the new international machinery which bore the hated stamp of Woodrow Wilson. A long history of Republican protectionism prompted a return to that restrictive tariff policy. The threat of hordes of would-be immigrants counseled establishment of a policy of drastic limitation, which had been clearly foreshadowed prior to the war. The idea of canceling loans made in good faith and with expectation that the debts thus incurred would be paid with equal honesty was at least a novel notion to a nation not accustomed to repudiation. And, though refusal to admit a connection between these debts and German reparations indicated a degree of stubborn ignorance, it was not entirely out of keeping with the thinking of the time.

All was not isolationism or stagnation, however. Change was real, albeit slow and often grudging; cooperation and, on occasion, even leadership, developed; involvement was frequent. Succeeding chapters will point up these generalizations in detail. Relations with the League of Nations, after a slow start, became effective in many nonpolitical areas and, toward the end of the period, grew momentarily close in the Manchurian episode. American leadership in disarmament was demonstrated at Washington in 1921–1922; involvement continued through 1930 in a tortuous succession of failures. The Latin-American story is one of heavy involvement and of considerable progress. America helped emancipate China from age-old limitations upon her sovereignty, but cooperation with the League of Nations failed to halt Japanese imperialism in Manchuria. The ill-fated Kellogg-Briand Pact was launched under vigorous American auspices.

The failure of efforts at disarmament, the final decision against membership in the World Court, and the collapse of the peace machinery before Japanese aggression should not be permitted to obscure the facts of Charles Evans Hughes' striking leadership at the Washington Conference or Frank B. Kellogg's constructive if reluctant sponsorship of the Kellogg-Briand Pact. Nor, in the realm of Latin-American relations, should the ameliorative efforts of Kellogg and of Calvin Coolidge, taken under pressure, or those of Herbert Hoover, taken somewhat more spontaneously, be entirely swallowed up in the more flamboyant Good Neighbor policy of Franklin Delano Roosevelt. In none of these episodes, however, did the Republicans carry cooperation, leadership, or involvement to the point of political commitment. It is here, in retrospect, that they may perhaps be most harshly criticized, and where the unfortunate consequences of greater boldness may be most temptingly suggested.

The following pages attempt to portray this odd combination of fits and starts, of not infrequent involvement which avoided wholehearted commitment. The reader, it is hoped, will first put himself in the author's frame of reference and try, as the latter has done, to see the Republicans in their own day and against their own background, honestly if not always effectively coping with new and often bewildering problems. Then, and only then, will he permit himself, as the author has done, the luxury of the historian's second guess.

As the Bibliographical Essay will indicate, the author owes a heavy debt to his fellow laborers, upon whose monographic works he has relied so heavily. If his approach, due to age or myopia, is at times more charitable than theirs, they will, he hopes, bear with him. The Research Council of Rutgers, The State University, awarded funds which enabled him, in retirement, to complete the study. This being the fourth of his books published by the University Press, the staff of that long-suffering organization should be accorded a word of thanks. Most long-suffering of all, generally in silence but always with comfort and encouragement, is his wife Elizabeth, to whom the volume is affectionately dedicated.

L. ETHAN ELLIS

Piscataway, New Jersey
November, 1967

Contents

Republican Foreign Policy, 1921-1933

I

Signs and Portents

Warren G. Harding's inaugural day (March 4, 1921) was clear and crisp. As he joined Woodrow Wilson for their journey to the Capitol, the outgoing President limped determinedly across forty feet of White House portico, but he was forced to accept help in entering the limousine which would bear the two to the ceremony. In the President's Room Wilson performed the last-minute duties of office, including a frigidly correct exchange with Henry Cabot Lodge, the architect of his great frustration. This so wearied him that he had to forego the inaugurals of Calvin Coolidge and of Harding, and he retired to his new home in S Street to nurse his frail frame and bitter memories. Thus ended eight years fraught with great events and with fateful portents, some apparent and some still unrecognized, of the years to come.

Neither events nor portents seemed to weigh heavily as Harding's sonorous phrases (they were his own at this point) heralded what would be twelve years of Republican stewardship. His address proclaimed a thorough divorce from international entanglements. Otherwise, most of its somewhat rambling sentences were concerned with domestic matters, a fitting posture for the apostle of that "normalcy" which he so vigorously proclaimed. Some who listened to him under the Washington sun or heard him over the newfangled radio (his was the first such address to be broadcast) may well have pondered on the current state of affairs and wondered what lay ahead.

Wilson's later months had witnessed severe disturbances, some of which were still unresolved. Prices had continued to a postwar peak in November 1920, with living costs 105 percent above the prewar level. The bottom then dropped out and in 1921 over 19,000 business failures occurred, involving an investment of almost a billion dollars. By 1922, according to estimates which were doubtless no more than approximate, as many as five million were unemployed. The farmer, too, was in the dumps. A victim of his war-induced surpluses, he was already finding it difficult to hold overseas markets, now filling with domestic goods. This problem and that of his heavily mortgaged acres, kept him unhappy through the period under review.

Labor had been highly organized and restive. Disturbances began early in 1919, and numerous strikes established a continuing feud with capital which greatly weakened the union movement. Labor's alleged political radicalism furnished a club with which to beat the organized as well as the unor-

4

ganized worker, and a "Red Scare," characterizing 1919 and much of 1920, continued for years to invest labor with a pinkish tinge in the public eye and to support the conservative attitudes which were rapidly developing. Prosperity would, of course, return, but courts and capital united to keep organized labor's lot unhappy and its numbers decreasing.

These were problems obvious to all. There is no evidence, however, that the President, as he downed his preprandial highball (Prohibition sat lightly on his convivial soul) and, perhaps, thought nostalgically of his senatorial clubmates, thought over what solutions he might propound. The problems had been posed nearly a year before, by *The New Republic*, that gadfly of the complacent in high places, which had opined on June 23, 1920, that the coming four years would confront the government

> with a group of political and economic problems of altogether exceptional stubbornness and difficulty. Only once before in the history of the nation, that is, in the years immediately preceding the election of Washington, has the American people been confronted with the necessity for an equally grave and complicated group of decisions.

Some problems, then, were present and urgent. Other factors, some important and some no more than ephemeral and amusing, were either poking over the horizon or still veiled from view. Some would make trouble for governments on all levels and some would bring pleasure, or pain, to millions of Americans. Only one who, like the present author, has lived through the period can fully appreciate the perceptiveness with which Frederick Lewis Allen's writings evoke the spirit of the times. In *The Big Change, Only Yesterday,* and *Since Yesterday,* he gives a delicately ironic touch to matters treated more seriously by the pundits.

On the lighter side, skirts were already elevated nine inches in 1920 and would go even higher for the inaugural. Knees, it was reported, were visible above rolled-down hose. The summer would witness the debut of the bathing-beauty contest, destined to become an American tribal rite before assuming global dimensions, with aspiring royalty displaying burgeoning anatomical charms on an ever-widening stage. A penniless Aimee Semple McPherson had arrived in Los Angeles in 1917. Her tabernacle of the "Four Square Gospel" would open in 1921; her artfully constructed edifice of religion and big business would only dissolve in a miasma of sex and deception in 1926, the year the Florida real estate boom reverberated into a roar. Jack Dempsey's fearsome scowl would overawe and his more fearsome fists annihilate Georges Carpentier, the "orchid man," in the summer of 1921. Harold Grange was still a schoolboy and the Four Horsemen were yet to desert Holy Writ for South Bend, Indiana, under the beckoning magic of Knute Rockne. The crossword puzzle was still an addiction of the few and Mah-Jongg a diversion of the Mandarins.

In the field of periodical letters Henry L. Mencken in 1921 combined his *pied-à-terre* on the Baltimore *Sunpapers* with collaboration with George Jean Nathan on *The Smart Set.* As this sophisticated journal encountered diminishing returns, Alfred A. Knopf persuaded the two to join him in launching *The American Mercury.* This first appeared in December

1923 and attained, during the remainder of the decade, a well-nigh scriptural status among the would-be cognoscenti. Himself unspoiled by college, Mencken became the darling of a hundred campuses, his style the pattern of a thousand diatribes against the Establishment. Were it Prohibition, anathema to a German Baltimorean, were it democracy on whatever bumbling level, were it revealed religion defended on a Tennessee rostrum by a sweaty William Jennings Bryan against a malevolently atheistic Clarence Darrow, Mencken's scalpel was there to dissect and reveal the weak, the venal, and the confused for all to see. Judgments have differed radically as to his more serious forays into philology in *The American Language;* none can challenge his effectiveness as a working reporter, an inspirer, however briefly, of devotion and emulation, a profound influence on the content and outlook of journalism and on the temper of his time. Mark Sullivan exaggerated only slightly, if at all, in calling him "a national character, and the magazine he edited . . . a national institution."

The same climate which produced an Aimee Semple Mc-Pherson and the crossword puzzle craze and supported Henry L. Mencken could nurture less benign phenomena. Among the hardier was the Ku Klux Klan, well on the move by March 4, 1921, after its establishment in Atlanta, Georgia, in 1915. The money-hunger of its professional organizers and the fanaticism of its members channeled its energies wherever there were objectives of local hatred in need of subjugation—the Negro, the Catholic, the Jew—and sheets and burning crosses served as outlets for personal frustration and fears for an imperiled Nordic Protestantism. Unlike its predecessor of Reconstruction days, its stronghold was never in the Old South. Though its organizers moved from place to place seeking where they might reap a fiscal harvest, its prime fortress was the Midwest, and its peak membership (in 1923) an estimated four million. It remained a factor throughout the decade and furnished precedents for Fascist groups in the next.

Prohibition, undertaken almost gaily in the Eighteenth Amendment and its implementing Volstead Act, was a hardy perennial which would bloom luxuriantly in the garden of each Republican President. Harding, advised by somewhat less than sapient drys, was a poor policeman of a situation little to his personal liking. Neither Congress nor Coolidge broke the cycle of inadequate enforcement, and inevitable consequences ensued. For example, rampant crime emerged from the profitable violation of the law. Chicago furnished more than usually bloody documentation of this point, though any large city would do almost as well; indeed, General Smedley D. Butler, a swashbuckling Marine, was loaned out in 1923 to clean up Philadelphia, but quit in September 1925, remarking ruefully that "liquor law enforcement in this city is virtually stopped."

In Chicago the name of Alphonse ("Scarface Al") Capone was written large. Imported from New York in 1920, he and a fellow worker took over after the murder of Big Jim Colosimo, whom he had once been hired to protect. From liquor he branched out rapidly and from his Cicero base exacted tribute from vice, gambling, and drugs. Open warfare presently broke out between the Capone forces and those whom he displaced or who sought to displace him. These struggles, it was reported, took over seven hundred lives between 1921 and the end of 1928, with a peak, of sorts, in the infamous St. Valentine's Day Massacre of 1929, in which seven men were gunned down in a garage. Meantime, Capone raked in the profits and defied the law. In fact, only through the profit angle was he eventually brought to book, for failure to share his take with the Internal Revenue Service. He went to prison in 1931 for income tax evasion, rather than for the bootlegging which had originally brought him fame and fortune.

So explosive an issue must have political repercussions, particularly embarrassing since both parties included wets and drys. Each, accordingly, adopted reversible tactics in the campaign of 1928. The Democrats nominated Alfred E. Smith, an avowed wet, on an enforcement platform, while Herbert Hoover's masterly circumlocutions comforted both sides. Once in office, Hoover took refuge in appointment (May 1929) of a Commission on Law Enforcement and Observance (the Wickersham Commission), whose report (in January 1931) appeared to lean toward the dry side, but revealed sharp differences of degree among the members. Thus by the end of the period both law and Constitution had been reduced to absurdity, and a full review had become a necessity.

This is no place to speak in detail of the Bull Market which was adumbrated as early as 1924, was an obvious phenomenon in 1927, was a worry to thoughtful observers of the economy in 1928, and expanded with frenetic energy before exploding in 1929. The boom and the ensuing Depression, throwing millions into abysmal poverty, are mentioned here

9

only as aspects of the backdrop against which the drama of the period was played. The perspicacity of the national political leadership in treating these manifestations may, however, be kept in mind as a sort of yardstick against which to measure total performance.

Political leadership in the United States was, in the 1920's as always, a product of relations between two of the three coordinate branches to which the Founding Fathers in their wisdom entrusted the conduct of national affairs. Our history has, in a political sense, been largely one of continuing adjustment between the executive and legislative arms. These have fought a continuous warfare, the outcome of which has depended, over the years, on the personalities, experience, and aggressiveness of successive members of each branch. Adding another variable to this never-stable equation, national emergencies such as war always enhance executive power at the expense of Congress, and postwar periods have always witnessed congressional efforts to recover lost ground. The moment for such a readjustment of interdepartmental relations was at hand on March 4, 1921, complicated further by the party shift which brought the Republicans into the White House with solid majorities in both Houses of Congress. Without attempting at this point a full characterization of Congress or the executive, a brief statement will give a partial setting for the diplomatic history of the coming era and suggest what domestic problems were influential in the area of foreign affairs.

There was as yet no peace, and many Americans had not

yet given up hopes for the League of Nations. Millions were unemployed and business desperately needed tax relief and tariff protection to lubricate rusty industrial machinery. Europe owed the United States many billions, and the complex question of pay-or-cancel remained to be resolved; tied intimately to this and to the tariff was the still hardly realized shift of the nation from debtor to creditor status. Europe's millions, furthermore, seemed determined to flow into the land of plenty. While solutions were being sought for these and other issues not brought into this brief discussion, still other issues perpetuated the problem of leadership and of interdepartmental relations. What, then, was the equipment of each contender for predominance?

The three chief executives during this period came to office with sharply contrasting backgrounds of political experience. Harding had come from the Marion *Star* and the fringes of Ohio politics—a hard school—to the Senate, where he had observed if not comprehended the national scene. Coolidge knew grass-roots and state politics as had few previous Presidents, but had never been to Washington or west of the Alleghenies prior to his election to the Vice-Presidency. It has often been pointed out that Hoover, despite his global business experience and expertise in high-level administration, was less familiar with the domestic political process than any President since Ulysses S. Grant. None of these three had had experience in international politics. Since, then, any latent talents had been hitherto completely obscured, there was slight augury of executive aggressiveness in any of the three Presidents.

Temperament or individual political theory augured little

11

more. Harding, not one to seek out dragons, had no positive program; besides, he believed that legislation should originate in the legislature. Nor was Coolidge one to disturb a happy equilibrium by stirring up the Congress; his *status-quo* genius instinctively avoided aggressive leadership as inimical to the prosperity which he cherished. Neither was Hoover an innately "strong" executive, but viewed himself more as a technician than a politician. A thin skin, poor press relations, a term which turned into a long nightmare of mounting crises, and an uncontrolled Congress in his latter years robbed him of whatever success a happier time and an abler temper might have brought him.

Certainly, none of the three did less than his best according to his lights. None can stand totally condemned for individual limitations of character and ability, and all must be judged in the light of the politics and standards of a day when, perhaps, tolerance of mediocrity in high places was fairly high.

Congress was little better. Some of the ablest figures, such as William E. Borah and George W. Norris, were too prone to be mavericks to inspire consistent followership. Many of the party wheelhorses, such as Boies Penrose, Lodge, and Philander C. Knox, passed off stage. Their successors were for the most part rather narrowly partisan and not largely endowed with statesmanship. Moreover, the fact of majority was not well established, due in part to factions among the regulars and in part to the remnants of Progressivism. These remnants, though nominally Republican, and frequently holding a balance between the regulars and the Democrats, could not be counted on to go down the party line. And both

Coolidge and Hoover were later plagued by a Democratic resurgence in their midterm elections.

Events would prove that the interaction of this combination of executive negativism with congressional mediocrity and factionalism would accomplish little in domestic legislation. Since the present account is directed mainly toward foreign relations, its general concern with internal matters will be terminated at this point. Some attention, however, should be given here to certain domestic factors, partly legislative and partly nonlegislative, which directly and immediately impinged upon external relations: immigration, the protective tariff, the shift from debtor to creditor status, and the Great Depression.

Acts of 1921 and 1924 embodied two marked changes in national immigration policy. Both laws abandoned the long held belief that the United States could melt and mold Europe's polyglot races into a new whole. The Act of 1924 gave statutory form to that Japanese exclusion which had since 1900 been practiced under a face-saving subterfuge. Since each innovation represented the exercise of undoubted sovereign rights, no legal objections could be raised against either. Europeans had had some warning that the melting pot was becoming an outmoded utensil and so adjusted, reluctantly, to the new state of affairs. To Japan, newly powerful, jealous of status, and wary of the West in general and of the United States in particular, exclusion, while not entirely unforeseen, was degradingly discriminatory.

The melting-pot concept had, in fact, come under attack

prior to World War I, as witness the severe setback to immigration registered in the literacy test adopted in 1917. In the postwar period factors, some old, some new, operated to modify it still further; indeed, the crucial question came to be not *whether* restrictions would be imposed, but *how severe* they would be. The depression of late 1920 coincided with the arrival of a new wave of immigrants who poured into New York at the rate of five thousand a day in early September. This inundation alarmed a labor force operating an increasingly sophisticated technology and thus increasingly wary of unskilled competition. It was becoming clear, too, by the end of 1919 that "foreigners" were intimately involved in the criminal aspects of Prohibition violation. Moreover, the enhanced world position of the United States resulting from the war gave birth to a new nationalism demanding a greater homogeneity than seemed to be emerging from the melting pot.* The stage was thus set for drastic change in the Act of 1921.

The Emergency Quota Act of May 19, 1921, designed for a single year but extended to 1924, established the basic principle of sharp restriction on a quota base. It provided that admissions from any country for each fiscal year be limited to 3 per cent of the foreign-born residents of such nationality according to the Census of 1910. Experience demonstrated the law's quantitative and qualitative shortcomings in reaching the restrictionists' objectives. Over 700,000 entered the

* These technological and nationalistic aspects have recently been stressed somewhat more heavily than the long-accepted idea that the legislation under review aimed primarily at the so-called "new" immigration from Southern and Eastern Europe; it would not appear that the two approaches are mutually exclusive.

14

United States in 1924, and too many of these were of the "wrong" sort. Sentiment for further restriction developed against this background of ineffectiveness and produced sharp debate during the life of the law.

Some issues in this debate were recurrent, but some were new or more heavily emphasized than before. Renewed prosperity brought industry and business out in defense of immigration as a source of cheap labor. The National Association of Manufacturers and the American Federation of Labor resumed their normal hostility in the dialogue before congressional committees. Nationalism, verging at times on racism, demanded ethnic homogeneity as a quality essential to realization of national destiny.

The Johnson-Lodge Act of 1924 retained the quota principle. It was designed to reduce the annual influx still further and to alter its character. This was to be done by lowering the percentage from three to two and by shifting the base back to the Census of 1890, when the "older" immigration still dominated the flow. Under its operation admissions averaged approximately 50,000 per year between 1924 and 1927. It ordained a still more restrictive technique for the future, since beginning on July 1, 1927 (postponed until 1929 due to the difficulty of establishing the necessary statistics), quotas would be determined by *national origin*. The first step here would be to ascertain the number of inhabitants of the United States in 1920 whose *birth or ancestry* related them to a particular area. The annual quota would then bear the same relation to 150,000 (fixed as the maximum number of admissions for any year) that the national origins group bore to the total population. European

15

contributions to the American amalgam would thus be conformed to a pattern unfavorable to immigrant groups recently dominant but, according to prevailing thought, less assimilable.

The feature giving the Act its greatest international repercussions was the application of statutory exclusion to Japan. In 1900 and again in 1907–1908 the government, unable to contain Western demands for exclusion, whipped up by William Randolph Hearst and smaller-caliber Japanophobes, had, in two so-called Gentlemen's Agreements, arranged an informal but effective stoppage at the source, whereby Japan denied exit to would-be emigrant laborers, thus honoring in the breach more liberal treaty provisions established in 1894. War and postwar developments reduced exclusion to a definitely racist level; the Washington Conference of 1921–1922 did not deal with immigration and calmed feelings only in part. A Supreme Court decision of November 11, 1922, ruling that Japanese were ineligible to citizenship, raised the issue in another light. It remained only to embody the decision in the statutes. This the Act of 1924 did.

Senators asked, in the course of a more-or-less routine debate, whether acceptance of Japanese determination of the eligibility of Japanese to emigrate was not a trespass upon American sovereignty. This query trod perilously close to the extra-legal Gentlemen's Agreement, whose details had hitherto been shrouded in secrecy though its net effect was well known. Then, on March 24, 1924, the House Committee on Immigration reported the bill with exclusion spelled out by forbidding entry to "aliens ineligible to citizenship." All this alarmed the Department of State, anxious to preserve the *status quo* as part of the mild glow still pervading post-Washington-Conference relations, and led to the disastrous Hughes/Hanihara *démarche*.

Ambassador Masanao Hanihara had repeatedly (on December 13, 1923, and on January 15 and 19, 1924) warned Secretary of State Charles Evans Hughes of the danger to Japanese-American relations inherent in the pending legislation.* Hughes in reply could only report that it was not an Administration measure, and urge the House Committee on Immigration, as he had done on February 8, 1924, that Japan be given quota treatment similar to that accorded European nations (it had been calculated that this would admit 150 Japanese per year), warning sternly that exclusion would "largely undo the work of the Washington Conference. . . ."

On the strength of the House exclusion proposal, Hughes and Hanihara went to work. At an interview on the 27th Hughes "said that he had an idea—he did not wish to make a definite proposal—that possibly the Ambassador could write a letter to the Secretary" in which the Gentlemen's Agreement "could be summarized in a brief and definite fashion and could be presented authoritatively. . . ." In it, too, "Japan could state the course that she had taken under the Agreement in the actual control of emigration to the United States. . . ." After referring the matter to Tokyo, Hanihara reported (April 3, 1924) that the idea had merit. Hughes then suggested that a Japanese draft memorandum be submitted to J. V. A. MacMurray, Chief of the Department's Far

---

* The account from this point relies largely on one of the *Beerits Memoranda* in the Charles Evans Hughes Papers in the Manuscripts Division of the Library of Congress.

Eastern Division, and to Sadao Saburi, Counselor of the Japanese Embassy, prior to another Hughes/Hanihara review.

Hughes saw the proposed letter on April 10. At this stage it concluded: "I realize, as I believe you do, the grave consequences which the enactment of the measure retaining that particular provision would inevitably bring upon the otherwise happy and mutually advantageous relations between our two countries." Hughes had apparently not previously seen the phrase "grave consequences" and, though embarrassed by it, did not foresee its results any more than did Hanihara, who later wrote that he used it "quite ingenuously."

Exigencies of timing called for its prompt submission to Congress, and it was transmitted and printed in *The Congressional Record* for April 11, 1924. On the 14th Senator Lodge took up the cudgels, referring to the note as a "veiled threat," and the lid was off. The bill was enacted with the exclusion provision intact, despite attempted intervention by President Coolidge while it was in conference between the two Houses. Congress had asserted its independence both of its own chief executive and of foreign interference, in an act of perfectly legal nationalism reflecting the undoubted sentiment of the majority of Americans—an act of almost unparalleled poor judgment in the long run. In Tokyo July 1 became a day of national mourning. The insult to Japanese pride continued to exacerbate Japanese-American relations, contributing considerably, if incalculably, to an antagonism which had never been entirely extinguished and which would grow over the years.

•

Republican tariff policy provided an economic counterpart to the ethnic nationalism embodied in the Johnson-Lodge Act. Again, the legislation accurately reflected the national mood, and again it played a mischievous role in international relations, both economic and political. It was, still again, a reversion to and refinement of the Republican policy of high protection moderated only twice since 1890 by Democratic interludes. The Wilson-Gorman Act of 1894 was an ineffective attack on the citadel; the Underwood-Simmons Act of 1913 breached the wall but was soon modified in practice by wartime abnormalities. Protectionists had rallied to the attack even prior to Wilson's departure, and he had vetoed a bill raising the rates on raw materials.

Republican eagerness found outlet in a special session called in 1921 to deal with tariff and immigration matters. Presidential ignorance matched congressional impatience in this as in other issues. Bruce Bliven, quizzing the Ohio statesman on his views, was surprised to hear him aver that "The United States should adopt a protective tariff of such a character as will best help the struggling industries of *Europe* to get on their feet"; Harding repeated this economic profundity at Bliven's horrified request and it furnished an interesting tidbit for readers of *The New Republic* for May 21, 1924.

Three pieces of legislation went on the books—the Emergency Tariff Act of May 27, 1921, the Fordney-McCumber Act of 1922, and the Hawley-Smoot Act of 1930. Farmers were beset, after March 4, by the same ills of high mortgage costs and lowered foreign markets which had troubled them on March 3 when Wilson had vetoed the bill placing higher duties on agricultural imports. Their pressure resulted in re-passage of the vetoed legislation and the raising of rates on corn, meat, sugar, and wool to the level of the Payne-Aldrich Act of 1909. This temporary measure, soon extended pending a full-dress revision, gave the farmer unnecessary protection on goods which were in exportable surplus; it also committed him to support similar increases on manufactures, which were promptly sought and eventually secured in the Fordney-McCumber Act of September 22, 1922.

This Act enfolded new commodities within the protection-ist blanket, and raised the rates on many already covered, including aluminum housewares, whose basic commodity was controlled by Secretary of the Treasury Andrew W. Mel-lon's Aluminum Company of America. At home, the results were no more than modest. The farmer, predictably, failed to profit from protection of his principal exports; his overhead continued high. He soon sought largesse in federal legisla-tion supporting prices, embodied in a parade of McNary-Haugen Bills, designed to relieve his depressed circumstances through government purchase of his exportable surpluses, at prices which would not depress the domestic market, for foreign resale at world prices. These bills were anathema to a succession of Republican Presidents who, with what must have seemed to contemporary economists to be willful obtuseness, drew a sharp distinction between this kind of government interference on behalf of a special agri-cultural interest and that involved in tariff legislation equally beneficial to its equally special industrial counterpart. Ex-cept in the case of chemical manufactures, the Fordney-Mc-Cumber Act did not greatly aid war-born industrial infants;

20

its principal beneficiaries were already well established and even some of these (textiles, for example) were not much helped.

In the international sphere the Act introduced the first phase of an economic astigmatism which would characterize the whole Republican period. In earlier years, while the United States was still a debtor, sales in European markets had helped to settle adverse balances due in part to debt service and liquidation. Now, with the debtor-creditor relation reversed, and with Americans still anxious to sell across the Atlantic, Europe's goods must find sale in this country to finance her obligations here. Joseph Fordney, Porter J. Mc-Cumber, and their henchmen in both Houses of Congress had laid heavy hands on this essential flow of commodities, necessitating resort to other techniques of settlement which will be examined briefly below. Immediately, Europe was angered at the legislation and, naturally enough, turned to retaliatory action.

Renewed pressure toward the end of the decade produced the Hawley-Smoot Act of June, 1930. It stemmed immediately from continued agricultural malaise, and Hoover hoped that the special session summoned to deal with this matter would confine itself to farm relief. After a bow to the farmer, however, other interests insisted on stopping up what few chinks were left in the protective wall around manufactures, and a log-rolling process normal to tariff discussions produced a bill which was reprobated in many quarters and passed only under the party spur. With Depression nine months under way when the bill passed, bankers and industrialists concerned with foreign operations feared its consequences on international trade. Economists, numbering over a thousand, denounced the bill; Hoover, denouncing the economists, signed it into law in what Professor Denna F. Fleming has called "a declaration of economic war by the strongest economic power against the whole of the civilized world."

Reaction was not long delayed. Indeed, thirty-four national protests had been added to the voice of the economists prior to passage of the law. By 1932 twenty-five governments had retaliated in one way or another. France set an example for other nations by establishing import quotas on hundreds of commodities. Britain, in part due to this legislation, abandoned the free-trade policy of decades, levied duties starting at 10 per cent *ad valorem* in 1931–1932, and established in the Ottawa Agreements of the latter year a system of Imperial Preference which cut deeply into British and Canadian markets for American goods. Reprisals, taken as a whole, have been estimated as halving the volume of exports. When it is considered that other nations were equally desperate for trade in the early thirties, the volume of ill will engendered by the Hawley-Smoot Act can only be guessed at, particularly in view of the fact that throughout the preceding decade the United States had been firmly insistent on payment of the war debts, a problem which should now be examined in connection with the emergence of the nation into a creditor position.

As has been indicated, the war period moved the United States from the red to the black side of the international ledger. A few statistics may be cited to indicate this shift, which would have developed war or no war but which, coming during a period of domestic and international disturbance, eased the transition no whit. Statistics vary with statisticians but, give or take a few hundred millions and taking outside figures in each instance, the picture is clear. In mid-1914 the United States owed some $3.5 billion; by the end of 1919 she was owed, on private account some $3.5 billion and on intergovernmental account nearly $10.5 billion more. The last figure is generally referred to as "war debts," though much of the money was devoted to postwar rehabilitation. The sums had been borrowed straightforwardly on the understanding that they were to be repaid; in this country they were represented by Liberty and Victory Bonds whose owners, if the debtors failed to pay, would expect their own government to insure reimbursement through higher taxation.*

This, then, is the situation which developed. The efficient American industrial machine produced an increasing volume of manufactures for export and sale in foreign markets—their value approximately doubled between 1922 and 1929. During these same years the amount due the United States on foreign debts averaged $339,000,000. Foreign purchasers of American manufactures, and foreign debtors, would alike hope to meet their obligations by selling goods in the United States, but were largely blocked by domestic tariff policy.

---

* No attempt will be made here to consider the connection between these debts and German reparations, a connection which the United States stubbornly refused to recognize. This problem will be noted later. See below, pp. 191–214.

This is what is meant by the refusal of the United States to accept its creditor position. Such a combination of circumstances might have produced a stalemate but for the fact that American capital, as well as goods, was in surplus supply and that foreign demand was high.

Thus the predepression twenties witnessed an outward movement of American capital at a rate which approximately balanced the excess of American exports over imports, plus the current payments on the war debts. The American investor thus established and preserved an equilibrium, but it was achieved at a considerable cost in ill will resulting from domestic tariff policies. It was, moreover, an uneasy equilibrium, since the market for most of the goods exported for sale would decline sharply in the face of reduced prosperity. The conjunction of circumstances represented by the Great Crash of 1929, followed in nine months by the Hawley-Smoot Tariff of 1930, strained the equilibrium to the utmost and posed for the Hoover Administration what was to prove an insoluble problem of adjusting national policy to a new Order of Disaster. The international side of this attempted adjustment will be the last aspect of this survey.

The economics, the drama, and the tragedy of the Great Depression have attracted many pens, as have its causes, its major manifestations, and approaches to its cure. Fittingly, most attention has been devoted to its domestic aspects. In all accounts the figure of Herbert Hoover looms large, frequently a target of critical shafts for alleged obtuseness, callousness, and egregious ineffectiveness. He has been charged with tardiness in admitting that anything was wrong, with reluctance to use the arm of federal authority to right the wrongs he finally admitted, and with favoring the rich, who suffered financially but still ate well, as against the poor, who were hungry.

Historians have begun to temper acrimony with justice in treating this shy, tortured man's earnest efforts to deal with his great burden. They generally agree, now, that he did more than any preceding chief executive to develop an affirmative approach through steps taken, some willingly, some reluctantly, and all too tardily to be of real avail. His more generous critics have pointed out, too, that there was more of the New Deal in his approach to domestic ills than either he or the New Dealers would willingly admit. Finally—the point of present interest—it may be pointed out that, once Hoover concluded (as he did late in 1930) that the Depression was an international phenomenon in which the United States was willy-nilly enmeshed, he elaborated an intelligent and temporarily effective remedy involving American participation—an attitude which the early New Deal eschewed in favor of arrant nationalism. This approach was, of course, the Hoover Moratorium, postponing for a year from July 1, 1931, Europe's obligation to meet either war-debt or reparations installments.*

After some ups and downs the European depression entered a desperate phase in the early summer of 1931. This was precipitated by an Austro-German move for economic

---

* Again, the question of war debts, in relation to reparations, will be postponed for later consideration. See below, pp. 191–214.

consolidation, which frightened France, wary of any German resurgence, even one designed primarily for self-preservation. French bankers' calling of short-term Austrian and German notes in March put an intolerable strain on the Viennese Kredit Anstalt, an economic pillar of Austria and of the Danube Valley economy. Gold shipments to meet French demands forced Germany to default her reparations payments, and the frightened President, Paul von Hindenburg, appealed to Hoover for help lest the Communists take over the Weimar Republic. The Moratorium followed, resulting from Hoover's hasty negotiations with congressional leaders (Congress was out of session, but had to be considered because it controlled national policy on war debts) and with the nations concerned. Congress reluctantly ratified his action in December with the clear understanding that reduction or cancellation of the debts was not to follow the Moratorium.

Professor Broadus Mitchell, no Republican, has called the scheme "economically intelligent and morally courageous, and . . . handled with political skill at home and diplomacy abroad." It was Hoover's closest approach to internationalism, taken under the spur of dire necessity. It brought him, as will be seen later, perilously close to admitting a connection between war debts and reparations, something no American in a position of authority had been willing to do. It was a palliative rather than a remedy and it ended in the midst of the presidential campaign of 1932 when no constructive sequel could be established. The verdict, then, on Hoover's approach to international depression must credit him with intelligent perception (clearer here than in the domestic area) and prompt action in an immediate crisis which neither he nor anyone else in that day could project to a successful solution.

This brief *précis* offers a glimpse of a lusty period wherein Americans adjusted, first belligerently to peace, then joyfully to prosperity, and then, painfully, to depression. These successive adjustments occurred under executive and congressional leadership reflective of the times and of the nation's position in them. The leadership has been roundly condemned and in retrospect justly so, for being callously indifferent to devious financial practices, for condoning large-scale corporate villainy and venality, and for ignoring obvious signs pointing to fiscal shoals in domestic and foreign waters. It should be remembered, however, that while the leadership was very modest, contemporaries found less fault with it (except for Hoover's handling of the Depression) than did later critics; indeed, the few voices raised in predepression plenty cried vainly in the wilderness. Congress and executive, each manned by figures of less than Homeric stature, spent time and wasted energy on a power struggle for control of affairs and in domestic housekeeping. Preoccupations in these directions diverted or warped the approach to issues which would be handled, or mishandled, mainly in the light of the contemporary conception of interests. The period was a stage of national development in which the United States, thus modestly led, entered, without fully realizing the fact, a world to which it accommodated reluctantly and incompletely. The story should be viewed through the eyes of those who sought to build according to what they considered, however shortsightedly, to be the national advantage, as well as of those who, looking back, so roundly condemn the shortcomings of their predecessors.

II

O Tempora, O Homines

It is a truism that the foreign policy of the modern state seeks to promote and defend the national welfare and security, and that it stems from concepts of national interest derived from sources varying according to the character of the government and people involved. In a democracy it derives from an amalgam of times (always changing), men (never permanently in power), and foreign influences (equally intent on realizing their own national objectives). Policy makers in a democracy face the problem of combining these variables to chart a course of action which will meet current needs and serve long-run objectives. Not blessed with second sight, they must approach both needs and objectives in terms of their own day and their estimate of the future. They thus place themselves in double jeopardy before their fellows,

29

who judge them at the ballot box, and their successors, who know how the game came out.

The preceding paragraph, perhaps, labors the obvious. It is designed to introduce another truism, that he who writes history is doubly vulnerable—he must observe his chosen period as nearly as possible through the eyes of its own actors, crowded by their own pressures, and then sit in judgment on their performance. If he fails in either task, he has not met his obligation. It is this writer's conviction, after years of study and a fairly careful review of the literature, that his period has been too much described in terms of what ought to have been done, in the light of later and unforeseeable events; that it has too often been treated simply as one in which weak leaders fumblingly failed to grapple with crucial issues which were in the making between the defeat of Wilson's internationalism and the "neutrality" complex of the mid-thirties.

In this conviction, and while reserving the right to an adverse final judgment, certain things should be pointed out in explanation, if not in exculpation, of Republican attitudes. Let it be remembered first that though Wilson had offered the men of the twenties a new role in world affairs, his proposals had been out of harmony with generations of American doctrine and experience, and that he and his party had alike been discredited. The Founding Fathers had coined and blessed the doctrine of avoiding foreign political entanglements and, though their sons had ignored it upon convenient occasions, it still carried the weight of tradition and authority. The facts of geography had, hitherto, made possible a reasonably successful and prosperous national experience

30

largely independent of Europe. There were, then, cogent reasons for letting well enough alone, particularly when the proposed new orientation bore the label of a defeated party.

Let it be remembered, too, that the period was one in which the nation was adjusting, a bit tardily and reluctantly, to a new order of magnitude in the world. A perennial debtor suddenly turned creditor to the tune of billions might be understandably suspicious of debtors anxious to cancel legally incurred obligations. A nation traditionally committed to high protection might be slow to realize that persistence on that course could clog the trade channels through which alone could flow the goods to pay the debts. A nation long accustomed to modest military expenditures might shy away from the huge outlays essential to a mercly adequate posture. A nation freshly recommitted to an independent course might be understandably nettled at overtures from a League of Nations which it had but recently abjured.

And finally, let it be remembered that most Americans of the day retained a perennial insularity of which war's momentary contacts with a larger world had not divested them. They turned joyfully to the business of business—of creating bigger and bigger if not better and better organs of finance capitalism, of production on the farms and in the factories, of acquiring cars, radios, and electric refrigerators, of exploring their land near and far, of making money, and of creating a better way of life. They pursued these objectives with whole-hearted abandon and finally with a fine frenzy which exploded into economic disaster of unparalleled proportions, after which they devoted themselves in misery to desperate adjustment to a poorer level of existence. Small wonder, then, that nation and people alike heard foreign affairs as no more than a minor obbligato against a louder and more insistent theme of domestic concern, or that they almost involuntarily cringed from foreign involvement.

A considerable dialogue has developed around the term "isolationism" as a characteristic of the period. Hardly a policy in the history of American foreign relations has had a larger or more venerable role. Thomas Paine, John Adams, George Washington, and Thomas Jefferson have been honorably connected with its early manifestations. Henry Cabot Lodge, William E. Borah, Hiram Johnson, and others joined their company under a somewhat different banner in 1919–1920. Leaders of the twenties would be similarly ticketed, and still other facets of the term's elastic meaning would include among its representatives Arthur H. Vandenberg and Burton K. Wheeler in the thirties and Robert A. Taft and Herbert Hoover in the forties.

Eminently respectable authority may be marshaled to prove that the country was, or was not, isolationist during the Republican years. Senator Lodge attacked the concept as early as 1924, asserting that "there never has been a period when the United States has been more active and its influence more felt internationally than between 1921 and 1924." William Appleman Williams avers, "The widely accepted assumption that the United States was isolationist from 1920 through 1932 is no more than a legend." And Samuel Lubell titles one of his chapters "The Myth of Isolationism." *Per contra,* others may be quoted in support of the isolationist tag as applied to the interwar years. Frank Simonds says that Americans never doubted "the wisdom of remaining faithful to the two principles of isolation and protection." Karl Schriftgiesser asserts that the Harding Administration "fostered a policy of deliberate isolation . . ." and that Harding himself "did his best to help America run away from the rest of the world." Walter Johnson has William Allen White seeing "the American conscience take a complete leave of absence—desert its world responsibility and ignore its own vital economic and social problems. . . ." Colonel G. A. Lincoln speaks of "our vacation from reality in the armistice between the wars." Selig Adler writes that the twenties witnessed a general, bipartisan swing to "the older concept that American self-interest demanded a return to insulation from Old World political entanglements." And a British observer, H. C. Allen, after describing American policy from 1921 to 1937 as "one of deliberate withdrawal from the affairs of the world," quotes the charge of his eminent countryman Winston Churchill, that the United States "simply gaped at the vast changes which were taking place in Europe, and imagined they were no concern of theirs."

The persistence of the dialogue regarding isolationism justifies some examination of the period in an attempt to appraise the temper of the time. The writer should, at the risk of compounding confusion, preface such an inquiry with a statement of his own conception of the term, based on cumulative study and reflection, and his application of it to the years under study. This will at once give his semantic position and forewarn the reader of the tenor of his conclusions. If isolationism be taken in its strict sense of avoiding outside political alliances, none can gainsay its applicability to the years 1921–1933; no responsible leader would have risked political suicide by sponsoring such heresy. A somewhat less rigid and, to the writer, more realistic yardstick makes possible a more satisfying analysis of the Republican years. If this yardstick be labeled "involvement without commitment," the possibility of greater flexibility emerges, and Republican policy makers come off much better on final balance. It seems to the writer that this is a fair approach. His narrative will therefore attempt to document his belief that the period manifested more of cooperation, less of arrant self-containment, than has usually been ascribed to it. It will thus be seen that he pictures the time as a mixed one, combining traditional self-concern and imperviousness to outside factors with occasional, perhaps exceptional, but very real willingness to participate in international action. It is thus a time of fits and starts, of hesitancy and of timid advance, to the study of which this and the following chapters are devoted.

A base point in analyzing the temper of the period, prior to examination of its detailed developments, must be sought in the country's very recent experience. The First World War had seen the United States move from complacent unconcern with Europe's faraway troubles through economic and ideological involvement to military participation. At the close of hostilities Woodrow Wilson had offered his countrymen, and the world, the apocalyptic vision of an order in which a

League of Nations would make old things pass away and all things become new. His fellow negotiators of the Treaty of Versailles had tailored the details of his dream to their more mundane and immediate considerations in return for allowing him to retain his Grand Design, and he brought home a combined League and Treaty which he presented in mid-1919 as an indivisible unit.

The midterm election of 1918 had confirmed a political resurgence under way since 1912 by returning a Republican majority in both Houses of Congress—slight, but sufficient to enable Wilson's enemies to organize the Senate and ensconce Lodge, his implacable foe, in the chair of the important Committee on Foreign Relations. Many senators shared Lodge's hostility to Wilson's packaged proposal on grounds variously compounded of personal animus and honest doubt. The imminence of a presidential campaign posed a tempting possibility: Successful opposition to the package might provide an important political issue. Calvinistic stubbornness and physical malaise prevented Wilson's making the compromises which might have earned sufficient bipartisan support to bring him victory.

The election of 1920, proclaimed by Wilson as a "great and solemn referendum" on American participation in world order, was more a verdict on Wilson, the Democrats, and all their works. It gave the Presidency to a Republican and returned stout majorities to both Houses. It is the work of this President and his successors, their advisers, and the Congresses with which they had to deal, which comprise the raw material for an assessment of foreign policy in the years

35

1921–1933. The assessment must, of course, be made in the light of an immediate past, which has here been sketched lightly, and of a public temper which can fairly be characterized as one initially concerned with the establishment of that "normalcy" heralded by the new President and never deeply concerned with world problems.

At the risk of laboring a point, attention must again be called to the position of the United States, and of American leadership, at the time of the Republican take-over. The nation had been catapulted into a position of tremendous power, for which it had made no preparation and of which it was only vaguely aware. Victory in the recent war had shifted the national position from debtor to creditor—a fact whose existence was known to few and its significance to still fewer. A struggle of unexampled bitterness had averted an international entanglement and the ensuing election had confirmed the decision. To the new leadership recent events might well appear to be a mandate to eschew unnecessary involvement in affairs against which three thousand miles of salt water still seemed a sufficient barrier. Under the circumstances, American leadership would have been bold indeed had it essayed a leading world role.

This leadership, be it remembered, was subject like all democratic leadership to the limiting dictates of public opinion. That opinion had just been registered vigorously against political involvement—a stand whose label "isolationism" has, unfortunately, been equated too closely with the question of membership in the League of Nations. The stage must be broadened to include the whole range of relationships with the outside world, and the frame of reference extended to cover the whole period under review before a judgment can be passed on the leadership of the time. In this sense "isolationism" becomes a relative term, to be removed from the shadow of the League battle and adjusted to the changing circumstances of a decade and more.

And in broadening the frame of reference the leadership must be judged, not only on its management of the immediate events of an incoming Administration, but by its perceptiveness of and adaptability to change and by its flexibility in the face of national and international pressures of a new and untried order. Measuring by such a standard, the writer believes that no amount of semantic acrobatics can rightly apply the term "isolationist" without qualification to the Republican years; nor can the term "negative" or "static" be indiscriminately employed. This is not meant to assert that the leadership met its opportunities or, indeed, its obligations, in full, or to deny a sigh of regret for opportunities not grasped; it is only intended to forestall an initial condemnation, and to urge that the judgment be based on the entire record.

The immediate criterion, certainly, was one of avoiding foreign political commitments and of considerable preoccupation with domestic affairs. The trend toward concern for the outside world never reached a point of serious political commitment, but did attain a fairly high level of cooperation before the end of the period. It will be the task of the next succeeding pages to comment on the character of the leadership and its equipment to guide the nation in a time of world change.

The Founding Fathers, conditioned by a recent period of weak government, assigned the President a dominant role in foreign affairs. A constitutional provision authorizing him to require the opinion of the heads of departments, in writing, justified the creation of the Department of State, headed by a Secretary, to provide the President high-level assistance. Legally, the President makes and is responsible for foreign-policy decisions. Historically and practically, President and Secretary divide the exercise of this enormous power according to the experience and temperament of the men occupying the two posts. Both operate within a domestic framework created by congressional attitudes and within the broad and sometimes capricious limits of a public opinion to which government policy must ultimately conform. They are guided, and sometimes circumscribed, by long-standing shibboleths, to be disregarded only under great provocation. Within these national guidelines, and under limits imposed by congressional and public pressures, President and Secretary tread a wary path, attempting maximum success in the conduct of national policy in dealing with opposite numbers whose often disparate national interests they must harmonize with their own.

Attention has already been called to the constant seesawing struggle between executive and legislative in our system of separated powers; Congress was ahead as our period opened, and remained so throughout, neither crisis nor personality sufficing to push the executive ahead. Thus successive Presidents and Secretaries, no matter what their respective talents, were initially handicapped in the development and application of foreign policy. Who were the men, and what their training and abilities, on whom this task was laid?

Perhaps the first fact to strike an observer is that the American political system provides those attaining high office with no sure training in international affairs. Presidents Harding, Coolidge, and Hoover, and their chief assistants, Hughes, Frank B. Kellogg, and Henry L. Stimson, together mustered a remarkably modest total of such experience. Only Kellogg and Stimson had even touched the periphery, the former briefly as Ambassador to the Court of St. James's and the latter as adviser on the Tacna-Arica affair, as presidential representative in Nicaragua, and as Governor General of the Philippines. Harding's senatorial career had given him a glimpse, albeit a myopic one, focused on the fight against the League of Nations, beyond the confines of Ohio, but Coolidge came to his lonely Vice-Presidency innocent of international concerns or contacts. Hoover's overseas interests had been long and deep, but had been directed to the acquisition of personal wealth and the distribution of national largesse in war and postwar relief operations, neither of which gave him training in or patience for the slow and tortuous processes of international negotiation. Hughes's talents, perhaps naturally the greatest of any of the group, had been devoted to law, domestic politics, and the judiciary. Much would depend, then, upon the rapport between successive Presidents and their Secretaries, the relation between the latter and their professional understrappers, the ability of these second-echelon operatives, and the capacity of the top men to establish effective relations with the press and to cajole or coerce the makers of congressional (particularly senatorial) opinion into following such leadership as might emanate from the lower reaches of Pennsylvania Avenue.

Harding and Hughes worked well together, simply because the President abdicated in favor of his impressive Secretary. No one has yet sought to build for this unhappy President a reputation for leadership in any area of activity. His utter parochialism, his abysmal ignorance outside a narrow range, his easy personal morals, the atrocities he perpetrated on the mother tongue he used so volubly and so lovingly, have been so often chronicled that repetition would be uncharitable. The only charity vouchsafed him, indeed, has been a verdict of "not guilty" of personal involvement in the crimes committed by his friends, who in his innocence he trusted too greatly.

Harding easily applied in foreign affairs an already developed talent for reversing himself, which will be noted below in connection with discussions of the League of Nations and the World Court. His chief merit in this area was his willingness to defer to others who he admitted knew more than himself. This is well illustrated by an anecdote related by Arthur S. Draper of *The New York Tribune* to Samuel Hopkins Adams. Harding asked the correspondent, just back from England, where he had talked with influential leaders, to tarry after a White House press conference. Expecting to be queried in depth, Draper was taken aback when Harding airily announced: "I don't know anything about this European stuff. You and Jud [Judson Welliver, his secretary] get together and he can tell me later; he handles these matters for me." In effect, he also applied this light-hearted approach to a higher level, leaving policy questions entirely to Hughes, of whom he stood in awe, referring to him always, along with Mellon and Hoover, as "Mr." No source the author has seen illuminates the discreet Secretary's private thoughts as he crossed from his office to the White House to submit carefully elaborated policies for presidential "decision."

Hughes thus entered office from Brown and the Columbia Law School, with long experience in the law and in state and national politics and on the nation's highest court, but without previous exposure to foreign affairs, to serve a President who shared no part of the burden, in a time when the local climate was inimical to such feelings for international cooperation as he once seems to have had. (He had been one of several Republican signers of an appeal to support American entry into the League, if this could be accomplished under Republican rather than Democratic auspices, and if something could be done about the objectionable Article X of the League Covenant.) He bowed to the seemingly inevitable and proceeded to do his best within the framework of the time. To the task he brought formidable talents and considerable ingenuity, circumscribed somewhat by a legalistic background and training and a naturally conservative bent of mind which merited part, but hardly all, of the acid criticism leveled at him by Louis D. Brandeis when he was a crusading reformer in New York State: "His is the most enlightened mind of the eighteenth century." * His austere carriage,

* It may here be noted that all three Secretaries of the period were trained and highly successful in the law, as have been so many occupants of their office. It is fashionable among students of foreign

adorned by a magnificent beard, aptly complemented Harding's easy informality. A high intelligence lay behind this imposing façade, which also covered, if it did not entirely conceal, a personality very sensitive to criticism and ill adjusted to the incidence of defeat. As an administrator he ran a tight ship but also a happy one. Hugh R. Wilson, looking back on a diplomatic career which had brought him into contact with most of the world's great figures, wrote that he had "found none to compare in wisdom and intelligence. . . ." Joseph C. Grew, his Undersecretary, told a retirement luncheon, and its honored guest, that under him the Department had "attained a cohesion, an enthusiasm and an esprit de corps which has never before been equalled." And William R. Castle, then a Division Chief, wrote that "the memory of your consistent kindness, of the inspiration you have given in your method of work, of the admirable justice of your conclusions will remain always. For the rest of my life you will be *The Secretary*."

Under all the circumstances, a Secretary blessed with large imagination and bold initiative would have fared badly in Hughes's day; lacking presidential support in any controversy with Congress and acutely aware of public opinion, he confined his activities (except for the Washington Conference) to a fairly restricted scope. Within this chosen area he parlayed able management of detail with adroitness in by-

---

relations to disparage the law as a school for diplomacy on the ground that its practitioners are trained to win cases, while the task of the diplomat is to reduce differences to a viable consensus. The stricture may be merited, but the fact remains.

passing congressional opposition into a successful incumbency. He could well pat himself on the back upon retirement; the relatively narrow range of problems with which he found it necessary to deal, in comparison with those faced by his two successors, might have given him cause, in 1933, to feel that his had been the ablest tenure of them all.

Death relieved Harding (August 2, 1923) of the pressures of impending calamity and provided the White House with a strikingly different tenant. Few have written of Calvin Coolidge in terms other than sharply critical.* Successive authors have belabored him for his slothfulness (he took long afternoon naps and spent brief hours in his office), his churlish taciturnity (which seems to have been a protective armor masking an innate shyness doffed only in the company of his few friends), and his almost total lack of initiative or imagination. None, however, has questioned his integrity, his courage (when forced to take a position, as in the Augean aftermath of his predecessor), or the political sagacity which brought him almost uninterrupted success at the polls. Indeed, it may be questioned whether the American political process could have produced a President more suited to the essentially interim character of his term, or one who could have better represented the economic interests which domi-

* His most recent biography was published after these pages had been penned; its author, having carefully sifted the available material, concludes modestly enough that he has written the biography of "a politician who was less than crafty, of a President who deserves some praise and much understanding along with criticism." His account forces no amendment of the present one in the area of foreign affairs.

nated both his Administration and the nation in a day when the handmaiden Prosperity waited worshipfully on the goddess Business.

It would have been strange indeed had this epitome of inertia evinced vigor in foreign affairs. He accepted the decision-making aspects of this area as an occupational hazard and kept a sharp eye on operations, bestowing more care and developing greater knowledge than had Harding, but he seldom meddled. If he did intervene, it was at specific points (often in a negative fashion). He was by-and-large content to accept a course of action reaching him through channels as representative of departmental and secretarial judgment, and to back Secretary and subordinates in its implementation. He achieved the singular distinction of writing an autobiography (for which he was paid handsomely on a per-word basis) without devoting a single syllable to diplomatic matters. It may be pointed out in mild extenuation, however, that his five years and seven months in office presented him with few issues of world-shaking import. Under these circumstances it was hardly disastrous that a man of his temperament largely entrusted policy formulation and conduct to his successive Secretaries of State.

At the start of Coolidge's full term in March, 1925, Frank Billings Kellogg succeeded Hughes, who retired to recoup his personal fortunes. Like Hughes, a lawyer, but with a sharply different background, he was a New Yorker early transplanted to Minnesota. No Ivy Leaguer like Hughes or Henry Lewis Stimson, who would succeed him, Kellogg's formal schooling had been interrupted early and his professional training obtained by "reading law" in the office of a practic-

ing attorney in Rochester. Lucrative corporate connections
furnished him a competence; the good fortune of connection
with important litigation brought a reputation which led to
presidency of the American Bar Association. Financial and
professional fulfillment caused him to look for new fields of
activity, leading to a foray into politics, which resulted in a
term in the Senate (1917–1923). These experiences, plus his
ambassadorial stint, broadened his outlook and his contacts,
but never entirely divested him of a sense of insufficiency
stemming from the fact that he had only a "common school"
education.

A short frame, white hair, a hand tremor, and one sightless
eye must have made him a disappointing replacement for
Hughes's magisterial presence. With these physical attributes he brought to the Department a compulsive nervous
energy which drove him, by his own witness, to "read every
word of the reports from our ambassadors and ministers" (a
devotion to duty which chained him to his desk while Coolidge basked in cooler climes), a hot temper, and a tendency
to vacillate on the way to a decision. On the strength of these
characteristics he probably merited the nickname "Nervous
Nellie," bestowed on him by some wag, but hardly the title
of "doddering political hack from the cow country," awarded
him by that laureate of invective Henry L. Mencken.

Kellogg worked with an abler chief executive than had
Hughes, but one still largely unconcerned with external matters. Their relationship was an easy one in which Kellogg,
like Hughes, took most of the pains and proffered most of the
policy proposals, which Coolidge normally accepted. There
was, however, a distinct master-servant attitude on Kellogg's

part in that any strong presidential stand gained almost obse-
quious acquiescence. He worked in a framework where isolationism was strong though being moderated, and where domestic concerns took precedence over foreign affairs; he, like
Hughes, had a fairly narrow area of maneuver. His own outlook no broader than Hughes's, he worked in a period when
the winds of change were beginning to blow in various directions, and he took, usually under pressure, modest advantage
of these currents, modifying for the better American relations with China and with Latin America, and laying a foundation for developments more prominently mentioned in
connection with the Hoover-Stimson period. Harmonizing
admirably with both his time and his chief, he took any move
violative of the *status quo* only under severe provocation and
with considerable reluctance, as the succeeding narrative
will show. He thus achieved what for his own day might be
considered a workmanlike performance but which a later
day would label short of first-rate.

Calvin Coolidge, departing for Northampton, might have
left much of his intellectual baggage in the White House for
his successor's use. Herbert Clark Hoover brought with him
the same admiration for the *status quo,* the same economic
paraphernalia of *laissez-faire,* the same trust in the goddess
Business, and the same confidence in her handmaiden Prosperity. He, like Coolidge, was shy and ill-at-ease with his enforced contacts, but he ignored the servants where Coolidge
had poked his nose into the housekeeping arrangements,
shuffled papers on his desk to avoid looking at visitors where
Coolidge had stared out the window through long stretches
of silence. Like Coolidge, he was not remarkable for the flexi-

bility of his ideas. This last was less a handicap to Coolidge, since ideas and times better coincided; it was Hoover's fate to possess ideas which the times subjected to intolerable strains. That he made a real effort, with some success, to moderate his ideas to suit the times, is being tardily recognized.

There were other differences, too. Unlike Coolidge, Hoover had no background in practical politics. His considerable wealth (he had been a rich man for twenty years and had hired his own assistants while Secretary of Commerce) and his large administrative experience had accustomed him to buying assistance rather than seeking advice and negotiating agreement. Where Coolidge conserved his energies, Hoover expended his incessantly; Stimson would reminisce somewhat enviously that Hoover was "capable of more intense and prolonged intellectual effort than any other man" of his acquaintance. Students have discovered only three possible presidential rivals for his industry, John Quincy Adams, James K. Polk, and Grover Cleveland. While sharing Coolidge's inexperience in foreign affairs, Hoover displayed a much more active interest; this area during his Administration came to occupy, proportionately, a larger share of presidential and popular attention than in the preceding years under review. If Coolidge worried about affairs of state, he concealed the fact; Hoover carried his burdens visibly, with obvious effects on his personality.

It is this matter of burdens that, perhaps, constituted at once the greatest contrast between the two men and Hoover's major problem. The Great Depression cast a shadow over the nation and the world, thrusting awry all the standards of economic though on which generations had built. For Hoover, it necessitated an anguished readjustment. During this reorientation Japan's Manchurian adventure shattered the relative stability of the post-Versailles world, pushing foreign affairs sharply upstage. It was Hoover's ill fortune to have to wrestle with two major disturbances of a *status quo* which had remained relatively tranquil for the best part of the preceding decade. Small wonder that he burned the midnight oil, seeming, to his Secretary of State, to be often fretful and sometimes almost impossible.

Henry Lewis Stimson shared some aspects of background with both his predecessors. Like both, he was a lawyer, leaning to a conviction that international controversies were cases to be won rather than differences to be composed. Like them, the law had brought him wealth. Like both, he had accumulated some fairly high-level experience, as an unsuccessful candidate for Governor of New York (1910) and as a colonel in the War of 1914–1918, where he created mild embarrassment for generals whose activities he had previously directed as Secretary of War under William Howard Taft (1911–1913). Like Hughes, his was an Eastern, Ivy League background of Phillips-Andover, Yale, and the Harvard Law School. Elihu Root, whose law firm he joined, was his early mentor and remained his idol. Like Kellogg, Stimson was hot-tempered. He exhibited a sense of class to which Kellogg could never aspire and which Hughes would not have deigned to display; he lived like a grand seigneur at Highhold, his Long Island estate, transferring some of the panoply to his Washington home at Woodley, which he purchased for $825,000 upon accepting Hoover's appointment.

Stimson was not the President's first choice; Hughes and Borah had rejected direct proffers and Kellogg a tentative one. In office he was cold, aloof, and difficult to work with, as illustrated by the anecdote which has his secretary cutting a peephole in the office door for the purpose of reconnaissance before entering the Presence; through it he learned to judge with some accuracy whether he was likely to be greeted amicably or by a book thrown at his head. For months he largely disregarded the able underlings in the Department and presently was able to bring in congenial spirits of his own choosing, including the first military aide to serve a Secretary of State.

As has perhaps been suggested, he was a man of spirit. He was, also, a man of ideas and one who found a much different atmosphere for their expression than had his predecessors. Harding, being a man of few if any views, had offered no impediment to Hughes's proposals. Coolidge had few ideas but found Kellogg completely subservient to such as he expressed. Stimson, the strong-minded, had the fortune to be associated with a man of equal determination, of far greater energy, and of greater caution.*

The result was a continual give and take, at first amicable but later increasingly irritating, which burned up many calories on both sides, brought each some victories, and often left Stimson unhappy and strangely unfulfilled, though the consensus seems to be that their differences had but slight influ-

---

* Stimson's physical stamina was not great and needed incessant renewal. He found desk work wearisome and to be borne only for short stretches interspersed with deck tennis or horseback riding and relieved by long vacations.

ence on the course of policy. These personal foibles, differences with his superior, and the innate difficulties of his period in office would leave him, as they have left students of his work, unhappy at the conclusion of a less than pleasant and somewhat less than effective experience. He himself recorded, in his third-person reminiscences, that his last years under Hoover were "the least happy of his public career" in an assignment "for the difficulties of which Stimson was least prepared."

Numerous factors condition the practical conduct of Presidents and their Secretaries of State in the formulation of foreign policy and the conduct of operations. Some, external to the executive department, stem from public and congressional interest in foreign affairs; others develop, so to speak, inside the governmental family. The former category includes the relations of Presidents and Secretaries with the press and public opinion, their relations with Congress and, particularly, with the powerful watchdog over the executive, the Senate Committee on Foreign Relations.

Internally, the efficiency of the Department of State as an instrument of effective government depends largely upon the caliber and personalities of the second- and third-echelon men who serve as Undersecretaries and Assistant Secretaries and their relations with their superiors. Improved means of communication available during the period under review tended to minimize somewhat the earlier importance of the men in the field by enabling Washington to exercise closer direction by cable and by international telephone; departmental contact with Europe by the latter device was inaugurated in 1927, Dwight W. Morrow used it extensively in his Mexican tour of duty beginning in the same year, and Stimson was an inveterate user of the instrument. As a result of this and other factors it is fair to say that the Republican years were ones in which the field men were closely shepherded from Washington except when, as in the cases of Morrow in Mexico and Stimson in Nicaragua, central control was relinquished to practical proconsuls.

Biographical accounts abound in asseverations of presidential and secretarial "sensitiveness" to the attitudes of the press and their individual and collective deference to public opinion. These truisms are difficult to measure with any precision, but brief comment will indicate considerable variation in tenor and approach. Harding attempted to apply his easy informality in relations with newsmen, but restrained himself after one or two egregiously mistaken statements had to be corrected. Coolidge met the press often, but his insistence upon submission of written questions prior to the conference permitted a selectivity of which some complained. Transcripts of his remarks, preserved in the Forbes Library at Northampton, reveal little that is new about this enigmatic character, but testify to his willingness to face the issues of the day and the caution with which he did so. Hoover launched his press relations successfully but the honeymoon was a brief one. Sensitive to criticism and burdened by the Depression and his self-imposed overload of work, he became peevish under attack, and his relations with reporters deteriorated to a point where Paul Y. Anderson of *The St. Louis Post-Dispatch* asserted (*The Nation*, October 14,

1931) that they had reached "a stage of unpleasantness without a parallel in the present century . . . characterized by mutual dislike, unconcealed suspicion, and downright bitterness."

On the secretarial level, Hughes saw the press twice daily except in the dull summer season, spoke freely, but permitted direct quotation only upon express authorization. He furnished, also, much usable background information without allowing attribution to the Department. Kellogg met the reporters four times weekly, read memoranda, and invited questions in a free give-and-take, maintaining Hughes's limitation on direct quotation. He was sufficiently pleased with his own performance to have mimeographed summaries of the conferences sent to Foreign Service officers. Stimson had difficulty with large groups of reporters, particularly at the London Naval Conference. This unhappy experience led to the holding of weekly conferences at Woodley, a device which conserved his energies and saved his temper. Here he briefed selected and veteran correspondents on current issues. This technique, not entirely dissimilar to Hoover's scheme of relieving hungry citizens by making large loans to bankers, doubtless pleased its beneficiaries more than the less favored members of the Fourth Estate.

As in the case of the press and public opinion, the literature amply documents presidential reluctance to put pressure on Congress beyond the constitutional obligation imposed by the annual State of the Union address. With each of the incumbents, restraint in this quarter was at least partly a matter of principle, of subscription to the doctrine of the separation of powers, and a belief that it is the business of the legislature to legislate; only rarely was any attempt made at outright pressure. Also, as has been pointed out above, this was a period of congressional ascendancy, and it would have taken abler, and certainly bolder, men to lock horns successfully with a resurgent Congress. The net result was years of executive nonaggression.

Though presidential pressure on Congress was rare, a force emanating from upper Pennsylvania Avenue influenced both Presidents and Secretaries. This was the stance which Congress, particularly the Senate, might adopt toward executive excursions in foreign affairs. The relationship was focused on the Senate Committee on Foreign Relations and pinpointed on the chairman of that powerful group, a position successively held by Lodge of Massachusetts and Borah, the Lion of Idaho, men as widely separated by temperament as by geography.

Lodge was the Back Bay Brahmin personified, unreconstructed since he teamed with Theodore Roosevelt to light the torch of Empire in the 1890's. He had been the epitome of party regularity on such issues as the tariff. Sardonic and imperturbable, he had led the opposition which wrecked Woodrow Wilson's League. But he was an old man in 1921, and his influence in the party waned before death took him in November, 1924. His chief contribution to the story to be told here is his part in the Washington Conference of 1921–1922, where Hughes took him hostage by making him a member of the American delegation, and his work in securing senatorial consent to the resulting treaties.

No Brahmin, Borah. No imperialist, either, nor yet a party regular. He spoke for Borah, and for Borah's concept of what, at any given moment, was for the good of that American people whose well-being and security were his highest aim. His peculiar makeup often led him into opposition to his own party, and he became a nay-sayer par excellence, more constructive in the negative, if that contradictory phrase may be used, than in the positive. His volatility, his volubility, and the power of his position made him a force always to be reckoned with, and all hands took him into full account.

He was, during the Coolidge era, one of the most frequent visitors to the White House; his relations with the President remained good, no matter how often he opposed the Administration. Kellogg was inordinately wary of his vagaries and consulted him constantly; the quip that he conducted American foreign relations by ringing Borah's doorbell had enough foundation to be plausible, but hardly enough to be true. Hoover sought to take him into camp by offering him the Secretaryship of State, but he refused, insisting that he had neither the cash nor the qualities to support the social side of the office. Perhaps as important was his fierce desire to remain his own man. As Secretary, he could either say Yes or resign, and he refused to subject himself to such confinement. His relations with Stimson continued to be cordial, and he permitted himself to be used, on occasion, as in the Manchurian business, as an agent in ferrying Administration policy from the Department to the public.

Reviewing this period when chief executives used little pressure and when congressional leadership displayed few constructive qualities, one may speculate somewhat ruefully as to what might have resulted had either party to the relationship possessed greater energy and understanding of international forces. Presidential initiative, in almost any direction, would undoubtedly have incurred congressional hostility; congressional initiative, though considerably confined within constitutional bounds, might well have spurred executive activity. One might speculate, fancifully, as to the possibilities had *both* branches possessed greater vision and more firmness. Then, conceivably, the Geneva Disarmament Conference of 1927, instead of dissolving in stalemate and recrimination, might have provided a constructive aftermath of the Washington Conference of 1921–1922 and a positive lead into the London Conference of 1930. Still more fancifully, had American initiative in 1931 been able to spur the League into positive steps to contain the Japanese adventure in Manchuria, the procession of possible consequences is an endless one. The facts, of course, remain to be described in later chapters.

Seven men held the position of Undersecretary during the period. Designed as a high policy-making post to be filled by a man of training and experience, it was occupied by a considerable variety of men who served with varying degrees of success. Hughes appointed three, one of whom held over for a time under Kellogg, who chose two; Stimson also chose two. Of the seven, five had had experience in the Department or in the field, and two were political appointees.

Henry P. Fletcher, a former Rough Rider and successively Ambassador to Chile and to Mexico, and William Phillips, a career man, served Hughes until the appointment of Joseph C. Grew, also a career man, in 1924. Kellogg retained Grew until 1927, but the relationship became increasingly uneasy. Hughes had kept him briefed on policy matters; Kellogg did not, but expected him to take over effectively in his own rare absences. A hearing difficulty hindered effective communication with the President on the occasions when he was in charge. A mutually agreeable solution was found in the offer, and acceptance, of the Ambassadorship to Turkey.

This change gave Kellogg an opportunity to advance Robert E. Olds (a former law partner) from the Assistant Secretaryship which he had held since 1925. This, Kellogg's only political appointment at the top level, filled the Secretary's long-felt need for a lawyer-adviser and gave a decisiveness hitherto lacking in departmental operations. When Olds left to join a New York law firm, Kellogg chose J. Reuben Clark, thus obtaining both a lawyer and a career man. Clark had previously occupied government posts and more recently had been in Mexico in the personal employ of Dwight Morrow. He remained a lawyer rather than a policy maker (except for his *Memorandum on the Monroe Doctrine*) to the end of the Kellogg period.

Stimson likewise chose a lawyer friend, Joseph P. Cotton, as his first understudy. Cotton's somewhat flippant manner failed to endear him to all his new associates, but he had the Secretary's complete confidence, and served him well until his untimely death in March, 1931. He was succeeded by William R. Castle, whose appointment Stimson was later to label a "mistake," though he was not averse to it at the time. This was on personal rather than professional grounds, as Castle was an old Department hand, had been Chief of the Division of Western European Affairs and, briefly, Ambassador to Japan, and was one of the most knowledgeable men of his day. It was his, and Stimson's, ill fortune that he attained his highest departmental post just as Stimson's relations with Hoover were deteriorating; since Hoover and Castle were friendly, the latter found himself torn by divided loyalties and, leaning toward the President, incurred the enmity of the Secretary.

Space precludes lenghty comment on the numerous men filling posts as Assistant Secretary and Chief of Division. They were for the most part experienced, the palm in this quarter belonging to the perennial Alvey A. Adee, who had entered the Department in 1882 and remained a walking compendium of protocol and proficiency until his death in 1924. Most of these men were professionals; Kellogg appointed Olds from the outside and Stimson brought in James Grafton Rogers, Harvey H. Bundy, and Allen Klots. Several of them, such as Castle, J. V. A. MacMurray, Nelson Trusler Johnson, Wilbur J. Carr, Francis White, and Stanley K. Hornbeck, were men of real distinction and ability; their effectiveness depended in large measure on the impression they were able to make upon their immediate superiors and the habits of these superiors in relying upon professional advice. It would perhaps not be unfair to conclude that their overall impact on affairs was generally somewhat less than their ability warranted.

This brief review of times and their men has described a period when national concerns were primarily domestic and when foreign relations were deeply tinged with memories of recent and unpleasant involvement in a world turmoil now happily removed from sight, if not entirely from sound. It opened with an almost aggressive noninvolvement, but as it proceeded (and this the subsequent narrative will more clearly show), an uneasy accommodation to the outside world became more and more the order of the day. The men in charge of affairs fitted into this changing pattern, reflected its main outlines to a degree, and, indeed, played a part in its alteration. Neither Harding nor Hughes could have carried the country into full membership in the world community. Coolidge and Kellogg edged closer to the current, and Hoover and Stimson were swept still closer to the brink. All were men of their time, and must be judged, finally, by the standards of the time, as well as by a broader one erected at a later day.

III

Europe:
In or Out?

No extended span of years can be treated within simple organizational boundaries, and any account of such a period traces threads which cross and recross. The men whose characteristics have been set forth above watched these multiple threads unwinding from the bobbins and moving toward the loom, and tried to keep them moving without snarls. When snarls occurred, they perforce worked at untangling them with a minimum of damage to the fabric, hopeful that the other threads would meantime continue to move smoothly. The resultant product, human hands being human hands, presents an uneven texture, punctuated by bumps and gaps. The later student, running his fingers over it, can mark his history by its unevennesses, sorting bumps and gaps and dividing them neatly into categories for descriptive purposes.

He must sort cautiously, however, constantly aware that a whole, as well as its parts, occupied the original weavers. He must remember to look, as they did, across the fabric as well as from beginning to end, and keep constantly in mind the fact that events were happening in multiples at a given moment, as well as in sequence along a time line. Trying to work within these cautionary guide lines, I have organized the following chapters roughly by areas and in time, with an attempt to treat successively each area where events of crucial importance developed, following these events through to their conclusion, then returning to pick up the next area, and so on. On this principle, problems primarily concerning Europe, Latin America, and the Far East will be approached in that order, with due effort to serve notice in each account of contemporaneously important developments in the others.

The present chapter deals successively with the American reaction to affairs centering largely in the European theater of political activity. Peace with defeated enemies, relations with the League of Nations and with the World Court, and refusal to recognize the Soviet Union are all aspects of the problem of American accommodation (or lack of it) to the new world of the 1920's. Their details combine insistence upon independent action and willingness to cooperate in about equal proportions, and thus fit into a pattern of not-in, not-out which tends to modify somewhat the label of isolaionism often attached to the Republican years.

Relations with erstwhile enemies were, to put it mildly, indeterminate when Harding and Hughes took over in 1921.

There was no peace, since in rejecting his League the Senate had also sidetracked this other aspect of Wilson's dream. The President, trusting to the upcoming election to bring the country to a sensible acceptance of his League and, consequently, of a return to peace, had vetoed, not without vindictiveness, a joint resolution by which in May, 1920, Congress had sought to end the war. Another joint resolution of July 2, 1921, declaring the war at an end and claiming for the United States all the rights which would have accrued through the Treaty, filled the vacuum only partially, creating an American claim but securing no German acceptance of obligation. Germany's renunciation of rights and interests at Versailles had become effective in favor of her other conquerors, but not the United States, and this defect, along with others, must needs be remedied. For example, the Armistice, to which the United States had been a party, had surrendered German overseas possessions to the five Allied and Associated Powers. The United States wanted no part of these territories, but needed to safeguard the national interest in their disposition. Neither had anything been done to compel performance of Germany's promise at Versailles to reimburse the United States for the cost of the Army of Occupation, a heavy drain on the national Treasury. Nor had there been any settlement of claims arising prior to American entry into the war in 1917 and outside the reparations framework.

Hughes sounded out a congressional group, including at least part of the so-called Irreconcilables of the Treaty fight, on the possibility of securing favorable Senate action on a revised treaty, but the signs were not propitious. To end this

61

anomalous situation of no-war, no-peace, he devised an omnibus scheme in which he embodied the joint resolution of July 2 in a new treaty with Germany, reserving all rights granted the United States in the Treaty of Versailles. This was signed in August, as were similar arrangements with Austria and with Hungary, and all three went into effect in due course. Thus somewhat ingloriously, but in proper accord with the realities of the day, the United States safeguarded her interests while sidestepping any responsibilities.

The treaty of peace brought the past into line with the present concerning the conquered enemy. Existence of the League of Nations, however, posed the much more delicate problem of bringing a present, in which the United States shared no formal part, into line with a future in which relations could hardly be avoided. There were, understandably, tender sensibilities on both sides. The officials of the League, charting a course necessarily circumscribed by American nonadherence, would at once be anxious for consideration and possible cooperation, and alert for slights. A substantial minority of Americans were still dazed and hurt at their country's failure to join the organization; the national voice, however, had sharply repudiated membership. Harding, the titular head of the party, reflected the opinion of the majority, having proclaimed in a campaign statement that "It is not interpretation but rejection that I am seeking" (at Des Moines, Iowa, October 7, 1920), and having announced, two days after his election, that the League was "now deceased." His Secretary of State had been less vigorously hostile; his principal objection had been to the guarantees of Article x, and he had joined a number of prominent Republicans in the appeal for acceptance of the Covenant with reservations. Having taken Harding's salt, he could hardly emphasize his previous point of view, but remained, as events would demonstrate, not completely impervious to contacts with the new organization; he would become, indeed, the chief architect of the scheme of cooperation without involvement which would characterize American policy for some years.

It is perhaps not too difficult, given the temper of the time and the recent popular verdict, to understand the attitude of the new Administration. The League itself was as yet untried, its direction and leadership still to be determined. Time would demonstrate its subservience to the political ends of its major members and their reluctance to put its machinery to the ultimate test. At the moment the possibility that it might develop into the super-government from which its opponents believed they had just saved the United States was, in their minds at least, a real one. No amount of reasoned wariness, however, can justify the cavalier note on which relations were originally inaugurated; the facts can only be explained in terms of inexcusable carelessness on lower bureaucratic levels and too great delay in discovery by responsible officials.

The facts have often been recited, not always accurately. As nearly as the writer can discover, they are as follows: The Wilson Administration, after replying to fifteen League communications, expired with eighteen still unanswered. These and successive documents remained unacknowledged by the Department of State. A League official took to sending material to Washington by registered mail, acquiring receipts upon delivery. Shortly after adoption of this practice, Hughes sent a cable to the American Consul at Geneva (June 24, 1921), for delivery to Sir Eric Drummond, Secretary General of the League: "I am instructed to say verbally and unofficially that the American Government has received your communications of Nov. 18 and May 22 but inasmuch as the American Government has no relations with the League of Nations there will be no reply to them." This somewhat less than gracious statement was apparently passed along to Sir Eric on June 30.

On July 18 *The New York Times* carried a front-page dispatch playing up American neglect of the proprieties and paraphrasing Hughes's cable of June 24. Exposed by such charges of incivility, Hughes began promptly acknowledging receipt of League communications. He also started an investigation of the previous situation, which turned up the fact that a clerk charged with opening mail had decided, without reference to a superior officer, that several pieces of League material, some of which were routine handouts, required neither acknowledgment nor reply, and had accordingly interred them in the files. These were duly exhumed and, toward the end of September, Drummond received fourteen acknowledgments in a single envelope, bearing various dates in August. With one exception, however, they ended with the stiffly formal statement: "Note has been taken of this information for any purpose of relevancy to the United States as a State which is not a member of the League of Nations." The plethora and rigid formality of the replies provided the Secretariat with a nominal victory and somewhat cold comfort. And there were other instances of ungraciousness before adoption of the "unofficial observer" technique. For example, in May, 1921, the League requested statistics for use in one of its publications. Neither figures nor a reply were forthcoming until January, 1922; at this point the American Consul in Geneva sidled up to a League desk and depositing "unobtrusively" an unsigned memorandum, on unidentifiable paper, but containing the requested data.

Previously, the Wilson Administration had insisted vigorously to the League Council in February, 1921, that the United States had a right to be consulted on mandates problems involving France, Great Britain, Italy, and Japan. The Council promptly proposed that an American delegate sit in on its deliberations. The matter was held up until after the change in command, but Hughes neither replied nor sent a representative, and in August, 1921, opened individual negotiations with the four powers. Such arms-length tactics proved too cumbersome, and he presently evolved the device of the "unofficial observer," which became a regular part of international paraphernalia. By December, 1922, Dr. Marion Dorset of the Bureau of Animal Husbandry of the Department of Agriculture was sitting in such capacity with the Anthrax Committee of the International Labor Organization; in January, 1923, Dr. Rupert Blue, Assistant Surgeon General in the Public Health Service, was at work with the League's Advisory Committee on Traffic in Opium. In March of the same year Miss Grace Abbott, Chief of the Children's Bureau of the Department of Labor, met with the League's Advisory Committee on the Traffic in Women and Children.

All these were official appointments, though the quoted

title continued to obtain. In the careful words of William C. Beerits, whose memoranda in the Hughes Papers were prepared in such a way as to make him practically an amanuensis, the Americans named, and many others who followed them, provided the United States with

> fitting contacts with agencies of the League in matters affecting American interests or in humanitarian measures that appealed to this country. These representatives were unofficial only in the sense that they were not official members of the League Committees or organs; they were official as far as the U.S. was concerned in the sense that they represented the Government for the purposes for which they were appointed. In effect, this system amounted to full American representation.

Even this carefully controlled contact gave Borah grounds for asserting that the United States was involved in the League in everything but name—hardly an accurate statement in view of the observers' inability to venture into the realm of policy leadership or to talk money, on which any policy would depend for effectuation.

Relations gradually became closer through this device, however. As early as the summer of 1923 two Americans, Colonel James A. Logan and Fred C. Dolbeare, appeared at Geneva, apparently uninvited but certainly not uninstructed, and participated with the Council, albeit somewhat extracurricularly, in the negotiation of a loan to aid Greek refugees. Not until 1928 did the Council again risk a formal invitation to participate in carrying out the provisions of the Opium Convention of that year. This time Mr. Kellogg replied, formally declining the invitation, and it was only in February, 1931, that Stimson acceded to a request that an

American sit with a committee of Council members dealing with slavery in Ethiopia. The story of American cooperation with League machinery in the Manchurian episode of 1931–1932, the high point in this aspect of affairs, will receive later treatment.

Other contacts developed apace, and after 1928 special officers were detailed to the American Consulate at Geneva to devote their entire time to observing League matters. By this time cooperation in run-of-the-mill League activities had become established, and in 1931 it was reported that over two hundred Americans had represented their country in League meetings. Relations had come a long way since Ambassador George Harvey had truculently warned the Pilgrim Society on May 19, 1921, that his country would not "have anything whatsoever to do with the League or with any commission or committee appointed by it or responsible to it, directly or indirectly, openly or furtively." The League, too, had gone a long way in the intervening years, along a path which greatly facilitated cooperation. Instead of becoming an organization of international force, operating through potential economic or military sanctions, it had developed along the less dangerous lines of arbitration and conciliation, rendering near-involvement less of a danger than in the early twenties. Near-involvement, be it noted, however, carried with it no implication of actual involvement; by 1931–1932 only the die-hard internationalists hoped for anything more than they presently enjoyed.

Looking back, one can only mildly commend the Republican high command for taking what, in the climate of their time, were perhaps as long steps toward the League as public opinion would have sanctioned. Much more easily, one may sympathize with the frustrated die-hards, and lament the fact that no Republican possessed the leadership to risk putting matters to a more crucial test.

The Permanent Court of International Justice (more popularly, the World Court) had been established to supplement League machinery in undergirding the postwar international order. Proposed American association with such a League-connected body would inevitably engender conflicting emotions similar to those involved in the struggle over the League itself; victorious isolationists would view with alarm, and defeated internationalists would look with hope, to the prospect of membership. The period witnessed repeated efforts, repeatedly unsuccessful, to take the nation into the Court, though ultimate defeat would be reserved until a new day of Democratic triumph. The failure to be chronicled just below may be ascribed to a variety of factors, including poor timing, ineffective leadership in the executive branch, and vigorous opposition adroit in the use of death-dealing amendments. It is a failure compassed by the Court's enemies in spite of what students have generally judged to be a favorable popular opinion.

The original American contact with the Court in the summer of 1921 was hardly auspicious. Elihu Root, Oscar Straus, George Gray, and John Bassett Moore, American jurists connected with the machinery of the Permanent Court of International Arbitration existing at The Hague, were asked to nominate judges for the new body, the original invitations being, as a matter of courtesy and information, directed to them via the Department of State. These found their way into the administrative backwater already described, when League communications were being filed without acknowledgment. They finally emerged, after word of them had reached Straus directly. Secretary Hughes, however, mindful of recent turmoil over the League, refused to answer affirmatively the jurists' query as to whether they should respond with nominations, and though Straus and Gray protested to Root, the Secretary's consistent but hardly positive approach prevailed and no nominations were forwarded—a *contretemps* hardly calculated to strengthen the still tenuous American contacts with the League. Neither would it particularly encourage internationalists, still seeking desperately to bring the United States into the environs of the League; indeed, it would be months before the Administration took its first tentative step toward membership in the Court.

This was not because of hostility on Hughes's part, but mainly for reasons of priority and strategy. The Secretary was on record as early as 1916, and repeatedly thereafter, as favoring an international judicial body. Once he was in office, deep and lengthy involvement in the Washington Conference led him to postpone action on the Court, but his papers show that by early October, 1922 (the Court's initial session had convened on January 30), he was beginning to move in that direction, having become convinced that public opinion was ready for such a maneuver. He paved the way for an interview with Lodge by forwarding a copy of a pro-Court speech he had delivered in Boston on the 30th; in the words of Beerits, Lodge "expressed no opposition to such a policy." Even Harding was "not at all opposed," though in December he urged Hughes to postpone the matter until Congress had disposed of a merchant-marine subsidy bill important to his domestic program.

Meantime Hughes drew up a series of four reservations designed to preserve his principle of noninvolvement in the League while establishing parity between the United States and League members in the Court's actual operations. Root raised no objection to these reservations, and Hughes elicited from Moore a judgment that membership in the Court constituted no commitment to the League. Thus armed, he wrote the President on February 23, 1923, urging action, but still feeling it necessary to impress upon Harding the fact that the Court was "an independent body," and not an agency of the League.

Thus armed and urged, Harding took the plunge and on February 24 recommended adherence to the Court Statute under the Hughes reservations. Although the first of these was designed specifically to divorce the Court from the League, Senator Borah, unconvinced, launched one of his many diatribes, insisting that Court and League bore the same relationship as water and H_2O. Here matters ended officially for the remainder of Harding's term; his recommendations slumbered in the Committee on Foreign Relations until the President executed one of his famous backtracks, announcing on June 1, 1923, that he now feared too close a connection between Court and League to continue support of membership. His death passed the problem on to Coolidge, who decided to back the Secretary rather than follow his predecessor.

70

Aroused pro-Court public opinion resulted in hearings in the spring of 1924 before a subcommittee consisting of George Wharton Pepper, Frank B. Brandegee, and Henrik Shipstead, none of whom had been conspicuously friendly to any form of international entanglement. A series of dilatory tactics ensued. In the light of the hearings Claude Swanson introduced (May 5, 1924) a resolution favoring adherence to the Court under the Harding-Hughes formula. Lodge and Pepper countered with a pair of proposals ignoring the Court or designed to divorce it more effectively from the League than the Administration's scheme. The Foreign Relations Committee voted down the Swanson resolution, but reported the imaginative but somewhat far-fetched Pepper scheme (May 24), calling for the League Assembly and Council to adjourn as League organs, reassembling on the call of the old Hague authority to choose judges of the World Court. Americans might sit on these properly decontaminated bodies and participate in the choice of judges, while remaining unspotted by League association. The quadrennial American electoral madness was now imminent, and the Court was too touchy a subject to handle; it rested at this point, with both parties feeling constrained to write pro-Court planks into their platforms.

Lodge gave way to Borah as Chairman of the Senate Foreign Relations Committee after the election, but prior to Coolidge's inauguration in March, 1925. Coolidge supported adherence in his inaugural address, the day after the House of Representatives had voted, 301/28, to join the Court. Before the revived Swanson resolution for adherence with the Hughes reservations could reach a scheduled debate on the

Senate floor in mid-December, 1925, opponents had concocted a new bugaboo in fear of the Court's power to issue advisory opinions upon request. John Bassett Moore, a member of the Court since its inception, had developed a fear that such opinions involving American interests might affect the United States adversely, and aided anti-Court Senators in framing a fifth reservation designed to safeguard these interests. This was added to the four originals, and after a bitter debate in which Borah took a prominent part, passed the Senate on January 27, 1926, by a vote of 76/17. In its ultimate form the fifth reservation contained a provision, added after conference between anti-Court Senators and Judge Moore, and generally attributed to his authorship, providing that

> the court shall not render any advisory opinion except publicly after due notice to all states adhering to the court and to all interested states and after public hearing or opportunity for hearing given to any state concerned; nor shall it, without the consent of the United States, entertain any request for an advisory opinion touching any dispute or question in which the United States has or claims an interest.

The resolution, giving the United States a unique veto on advisory opinions, had to be accepted by all members of the Court before American adherence would become effective.

Doubtless taken aback by this vigorous stand, the League Council in March, 1926, nevertheless called a conference of League members to meet in September to discuss the situation, and requested American participation. Kellogg advised Coolidge against attendance, and declined the invitation, taking refuge in a senatorial insistence that acceptance of American membership be entirely divorced from League machinery, and be ratified by a direct exchange of American notes with each of the forty-eight signatories of the Statute. The September meeting, attended by twenty-two signatory states, was thus doomed to act in the absence of American delegates. It held six sessions mainly devoted to the last clause of the fifth American reservation. Several alternatives were suggested, but the meeting adjourned to make way for the opening of the League Assembly on the indecisive note of appointing a committee charged with defining "the exact meaning of the fifth reservation." Its final act failed to accept fully the United States position, though going some distance in the direction of that *Diktat*. It refused, however, to go the whole way and yield to the demand for an American veto on examination of issues to which it was not itself a party. Having thus failed to secure unanimous agreement to American demands (though several nations had acquiesced individually), Kellogg advised Coolidge (November 8, 1926) to give up; three days later the President's Armistice Day address underwrote the recommendation, Coolidge announcing that he would not ask the Senate to change its position.

Other matters engaged Kellogg's attention during 1927 and the Court issued languished during much of the year. Public interest revived early in 1928 to a point where Senator Frederick H. Gillett introduced (February 6) a resolution urging the President to renew conversations with signatory states. The Committee on Foreign Relations voted (May 23) to postpone further consideration until December. Coolidge intimated in November that something might be done to reopen negotiations, and in mid-December the League Council established a Committee of Experts to study revision of the Court Statute. Taking advantage of this opening, the aged and ailing Elihu Root was persuaded to join in the enterprise and embarked for Europe on his eighty-fourth birthday (February 15, 1929), after conferring with Coolidge, Kellogg, and leading Senators, for his final essay at a conciliation which might bring his country into the Court.

Kellogg presently dispatched a note (which Root had helped to draft) to the Court's member nations, using a loophole in the Final Act of September, 1926, to reopen discussion of American membership. The note was so ambiguous that the French Ambassador had to inquire whether it was positive or negative; Kellogg insisted that it was positive and was intended to show that the United States "would welcome membership in the Court." The Committee worked eight days and produced the so-called "Root Formula," another attempt to placate the United States on the touchy advisory opinion question. It proposed machinery enabling the United States to pose a protest when the Court was asked for an advisory opinion on any question in which it professed an interest. If in the face of such protest an advisory opinion were still demanded, the United States might leave the Court without prejudice.

The Root Formula, somewhat simplified, went into the report of the Committee of Experts to the League Council in March, 1929, was accepted by a Conference of Signatories on September 4, and by the League Assembly on September 14. A Protocol of adherence was accepted by fifty-four states, including the United States, during 1929–1930, but it was only on December 10, 1930, that Hoover presented the proposal formally to the Senate. By this time the Depression had laid its heavy hand on the nation; Borah's hand was as heavy as usual in opposition, and he was instrumental in having his committee postpone action until the spring of 1932. On June 1 a resolution of adherence reached the floor, only to be overwhelmed once more in the competitions of a presidential year. The indications are that Hoover was less than enthusiastic about his proposal of December 10, and that he made it largely in response to Stimson's insistence. Here, though endorsed by both party platforms, the matter rested, only to be given the *coup de grace* in 1935 by an overwhelmingly Democratic Senate. Thus a tentative move toward international cooperation, paralleling in time the gradual *rapprochement* with the League of Nations, surrounded by safeguards surely sufficient to reassure any but the hyper-timorous, failed, despite strong evidence of popular support, a failure due to a dearth of positive leadership at crucial moments and to the overt and covert hostility of such men as Borah, whose powerful influence was at all times in opposition.

Republican leadership faced a continuing problem of what to do about Russia, where a newly dominant dictatorship of the proletariat had overthrown the existing regime during World War I, repudiated its debts and taken the nation out of the war, and in the postwar years was propagandizing for a brand of politico-economic doctrine which few Americans found palatable. This exportation of ideas, indeed, with its threat to the stability of the established order, had made the recent Red Scare a more frightening phenomenon than Communist influence in the country really warranted. Administration policy would be framed in the light of these events, as well as the general attitude of aloofness which pervaded the nation in 1921. Though various pressures would become apparent, the Democratic policy of nonrecognition would remain in effect until another Democrat entered the White House in 1933.

Hughes received an overture even before taking office. While visiting Harding in Florida in February, 1921, he was approached by an official Russian agent desirous of creating a syndicate of American business leaders to help Russia out of the economic doldrums. Hughes was of course in no position to do more than listen. Before the end of March, however, another move was made, looking to the sending of a Russian delegation to negotiate a trade agreement. These two feelers will make clear that the chief Russian interest of the day was in trade matters rather than in politics, a situation which obtained during the remainder of the decade. Forced to give serious consideration to the Russian problem, Hughes developed a list of reasons which made recognition unwise, chief among which was "the persistent propaganda spread throughout this country by the Soviet regime. . . ."

Nothing further of note occurred during the Harding period, but Coolidge, in his first State of the Union message (December 6, 1923) set forth a list of criteria which might make recognition possible—not an encouraging list from the Soviet point of view:

Whenever there appears any disposition to compensate our citizens who were despoiled, and to recognize that debt con-

tracted with our Government, not by the Czar but the newly
formed Republic of Russia; whenever the active spirit of enmity
to our institutions is abated; whenever there appear works meet
for repentance, our country ought to be the first to go to the
economic and moral rescue of Russia.

Undiscouraged by these formidable hurdles, a Russian overture for negotiation ensued (December 16), but it was
couched in such terms that Hughes replied that there was
"no reason for negotiations," and there the matter rested, formally, until picked up by Franklin Delano Roosevelt in 1933.
Some interim developments, however, helped to set the stage
for action, after an unpleasant moment in 1929, during the
Sino-Soviet dispute over Manchuria, which will be noted
later. As that crisis was nearing its end, Stimson undertook to
lecture Maxim Litvinov, Russian Minister of Foreign Affairs,
for Russia's part in it, though he seems to have been partial
to that side of the controversy. His reproof elicited a sharp
rejoinder which was more prominently paraded than were
more important developments then transpiring in other
areas.

It was pointed out above that Russian interests were early
oriented toward trade rather than toward political contacts;
Russians bought considerably in the United States, and the
curve of purchases continued to rise until after the Depression was well under way, when they dropped sharply. This
induced some American interests to press for political contacts as a means of improving one of the best remaining trade
outlets. Shortly thereafter the Japanese adventure in Manchuria caused both Russia and the United States to think of
recognition in political terms as an offset to Japanese imperi-

alism; Stimson, in fact, instructed the Division of Far Eastern Affairs in the spring of 1932 to draw up a memorandum listing the pros and cons of recognition. However, after careful scrutiny of developments during the summer he decided to drop the matter. Here, in the final episode in this series dealing with gradual American accommodation to the realities of the European world, policy remained unaltered throughout the period, though some signs of change were in the offing.

The episodes just chronicled reflect a highly developed Administration wariness of the dangers of too-close communion with trans-Atlantic developments—a wariness at times bordering on childishness. Today, such fears of involvement seem slightly ridiculous. The League would fail its first major political test; the Court adjudicated few cases of startling import; and recognition of Russia would probably not have conspicuously altered predepression or postdepression trade balances. Policy, moreover, except in the case of the Court, undoubtedly followed public opinion. There remains, however, the unanswerable question raised so often by a backward look at these days of aloofness of how much better, had the Republican leaders been more vigorous and perceptive, the record might have been. Nor can it be forgotten, finally, that though aloofness persisted into 1933, it had greatly moderated since George Harvey's blast to the Society of Pilgrims in 1921.

IV

Disarmament:
The Washington Conference

Republican leadership had thwarted a Democratic approach to the perennial goal of security, sought by Woodrow Wilson through international organization. Avoidance provided no solution, and the problem became even more acute as the nation continued to stand aloof from the common instrument through which most of the world sought security. Despite the clamor of domestic concerns, the desire for security would not subside, and administrations pledged to normalcy, the promotion of big business, and prosperity found themselves, perforce, devoting considerable energy to disarmament matters, which might be called an American substitute for involvement in League affairs.

Ironically enough, the Washington Conference on the Limitation of Armaments, the Geneva Conference for the

Limitation of Naval Armaments, the London Naval Conference, the League of Nations Preparatory Commission on the
Disarmament Conference, the Disarmament Conference itself, and their ancillary negotiations, found the United
States, which had repudiated the League, heavily involved
in the alternative approach to security. Here, too, involvement produced a closer approach to commitment than in any
area to be covered in this story, and at a relatively early period when unfavorable reaction to either involvement or
commitment was at a high point—a commentary, indeed, on
the thesis of isolationism as a characteristic of the Republican years.

Perhaps no single diplomatic problem was more pervasive
than this, thrust upon Hughes and Harding early in 1921 and
engaging them and their successors at intervals until well
into 1932. The end product resulting from this enormous expenditure of diplomatic energy was highly disappointing to
contemporary seekers after peace and to later students of
these years. The high hopes raised by Hughes's Washington
proposals of November, 1921, were not realized, a failure to
which American policy unfortunately made no small contribution; and a later generation came to view the proposals
themselves as a narrow and inflexible approach to an expanding and changing problem. If a backward look is disappointing, however, a forward one is hardly more reassuring, and
the drama and high hopes of 1921–1922 should not be forgotten in the study of later and no more successful efforts in
the same area.

The first approach to disarmament in the Washington Conference (November 12, 1921–February 6, 1922), brought

together in primary concern the United States, Great Britain, and Japan, with China, France, Italy, the Netherlands, Portugal, and Belgium occupying a receding periphery. It brought to focus immensely complicated and far-flung national interests, some long in conflict, some warborn, and some exacerbated by war and postwar developments. Any attempt at this point to assign primacy to a single factor of causation or to balance an equation full of so many variables would inevitably leave the author frustrated and the reader dissatisfied. The complex considerations actuating the three principal protagonists will be set forth first, followed by a recital of the alternate drama and drudgery through which the Conference, dominated at all stages by Charles Evans Hughes, evolved solutions reflective of an American sense of reality and viable for their own day, though, in the longer view and in the light of new variables, they were judged to be of more modest success.

Now obvious, but at the time realized only dimly if at all, was a rearrangement of the structure of world power and strategy—a rearrangement inevitably accompanied by considerable stress and strain. Britain, bled white by war, faced the grim prospect of yielding that naval supremacy on which her power had long rested. Her problem was to salvage the maximum of prestige and security while making this humiliating accommodation. Japan, greatly the gainer in power and territory, but still dissatisfied with her international status, would shy at any developments which might decrease the one or diminish the other. And the United States, recently become most powerful of the three but unaccustomed to the new pre-eminence, was proud of her new naval muscle, was concerned about Far Eastern matters, and had many vocal advocates of peace and of economy who pointed accusing fingers at the naval expenditures. The ramifications of these national problems stirred an international ferment which culminated at Washington.

American advocates of disarmament had filled the postwar period with sound and fury.* Their sentiment derived from numerous quarters. Peace advocates, always vocal in the wake of destructive warfare, were prominent. Their pressure generated a deal of congressional oratory and some congressional attention. Less vocal, but important at the polls, were taxpayers supporting a huge naval establishment which threatened to grow larger; their representatives in Washington watched and heeded as demands for tax reduction and for curbing naval expenditures reached their desks. Never one to forego an opportunity, Senator Borah sought to commit the new Administration to a course of action by introducing in the lame duck session (December 14, 1920) a resolution embodying his own ideas of proper procedure, as a matter of record, pending accession of the new Administration.

He proposed to authorize (i.e., urge) the President to take the lead in convening a meeting at which the three leading naval powers would seek agreement to reduce naval armament expenditures by 50 per cent of current estimates over a

---

* "Disarmament," in American parlance, concerned primarily the naval arm, since land forces, rapidly liquidated after the war, were hardly deemed essential to national security in the 1920's.

five-year period. The President-elect had established in his own mind an order of priority in which naval supremacy must precede disarmament and, moreover, he resented this senatorial attempt to usurp the executive function. Even less enthusiastic were the naval professionals and their political supporters, who had for some time been in the ascendancy and who desired, in the interests of their own concepts of national security and of private economic welfare, to project their building programs into the indefinite future.

The growth of navalism in the United States was a relatively recent phenomenon but one vastly disturbing to many Americans as well as to the other leading naval powers. Accepting with some modifications a report of the General Board of the Navy, Wilson had asked (in December, 1915) for legislative authorization of a huge construction program. Congress complied, but only after bitter debate and with still further amendments, in an Act passed June 2, 1916. The origin of the "1916 Program" is a subject of dispute among scholars, being variously attributed to fear of German sea power, to Japanese wartime antics in the Far East, and to British exactions on American commerce in the neutrality period. Whatever the motivations, Congress followed Wilson's lead and enacted the so-called 1916 Program into law. American entry into the war, however, postponed its implementation in favor of urgently needed merchant carriers. Congress enacted new implementing legislation in 1919, and demands for further authorizations would be high on the agenda after March 4, 1921.

Despite Anglo-American association in war, many Americans were normally Anglophobes. These looked with anxiety to a postwar day when Britain, relieved of Austrian and German naval menace, and with near-exhaustion preventing either France or Italy from acting as a curb, would develop a strategic superiority which might extend its threat across the Atlantic. Then, too, an argument for naval expansion stemmed naturally from the need to protect American interests against the aggressions which had characterized Japan's wartime activities and which might, it was argued, be extended postwar to a point where force might be necessary to protect them. Professional naval opinion, in fact, was convinced by the end of 1919 that Japan constituted a real danger in the Far East, though there is no indication that this opinion was effectively impressed on other departments of the government. This trepidation concerning Japan was hardly relieved by the existence of the Anglo-Japanese Alliance of 1902, renewed in 1911, and presumably to expire in 1921 unless renewed. This bound Britain to go to Japan's aid in case that nation became involved in war, thus posing a formal threat of British attack on the United States in the event of Japanese-American hostilities. Although it was understood at the time of renewal in 1911 that Britain would not be expected to activate the Alliance against the United States, the existence of the Alliance furnished grounds for suspecting both parties, and its dissolution became an end of American policy; it stood, in American thinking, indeed, as a British link with Japanese imperialism.

Suspicion of Japan was not confined to naval circles. Almost everything that nation had done in recent years seemed to endanger some American interest or policy. The war furnished Japan's imperialists a golden opportunity, exploited

84

to the full, to extend the national influence in the western Pacific. On the mainland she promptly occupied the German sphere of influence in Shantung Province, and presently confronted China with the "Twenty-One Demands," violative alike of Chinese sovereignty, of the rights of other foreigners on the mainland, and of the Open Door principle so long part of American Far Eastern paraphernalia, though never given all-out support. Japan shared with Great Britain in a takeover of Germany's Pacific possessions, receiving the Marshall, Caroline, and Mariana Islands. This insular establishment placed her in a flanking position *vis-à-vis* American territory and communication lines to Hawaii, Guam, and the Philippines, rendering these hostages to fortune more than ever vulnerable to attack. The war's end found Japanese troops in Manchuria and Siberia, threatening further territorial aggression on the mainland. These measures roused a high degree of suspicion and hostility, but evoked neither vigorous nor effective countermeasures.

The Versailles Conference increased the tension. Wilson was unable to break the Japanese hold on Shantung; his best effort secured only an open-ended promise that the province would ultimately be returned to China. Nor could he shake her hold on former German islands, and eventually accepted a half-loaf in the form of a mandate system carrying a promise not to fortify or erect bases; the facts of geography remained against him, with Japan still physically athwart the sea lanes. He failed, too, in efforts to extinguish her claim to the Island of Yap, a strategic pinpoint 700 miles from the Philippines and 1,600 miles from Yokohama which served as a landing stage for one of the two Pacific cables. Small wonder, then, that Americans, civilians as well as naval officers, viewing past Japanese actions with alarm and looking to the future with misgivings, hoped against hope that something might be done to moderate Japanese ambition.

Britain shared the fears and suspicions of the day. Victory had left her facing a future far from rosy. She had lent heavily to her Continental allies and dependents in the early stages of the war and had borrowed heavily from the United States toward its end; her credits were uncollectable while her debts remained payable. To complicate this unpleasant prospect, her fiscal primacy, long a solid feature of the economic landscape, had passed to the United States. Her Empire, too, was in a state of strain, with India striving for independence and other elements demanding status. The German menace had been crushed and neither France nor Italy was able for the moment to disturb the local equilibrium, but a trans-Atlantic cloud was rising to darken this tranquility.

The war had witnessed the erection of a somewhat shaky Anglo-American entente founded on common necessities but shadowed by memories of American desire to trade with Britain's enemies and by unpleasant, costly, and, to American eyes, illegal British interference with these neutral rights. British desire to nourish this delicate plant of Anglo-American accord faced heavy obstacles, particularly in the prospect of huge American naval construction which loomed ominously on the horizon. Britain could only view the current American formula of naval equality as a threat to her own position; alarm and resentment resulted in about equal proportions. The American move seemed particularly ungracious in light of Britain's sharply reduced building program and her repeated and public announcement (by First Lord of the Admiralty Walter Long in Parliament in March, 1920, and again by His Majesty in November of the same year) of acceptance of the principle of naval parity with the United States. It was difficult, too, for Britain to understand American insistence that she abandon the Anglo-Japanese Alliance which served her as an anchor to windward in the Far East, minimizing the likelihood that Japan might turn to Germany or Russia, thus forcing Britain to maintain a correspondingly large and expensive Pacific establishment.

Conflicting pressures thus impelled Britain to maintain her naval status in the face of dwindling resources, keep alive the Anglo-American entente, and avoid antagonizing her Far Eastern ally. Considerations of prestige momentarily outweighed monetary factors, and in the winter of 1920–1921 a decision was taken to damn the expense and return to battleship construction. This was undertaken, however, with a weather eye on the possibility of persuading the United States to modify its own announced program of naval expansion.

Nor was Japan without past grievances or fears for the future, directed mainly at the United States, which seemed bent on humiliating her and thwarting what she considered her legitimate interests. Driven by economic pressures and, be it admitted, by Western example, she had developed what she deemed legitimate interests on the Asiatic mainland. She expanded these interests vigorously during the war, on a pattern well established by the West, but which Americans viewed, somewhat self-righteously, as imperialistic aggression and, moreover, contrary to the Open Door shibboleth. The Twenty-One Demands found the United States too busy with Mexico, the *Lusitania* crisis, and British trade restrictions to offer more than perfunctory opposition, but it was the only opposition Japan encountered to this and her other wartime territorial adventures. Continued American unhappiness with her course constrained Japan, in the autumn of 1917, to send Viscount Kikujiro Ishii to Washington for a verbal sparring match with Secretary of State Robert Lansing. The result was the Lansing-Ishii Agreement, an exercise in semantics which afforded both nations verbal satisfaction and left each confident that it had contained the other, but offered neither a permanent solution to the problem of Japanese rights on the Asiatic mainland. War, then, did nothing to allay, and much to aggravate, Japanese-American tensions.

Tensions increased at Versailles and during the succeeding months. Wilson's principles led him to seek Japan's expulsion from Shantung; his failure to eject her from this treaty-sanctioned landhold focused a resentment holding over from wartime interference. He had a hand too, albeit unhappily, in thwarting one of Japan's great objectives, the adoption of a conference declaration that all races were equal, when, as Chairman of the League of Nations Commission he had ruled that the declaration, supported by all but two of its members, could be adopted only by unanimous vote. Finally he fought, he supposed successfully, for the internationalization of Yap, only to see it turn up as a Japanese mandate. Neither he nor Harding had recognized this disposition, and hard feelings obtained over this minuscule but important bit of tropical sand.

Post-Versailles American actions, both in the Pacific and at home, further exacerbated the situation. The American expeditionary force in Siberia, which Japan suspected was designed to counter Japanese forces there, retained its obnoxious foothold until 1920. American reentry into a financial consortium, advocated by Wilson in 1917 and finally signed late in 1920, was taken quite correctly as a move to invade Japan's financial hunting ground in the Chinese Republic. At home, western states were passing laws even more galling to alien landholders than their prewar versions. Japanese laborers were subjected to physical violence, and the picture-bride device, which had enabled a sprinkling of Japanese women to enter the country, was under heavy fire. In the West, too, there was strong hostility to legal but virtually nonexistent Japanese immigration which, as has been seen, would bear legislative fruit in 1924. Added to all these factors were the American attempt to drive a wedge in the Anglo-Japanese Alliance, the push for new battleships, and the talk of further fortification of American possessions in the Pacific. Then, in the spring of 1921, the new Harding Administration announced that it would base the bulk of the Battle Fleet permanently in that ocean. Small wonder that Japan felt constrained to embark, like Britain, upon a naval construction program that would strain her resources to the limit.

Here, then, was a complex of factors involving the prime naval powers, all of which stood committed, by mixed pride and fear, to building programs which met vigorous domestic opposition and threatened the financial structure of all but the United States. That nation, of the three, was best equipped to proceed on course—money was more plentiful, the new Administration appeared favorably disposed, and the opposition, though vocal, was not presently in the ascendant. There was, in short, no immediately compelling reason for affirmative action on disarmament. Fear pushed Britain, ridden by debts and taxes, to assume a burden which she would gladly see eased if the price were not too high; she would be alert for a way to get off the treadmill. Japan had, on the whole, most of what she wanted, though at the cost of some international grumbling, particularly from the United States. Of the three nations her position was perhaps the simplest. All she needed was to preserve the relatively favorable *status quo* or exact a good price for any alteration. Out of this delicately balanced situation emerged, quite suddenly but not without considerable background, the Harding invitation of July 8 to Britain, Japan, France, and Italy to a discussion of both naval and Far Eastern affairs.

The narrative may well proceed from the dichotomy, presented during the lame duck period in December, 1920, of a large construction program offered by navalists and the Borah Resolution proposing a tripartite conference to consider drastic naval cuts. Borah returned to the charge in January, proposing (on the 25th) a resolution which would suspend naval construction for six months to permit study of the utility of the battleship and the question of "what constitutes a modern fighting navy." Still in the lame duck period, the House passed the appropriation bill after reducing the requests considerably, obviously marking time until the new Administration should make its wishes known. With the Senate starting discussion of naval matters, Borah promptly moved his original resolution as an amendment to the House bill and aided in a filibuster which ended action for the session.

All awaited the advent of the Harding Administration and the special session of the new Congress. Harding for a time encouraged the big-navy element by standing pat on his previously announced position that the establishment of naval supremacy must precede disarmament discussions. Backstage, however, Hughes proposed to the President, "Shortly after entering upon his official duties . . ." that the United States call a conference of the "principal Powers" on general disarmament; Harding acquiesced, telling the Secretary to choose his own time for the maneuver. A complex of problems (Yap, a Costa Rica-Panama boundary dispute, peace with Germany) occupied Hughes's time so fully as to prevent early action.

Meantime, congressional debate on the naval appropriation bill served as a vehicle for discussion of the original Borah Resolution and for the airing of strong views pro and con the disarmament question. Late in April (the 28th) the House passed the bill (which had been reintroduced into the special session of the new Congress) without the Borah Resolution, thus following the presidential order of priority—supremacy before disarmament. Harding, who had been holding his own counsel while watching the debate, admitted to

91

some senators (on May 3) that he was opposed to the Borah Resolution, and the Senate Committee on Naval Affairs proceeded to add a billion dollars to the generous House measure.

Senators, the while, were listening to grass-roots pressure for disarmament, and sentiment for the Borah Resolution waxed apace despite continued Administration opposition. Eventually a deal seems to have been evolved whereby Borah dropped his formidable opposition to the extra billion of naval money and the Administration ceased opposing his Resolution, which passed on May 25 by 74/0, its opponents counting on the House, incorrectly as events would show, to defeat it. The House cut appropriations sharply, defeated a resolution by Representative Stephen G. Porter watering down Borah's proposal, and passed the bill (June 29) after approving the Borah Resolution by 332/4. Harding had meantime reversed himself and given his supporters permission to support the Borah Resolution, claiming somewhat lamely that his branch of the government had "already been seeking information with regard to the attitude of foreign nations on the general subject of disarmament." The two Houses reached agreement on its provisions and Harding signed it into law on July 12. Whether domestic pressures alone would have converted him to the Borah approach will never be determined, since external events, to be outlined below, had already forced the Administration's hand. However, no student of the story can deny that Borah, and the forces which he represented, exercised considerable influence on the event.

These external forces, primarily British but with Japanese

overtones, had been building for months and came to a focus in early July, while the naval appropriation bill was on Harding's desk. Their principal gravamen was a British effort to forestall an arms race by mutual concessions; the injection of Far Eastern matters both complicated and facilitated the calling of a Conference. The British action opened in February with the promotion (on the 22nd) of Lord Lee of Fareham to the important post of First Lord of the Admiralty. Lee had been in Cuba with Theodore Roosevelt's Rough Riders and in Canada as Professor of Military Science and Tactics at the Royal Military Academy, and had affirmed his friendship by taking an American to wife. There seems ground to believe that his appointment was a move to establish disarmament contacts without involving the Foreign Office. At any rate, shortly after Harding's inaugural address had carried a vague statement on the subject, Lee told the British Institute of Naval Architects (March 16) that an Anglo-American understanding obviating a naval race was in order; he repeated the substance of earlier British statements of willingness to accept fleet equality.

With Harding still in his primacy-before-disarmament phase, there was naturally no reply to this extracurricular approach, so Lee tried another, more confidential but no more successful in the immediate event—one which, however, probably added a cumulative influence. The following story bases on memoranda by Adolph S. Ochs, publisher of *The New York Times,* and his London representative Ernest Marshall, which were presented to Lord Lee in 1933 and accepted by him at that time as according with his recollection of the events described. On April 22 Prime Minister David

Lloyd George entertained Ochs at breakfast, paving the way for an interview between Ochs and Lee. During their conversation Lee suggested his desire to have Washington notified informally that Britain was willing to abandon her long-standing policy of a two-power navy and agree upon equality with the United States. Lee wished the matter put in train prior to the British Imperial Conference scheduled to assemble in June, in order to keep naval matters off the agenda of that meeting.

Marshall came to the States and presented the Lee proposal to Edwin Denby, Harding's Secretary of the Navy, apparently including a British suggestion that reduction of naval armaments might permit the establishment of a sort of Anglo-American hegemony over the seas, with Britain policing the Atlantic and the United States the Pacific, thus relieving Britain of the need for a strong force in that area—an interesting suggestion, at the least, from a partner in the Anglo-Japanese Alliance. Denby, evidently after intragovernmental discussions, expressed interest in the proposal at a second interview with Marshall. The Ochs-Lee *démarche* seems to have had no further immediate impact, and Lee's two fishing expeditions failed to elicit the invitation which he obviously desired. However, the twin maneuvers clearly indicated the existence of a cooperative spirit at 10 Downing Street.

Official American opposition to renewal of the Anglo-Japanese Alliance, developing rapidly against this background, found Britain willing to listen and the Dominions prepared to accommodate. The Canadian Prime Minister, Arthur Meighen, came to the Imperial Conference fired with

94

a desire to abrogate the Alliance, with its danger, however remote, that Canada might become involved in Japanese-American hostilities. Australia and New Zealand at first opposed him, being anxious to retain the Alliance as a damper on Japanese pretensions on such terms as would not jeopardize American interests. Direct Anglo-American conversations developed against the background of this temporary deadlock.

Hughes held an important interview with Sir Auckland Geddes, the British Ambassador, on June 23 (the Imperial Conference had opened on the 20th) in the course of which delicate threats were exchanged, Geddes indicating that the Alliance, with its provisions obnoxious to the United States, might be continued for another year beyond July 13, 1921, the generally accepted date of its expiration. Hughes riposted by intimating that, unless steps were taken to moderate the Alliance threat, Congress might create unpleasantness in discussing a pending resolution for the recognition of the Irish Republic. More significant than these sparring gestures was Hughes's exposition, taking advantage of an opportunity presented by Geddes, of the American ground of opposition to the Alliance. Carefully omitting mention of its unpleasant military implications, he concentrated on fear that its renewal might underwrite Japan's imperialistic ambitions in the Far East. Expressing concern at the proposed renewal of the Pact, Hughes indicated his personal approval of Geddes' somewhat roundabout suggestion of a tripartite Anglo-Japanese-American cooperation on Far Eastern questions; such cooperation would, of course, be a substitute for the Anglo-Japanese Alliance. After consultation with Mac-

Murray he insisted that any such document must not be considered an alliance.

Here matters stood until the end of June, by which time Harding had reversed himself to allow passage of the navy bill carrying the Borah Resolution, and the Imperial Conference had agreed on modification of the Anglo-Japanese Alliance and its continuance until July 13, 1922. On July 2 the Conference agreed that a Far Eastern conference should assemble meantime to redraft the Alliance in the light of the total Far Eastern situation. The British Foreign Office was instructed to explore this possibility with Japan, China, and the United States, and on Tuesday, July 5, Lord Curzon raised the Far Eastern question in a conversation with George Harvey. The latter, unaware of the developing urgency of affairs, sought and obtained Curzon's permission to propose the Far Eastern conference by mail instead of by cable in order to present the matter more fully.* The Ambassador was tardy in composition and it was only on Friday, the 8th, that, pushed by Curzon and by developments of the 7th, he dispatched a cable telling Hughes that he must act rapidly if he wished to hold the initiative in calling a Far Eastern conference.

On Thursday, the 7th, Lloyd George announced in Parliament that he was awaiting "replies" from the United States, Japan, and China before making a statement concerning the Anglo-Japanese Alliance. Although at the moment there was

* Most writers have repeated Geddes' charge that Harvey misrepresented his Government's position at the interview with Curzon by stating that the Alliance was of "no concern" to the United States. The pertinent Beerits Memorandum points out that an exchange of cables absolved him of the charge.

nothing to which the United States could "reply," Hughes was besieged by the press on the 8th and realized that Britain was moving toward a Pacific conference in London, which he deprecated. Seeking at once to circumvent this and to secure the initiative, he obtained Harding's permission to invite Britain, Japan, France, and Italy to Washington to discuss general arms limitation. His cable crossed Harvey's dispatch, which was directed at Far Eastern matters. On Saturday, the 9th, with both proposals now under consideration, Hughes stood pat on his disarmament proposal but agreed to broaden it to include Far Eastern affairs. Harding's acquiescence offered no problem; Lloyd George agreed over the weekend and on Monday, July 11, Harding informed the press that informal invitations had gone forward to the four powers for a meeting in Washington to discuss arms limitation, which would also, he indicated almost incidentally, deal with Far Eastern affairs; for this reason China had also been invited.*

Months of national anxiety, of domestic pressures, and of international maneuvering had thus conduced to the calling of a multipurpose conference which neither of the chief parties to the call had originally envisioned. Sparked by Borah and public disarmament sentiment in the United States, the idea of a meeting gathered headway only slowly west of the Atlantic despite repeated British gestures in that direction; it can only be guessed whether, or how soon, these pressures

---

* Formal invitations to the five powers went out on August 11 after acceptance of the informal ones had been received. Because of their interest in the Far East, Belgium, The Netherlands, and Portugal were invited on October 4 to participate in that aspect of the conference.

by themselves would have generated action. At the same time American dissatisfaction with the Anglo-Japanese Alliance coincided with imperial debate over this commitment to a point enabling Britain to move toward a Far Eastern conference to explore a substitute. Hughes's belief that a resolution of Far Eastern differences was essential to a successful disarmament settlement, and his reluctance to yield primacy to Britain in either quarter led him to combine the two in a fashion highly agreeable to Britain. How this would appeal to William E. Borah and to Japan remained to be seen.

The conference call involved the Secretary in a series of problems which would occupy his attention increasingly until November. He had first to fend off three British moves to hold preliminary Anglo-American talks on Far Eastern matters in London. This, said Lloyd George, Harding had suggested. These would make it easier, in the British view, to eliminate the Anglo-Japanese Alliance without offending Britain's partner. Denying that an invitation for a preliminary conference had been extended, Hughes firmly and successfully opposed the meeting, even when Curzon offered to bring the Dominion Prime Ministers to the States for its sessions. His professed ground was that such discussions would inspire domestic charges that the Administration was trying to siphon off attention from naval affairs. It may be surmised, also, that he was not anxious to have either Britain or the Dominions elbowing their way into what was becoming increasingly a Washington performance.

Harding's invitation posed a delicate problem for Japan. She, like others, would welcome the tax relief which armament reduction would afford. This, however, might be a dear price to pay for the threat a conference might level at the comfortable political and economic entrenchment which she had established and had no desire to jeopardize. The Anglo-Japanese Alliance, the Twenty-One Demands, and her territorial and economic foothold on the Asiatic mainland and the Pacific Isles would all come in question, and she had no illusions as to how the United States and China, at least, would view these essentials of her continued well-being. On the other hand, a refusal to parley could only brand her as churlishly uncooperative, and this she could hardly afford.

Japan's technique was to try to ascertain the scope of the proposed gathering and if possible shunt some problems into extraconference channels. She expended some effort, unsuccessfully, in trying to use Hughes in bringing about direct Sino-Japanese discussion of Shantung prior to the assembling of the conference. Hughes being cagey and China suspicious, the matter was left suspended, though in midsummer Hughes did suggest to China the possibility of direct negotiation with Japan, and told the Chinese Minister, Sao-ke Alfred Sze, late in October that the Shantung question must be settled before the conference ended. Tentative Japanese-American discussions over Yap likewise proved abortive. Some weeks of debate in Tokyo, conducted against this background of maneuver, produced a decision to accept membership in the conference, subject to two limitations designed to safeguard Japan's position. Her acceptance carried insistence that the conference agenda be kept free of "problems such as are of *sole concern* to certain particular powers or such matters that may be regarded as *accomplished facts* . . ." (emphasis supplied); thus she sought to keep off limits such ticklish items as Manchuria, Shantung, and the Twenty-One Demands, leaving Hughes with Japan's participation assured but only after considerable pains and with sharp limitations on her position *vis-à-vis* the other conferees.

The personnel of the American delegation was also a matter of some delicacy, from the standpoint of exclusion as well as inclusion. Borah deserved a place by all rights of interest in the problem and his prominence in the Senate, but his established allergy to team effort promptly earned him a seat on the sidelines. Representation of the Senate was a must, however, in the light of Wilson's bitter experience at Versailles. The problem was to justify other appointments after passing over Borah; the solution came in the choice of Henry Cabot Lodge and Oscar W. Underwood, chairman and ranking minority member of the Senate Committee on Foreign Relations respectively and thus almost *ex officio* nominees whose selection Borah could hardly contest publicly. There were ironical aspects in the naming of Lodge, who had been known as a big-navy man, to participate in an international gathering looking to reduced naval armaments, but he proved a good insurance policy. At Hughes's insistence and in the face of one of Harding's few objections to the Secretary's wishes, Elihu Root (known as friendly to Japan) rounded out the group. Hughes thus deliberately risked a delegation composed of two strong men who might, together, tilt a balance against his own wishes.

In another way, however, the Secretary safeguarded his own position, and that of the civilian arm of government, by relegating all members of the armed services to a strictly subservient and advisory capacity. Not only did he subordinate professional personnel in the delegation; though he carefully solicited their opinions, he disregarded or rejected these when offered, and used the naval contingent simply as hewers of wood and drawers of water to furnish the statistics undergirding his essentially political approach to the problems of the conference.

This divorcement of military and naval professionals from the political arm of government would characterize most of the Republican period, forcing the armed services to plan the deployment of a declining military force with no more than accidental knowledge of governmental political thinking. Experience in World War II and its Cold War aftermath in Europe and the Far East would conduce to a much closer coordination of military and political thinking. Indeed, it would be charged from time to time that "The Pentagon," the sprawling administrative center of military machinery unimagined in the 1920's, was exerting influence on policy proportionate to its size but out of harmony with the constitutional position of the military in a democracy. No sources which the writer has seen record accurately the effect of Hughes's cavalier treatment on professional blood pressure. His disregard of their advice, however, was as essential to his plans as it was galling to their sensibilities, though the example which he set was not necessarily a good pattern for the long run.

On July 7 Assistant Secretary of the Navy Theodore Roosevelt, Jr., who worked closely with Hughes during the planning of the Secretary's approach, instructed the Navy's General Board to undertake "a preliminary investigation of limitation of armament by general agreement. . . ." This directive of course countered the Navy's desire for more tonnage. Hughes himself wrote Secretary Denby on September 1 that he was encountering difficulty in establishing a "yardstick" for measuring existing armaments—one which, more ominously, could "also be applied as a standard of measurement in any general plan of reduction." The General Board's partial reply (of September 12) avoided the problem of general disarmament and talked in terms of its own concept of national needs, which involved parity with Britain and necessitated a two-for-one ratio with Japan to cover adequately the American position in the Far East.

Early in October Hughes seems to have concluded that the existing ratio of naval strength among the great powers (as measured by the Navy's yardstick of displacement tonnage) rather than the naval approach through national need, must be the starting point of negotiation, and after talking with the President and the American delegation (Root had arrived independently at the same judgment) began pushing the General Board for figures to support such a policy. On the 25th he repeated formally to Secretary Denby an earlier and informal query as to what Britain and Japan would need to do to match a possible abandonment of the entire American capital-ship building program. The General Board protested loudly and promptly against the dangers of such a course, but on October 30 the delegation, defying the Navy, agreed to propose a naval holiday and the scrapping of all vessels under construction. Since Lodge and Underwood had already informed the delegation that Congress would not pay for what the Navy wanted, this was a less drastic move than might appear at first glance. Properly subdued, if somewhat less than happy, the technicians went to work supplying Hughes with his tonnage figures, and the Secretary had won the domestic side of his fight for reduction.

Having set his course and secured supporting statistics from his unhappy naval bondservants, Hughes adopted a most unusual procedure for the opening session, one which offered several tactical advantages, and which he hoped might start the conference on a more useful bent than previous and fruitless moves in the area of disarmament. In addition to delivering himself of the expected platitudes, he would offer a reasoned and detailed proposal for drastic naval limitation. This would secure him the initiative, would fix him firmly on the crest of the wave of popular sentiment for arms reduction, would disarm possible senatorial criticism, would put the Navy rather than the Far East to the fore, would cut through several stages of conference procedure, and would narrow considerably the area of maneuver open to other participants. Such a scheme necessitated holding the first plenary session on a Saturday, and required the adoption of tight security measures against possible leaks. Hughes's remarks were submitted to the delegation (but not to the President, who was of course privy to their objective), mimeographed by an admiral, locked in the Secretary's safe, and turned over to the government printer on the morning of the address.

Hughes spoke in Constitution Hall on November 12 (the 11th had been ceremonially devoted to burial of the Unknown Soldier at Arlington National Cemetery) to an invited audience of about one thousand, plus three hundred newspapermen, including William Jennings Bryan, who caused some commotion by attempting to take a bow for applause directed toward the French delegate Aristide Briand. Mark Sullivan, then a working newspaperman, described the scene dramatically in *The Great Adventure at Washington* (1922), on which all subsequent narratives rely heavily. Harding had delivered his commonplaces and taken his departure when Hughes arose. His auditors shifted position, preparing for further generalities; in the early stages they were not disappointed—Hughes approached his objective circuitously and it was only after he had reached the normal terminus of such an address that he turned the occasion into what William Allen White, an old hand at high excitement, would retrospectively call "the most intensely dramatic moment I have ever witnessed." Calling for an immediate cessation of the current dangerous and unmanageable naval competition, he urged all hands to unite in the sacrifices required to end it.

He then laid down general principles of procedure, well calculated to horrify his navy-oriented listeners:

(1) That all capital shipbuilding programs, either actual or projected, should be abandoned;

(2) That further reduction should be made through the scrapping of certain of the older ships;

(3) That in general regard should be had to the existing naval strength of the Powers concerned;

(4) That the capital ship tonnage should be used as the

104

measurement of strength for navies and a proportionate allowance of auxiliary combatant craft prescribed.

Having sketched the outline, he then proceeded to blue-
print its implementation, documenting the plan's concrete
application to each of the three great naval powers. Broadly
put, he proposed a ten-year holiday on capital-ship construction, accompanied by wholesale elimination of capital ships
already built or less than 85 percent complete, designed to
reduce the level of naval strength in all categories and leave
the three great powers standing roughly at a ratio of 500,000
tons each for Britain and the United States and 300,000 tons
for Japan (France and Italy were eventually assigned the
ratio of 1.75 as compared with 5/5/3 for the major powers).

Naming specific vessels, he showed how the United States
would sacrifice 845,740 tons, Great Britain 583,375, and Japan 448,928, a total of 1,878,043 tons. Most American naval
officers were as unprepared as their opposite numbers for
this wholesale sacrifice of their interest. Long accustomed to
mastery of the seas, British statesmen and naval leaders received an extra shock as they watched Hughes, in the words
of one of their reporters, sink "in thirty-five minutes more
ships than all the admirals of the world have sunk in a cycle
of centuries." Eliminated, too, were four super-*Hoods*, great
battleships authorized but not yet laid down. Japan, asked to
sacrifice less, was yet to be deprived of *Mutsu*, well on to
completion through gifts of schoolchildren's yen. Hughes
thus demanded sacrifices of power and pride in the interest
of stabilization on a lower level, but was prepared for his own
country to make the heaviest sacrifice. The session adjourned

on this exciting if ominous note, to reassemble on Tuesday, the 15th.

By this time the first shock of Hughes's proposals had worn off and the chiefs of other delegations responded guardedly. The hugely favorable popular reaction forbade outright repudiation, and all hands perforce accepted the Hughes *démarche* "in principle" before taking refuge in qualifications. Mr. Arthur J. Balfour blandly pointed out that Britain could hardly be expected to surrender her two-for-one position relative to her strongest European rival, to risk impoverishment of British shipbuilders by immediate acceptance of the ten-year naval holiday, or to swallow without examination Hughes's proposals on cruisers and destroyers. Admiral Tomosaburo Kato let it be known that Japan would desire "a few modifications," which he was not yet prepared to spell out. Senator Carlo Schanzer warned that Italy must not be expected to drop behind France, and Briand foreshadowed what would become a more and more evident suspicion of both Britain and the United States. Thus the lines were drawn for the infighting that would characterize the remainder of the meeting.

Conference machinery followed the normal pattern in which occasional plenary sessions offered a forum for the presentation and ratification of decisions already made on a working level. Hughes, whom Balfour had already courteously nominated as presiding officer, served as *ex officio* chairman of all the operative committees and spread himself as broadly as possible over their numerous sessions. Delegation chiefs constituted themselves an unofficial steering committee, but the real decisions were made by the Big Three, Hughes, Balfour, and Kato. Within this framework Hughes, seeing the President daily and meeting the delegation almost as often, kept action within limits generally satisfactory to both. As always, the committees split into subcommittees which in turn were served by the technical and professional experts who furnished the factual basis for the arguments which were hammered into decisions on succeeding levels.

Three major multipartite agreements resulted: the Four-Power Pact between Britain, France, the United States, and Japan; the Five-Power Pact, including Italy as well as the parties to the Four-Power treaty; and the Nine-Power Pact, including all Conference members. Cognate documents were a Sino-Japanese Treaty on Shantung, a Japanese-American Treaty settling the Yap disagreement (signed February 11, 1922, after the Conference had adjourned), a Japanese promise to evacuate Siberia, and the later abrogation (April 14, 1923) of the Lansing-Ishii Agreement. The bewildering array of overlapping negotiations which produced these arrangements greatly moderated immediate tensions while contributing to others which would appear during the ensuing years. The picture eventually emerging resulted from a procession of gigantic horse trades in which each power sought to buy maximum security at minimum expense. Concessions in one treaty were paid for in others, until the complex process of give and take had been completed. Against this background, also, Japan and China were brought, under joint Anglo-American pressure, to compose some of their own difficulties.

The Four-Power Pact, basic to the bargaining progression, substituted a multilateral consultative treaty for the Anglo-Japanese Alliance. It eased American suspicions of possible machinations in which Japan might use her British connection to cover further Asiatic aggression, but kept Britain as a working partner in the peace-keeping machinery and in effect served as a reinsurance of American suzerainty over the Philippines. By paving the way for the nonfortification agreement in Article XIX of the Five-Power Pact, it also helped to break down Japan's obstinate opposition to acceptance of an inferior tonnage ratio.

It appears to have been Hughes's technique to avoid taking the initiative in this essentially Anglo-Japanese problem, though he, and informed American opinion, greatly desired to end the Alliance. He had not long to wait. It will be recalled that in June Hughes and Sir Auckland Geddes had discussed, inconclusively, a substitute for it. Hardly was the Unknown Hero interred on November 11 when Balfour appeared in Hughes's office to submit, personally, unofficially, and not under instructions, a memorandum suggesting a tripartite Far Eastern treaty which would have virtually incorporated the United States into the Alliance. Hughes played coy, preferring to substitute a broad statement of principles and policies for the Root-Takahira Agreement of 1908, the Lansing-Ishii Agreement of 1917, and the Alliance.

Though Balfour was willing to substitute "arrangements" for the "Treaty" of his original draft, Hughes was still wary, later pointing out that the Balfour scheme did not definitely cancel the Alliance, and that the two could at any time depart the proposed tripartite arrangement and renew their alliance, to the detriment of American interests. At the first interview Hughes adroitly suggested his preference for a four-power arrangement, including France; involving a fourth partner would serve to offset possible Anglo-Japanese maneuvers inimical to American interests.

Hughes disapproved of a four-power agreement, drafted by American legal advisers, which reached him on November 22 because it did not cancel the Alliance. A Japanese draft of November 26 was also unsatisfactory because it did not include France. Both the Balfour proposal of November 11 and the Japanese draft contained mutual pledges of non-aggression, but included East Asia and the Pacific Ocean in their purview. Acceptance would have condoned existing Japanese aggressions and estopped American opposition to further Japanese expansion, and Hughes refused to do either. At first using members of the American delegation in preparing an alternative draft, he soon dropped this approach, and the final document, mainly his own handiwork, emerged from sessions of the delegation chiefs; he later apologized to Chandler P. Anderson of his legal staff, who had tried unsuccessfully to correct apparent faults in the earlier document, for thus bypassing his technical experts. Among his own contributions to the finished product were inclusion of France, upon which he had insisted from the beginning, and narrowing the agreement's geographical scope. The British and Japanese plans applied the proposed pledges to rights and interests in Asia as well as to the Pacific Islands; Hughes refused to recognize this acceptance of Japan's position in Shantung, and succeeded in narrowing the treaty's application to "insular possessions and dominions in the Pacific Ocean." Thus, instead of underwriting Japanese expansionism, the treaty secured recognition of American dominion over the Philippines.

Japan, unhappy at this American refusal to admit the facts of life on the Asiatic mainland, successfully sought recompense in another direction. Toward the end of November, while four-power negotiations made little headway, naval discussions dragged because of Japanese reluctance to accept the inferiority imposed by the 10/6 ratio of the Hughes proposals. On December 1 Admiral Kato proposed what eventually emerged as Article xix of the Five-Power Pact, limiting Anglo-American as well as Japanese rights to fortify their Pacific possessions in return for Japanese acceptance of tonnage inferiority. As this proposal began to materialize, Japan's opposition to the consultative pact diminished. Meantime, France was restive at being excluded from participation in naval conversations, and Hughes was anxious to throw her a crumb by alerting her to the possibility of membership in the proposed four-power agreement.

On December 2, the day after Kato's nonfortification proposal reached him, Hughes asked the Admiral how things stood on the consultative pact and was told that Japan would probably sign. Congestion on the cables delayed by several days Japan's final acceptance, but on December 7 Hughes took a draft agreement, already acceptable to Balfour and

Kijuro Shidehara, to René Viviani of the French delegation. Viviani, delighted at this tardy recognition of French importance, bestowed a Gallic embrace on both wings of Hughes's beard. Matters came rapidly to a head. On December 10 Henry Cabot Lodge, innocent of participation in its composition but important for his potential influence in securing senatorial approval, loyally presented the agreement to the Fourth Plenary Session of the Conference, and formal signature occurred three days later.

The treaty specifically terminated the Anglo-Japanese Alliance, committed its signatories to respect each others' rights "in relation to their insular possessions and insular dominions in the region of the Pacific Ocean," to confer in case dispute over those rights arose among the Four, and to consult in case outsiders threatened the *status quo*. Failure to include sanctions was later attacked as a fatal weakness, but no amount of energy or propaganda could have included such an article in the treaty or sold it to the Senate at that time. As things stood, the Hughes strategy had shunted Britain from a bilateral partnership, bound to condone Japanese depredations and perhaps support further aggression, into a multilateral pact designed to maintain the *status quo* in an area where Japanese positions in the Carolines, Marshalls, and Marianas dominated the sea-lanes to Manila. Thus was enacted the first great horse trade of the conference, in which the nonfortification clause of one treaty facilitated Japanese acceptance of another—a trade which Borah, after three hours' examination of its terms would dub a bad deal and which he would charge, after longer study, concealed a secret alliance with Britain.

111

One matter remained in contention to the very end of the conference. Shidehara had wanted Japan's home islands specifically excluded from the Pact's applicability to the "insular possessions and insular dominions" of the four signatory powers, on the grounds (a) that such might be interpreted as international meddling in Japan's domestic affairs; and (b) that it set Japan apart from the other principal partners, since it applied to neither the British nor the American homelands. Balfour had pooh-poohed Shidehara's fears, arguing that there was no more point to excluding the Japanese home islands than to making a specific exception on behalf of Australia and New Zealand, but Shidehara remained firm. The next morning, however, he reversed himself and agreed to have the Pact include Japan's main islands and, as of the December 10 date of announcement, it was generally understood that the main islands were included, and there was an informal and confidential but not-too-definite understanding that Karafuto (the Japanese portion of Sakhalin), the Pescadores, Oshima, and Formosa would be placed in the nonfortified category. The matter remained one for comment, however, and a presidential *faux pas* kept it alive when Harding, pressed by reporters for comment but ignorant of the facts, asserted (on December 20) that the home islands were *not* included; when Hughes set him straight, he apologized honestly but lamely: "I didn't want to appear to be a dub." Neither did Shidehara; acting under orders he returned to the charge and secured signature (on February 6, 1922) of an agreement supplementary to the Four-Power Pact specifically stating that the "insular possessions and insular dominions" of the Pact, as far as Japan was concerned, should be

112

confined to Karafuto, Formosa, the Pescadores, and the mandated islands, leaving the Pact inapplicable to the main islands. (See below, pp. 122–124.)

The Four-Power Pact enabled the politicians, dominant at Washington, to turn a potential stalemate over dissolution of the Anglo-Japanese Alliance into a pathway to limited agreement on naval armaments in the Five-Power Pact, the major achievement of the Conference. Here, as before, the principal issues arose and were worked out among the three major powers, and again the chief problem was to persuade Japan to accept what at first blush seemed a situation less favorable than the existing one but which, when coupled with other developments and tested by time, redounded to her advantage. Paralleling the consultative pact discussions in time, the naval conversations outranked the former in length, in bitterness, and in immediate importance. Hughes and Kato were the principal antagonists, with Balfour actively mediating while seeking to salvage any possible portion of British advantage.

Japan's demands of November 16 delineated the area of conflict. Included were a ratio of 10/10/7 in capital ships instead of the 10/10/6 suggested by Hughes, parity in aircraft carriers, and retention of the *Mutsu*, which Hughes had consigned to the scrap heap. The *Mutsu*, it was argued, was completed and so entitled to remain the pride of Japan's fleet. Realistically, her retention, along with the other demands, would guarantee that dominance in western Pacific waters which Japan believed essential to her security; it was, too, important for domestic political reasons. Days of technical argument followed, with Japan's experts marshaling evidence to support her strategic and political necessities, with Britain supporting American opposition to Japanese claims, and with the Americans standing pat, apparently hoping that the extra expenditures involved in supporting the higher ratio would give Japan pause. These technical discussions reached a deadlock by the end of November, but a political approach, developing early in December, paved the way to ultimate agreement on the 10/10/6 level, though only after long-drawn-out and at times acrimonious argument.

It will be recalled that Japan was simultaneously balking at trading her British alliance for a less prestigious consultative pact. On December 1 a Kato proposal to Balfour was promptly relayed to Hughes, and a three-way discussion took place on the following day. This proposal, mentioned above, was to trade Japanese acceptance of 10/10/6 for retention of the *Mutsu* and an American promise not to fortify further her Pacific possessions—the one which, in its ultimate form, eased the adoption of the Four-Power Pact. A lively conference ensued. Kato argued that the *Mutsu* was in commission and had already gone five hundred miles under her own steam. In his great determination to improve Japanese-American relations he would, however, support the 10/10/6 ratio. An American promise to forego further fortification of Guam, the Philippines, and Hawaii would aid him greatly in this unpopular task; in return he would urge non-fortification of Formosa, the Pescadores and Oshima. Hughes argued vigorously that the 10/10/6 apportionment favored Japan, with no strong naval neighbors, as against the

United States with two vulnerable coastlines to defend, and Britain with long commerce lanes to guard.

Although Kato made the original proposal, it was Hughes who tied it to the consultative pact; as a memorandum in the Hughes Papers points out, the Secretary insisted that it would be

> impossible for him to consider these matters except as a part of the acceptance by Baron Kato of a general agreement which would also embrace the proposed quadruple entente in the Pacific. . . . It was impossible for him, after the great concessions involved in the proposals for the limitation of armaments, to go on making further concessions without some return.

He refused, furthermore, to include Hawaii in the self-denying ordinance, arguing that its posture was a purely defensive one. Balfour supported Hughes, insisting that Japan was "perfectly secure under this ratio." Kato, obviously impressed by the Anglo-American arguments, was obliged to consult Tokyo, which, with the limited cable facilities available, he estimated would take at least a week.

Other matters occupied the principals for some days and it was only after the Four-Power Pact had been agreed upon and submitted to a plenary session and Kato had heard from home that they resumed negotiation on December 12. The Baron reported that he could accept 10/10/6, but insisted on retention of the *Mutsu,* which had been busily steaming about in the interim and had now logged 2,500 miles; in return he proposed to scrap the *Settsu,* another prized Japanese unit. Hughes agreed to the *status quo* on Guam and the

115

Philippines, but again excepted Hawaii, to which Kato agreed. Hughes and Balfour united in attempting to bully Kato into giving up the *Mutsu,* by insisting that her retention would force both powers into further building. Kato stuck to his guns, and an adjournment was taken to consult the experts in an effort to fit the *Mutsu* into the 10/10/6 ratio. These figures, proffered on the 13th, essentially preserved the ratio, leaving the United States slightly above and Japan slightly below. At this point Balfour, sensing an opportunity to bargain, proposed to retain two post-Jutland battleships, designed but not yet built, and heavier than the 35,000-ton top called for in the Hughes proposals; for these he would scrap extra tonnage of older vessels. Another adjournment for consultation with experts followed an exchange of acerbities between the westerners.

The 14th witnessed further haggling over British tonnage, with Balfour holding out for construction of two super-*Hoods* at 49,000 tons each in return for scrapping older tonnage. Hughes and Kato unitedly opposed this attempt to exceed the 35,000-ton limit as giving Britain an undue advantage which would simply escalate existing rivalry to a higher tonnage level. After two fruitless sessions, another adjournment passed the controversy back to the technicians. These were evidently adamant, as Balfour continued to insist on the two super-*Hoods* on the 15th. Hughes sustained his pressure and, after crossing the hall to confer with his naval adviser, Balfour returned to the conference and announced dramatically that he would overrule his experts and commit his Government to substituting two 35,000-ton battleships for the larger vessels. Commentators have generally acclaimed his courage in giving a political accommodation precedence over a naval necessity. It may be pointed out, however, that the entire American program was based on a negation of professional naval opinion; Hughes's technicians had been in limbo since October. The variant attitudes are doubtless reflective of the relative importance of sea power to the two nations and, critics of the settlement would argue, reflective likewise of the realities of power.

Hughes's day of drama was not yet finished. Japanese-American cooperation having disposed of this British threat, a French menace appeared. French unhappiness had mounted from the moment when Aristide Briand had found himself at the opening ceremonies seated around the bend of the U-shaped table, instead of at its base with the other chiefs of delegation. This minor irritation increased when it became apparent that the agenda would not permit discussion of limiting land armaments, vastly important to France. With the conference more than a month old, she had been involved only nominally in naval discussions. It had already been Hughes's task to bring this noninvolvement to an unhappy end, and he faced two angry and excited Frenchmen after the three-power conference had ended in agreement.

Some consideration had already been given to the naval potential to be accorded France and Italy, and the American experts had suggested 175,000 tons (1.75, in terms of ratio) as a proper figure for each power. When these figures were proposed (on December 12) a French-style hurricane blew up. Both Briand and Viviani had gone home late in November to look after their domestic chores, leaving French interests in charge of Jules Jusserand and Albert Sarraut.

117

Hughes had avoided discussion of this blow to Gallic pride while completing discussions with Britain and Japan, contenting himself with inquiries, hitherto ignored, as to what tonnage France felt would meet her needs. Further avoidance was impossible, however, and he saw the two Frenchmen after Balfour and Kato had departed and reported to them Big Three agreement on 10/10/6. Again requesting a figure, he was "astounded" when Sarraut replied that France would need 350,000 tons. He pointed out, quite correctly, that this was a larger figure than Japan's and added, equally correctly but less diplomatically, that France, unable to pay her war debts, could ill afford the consequent financial burden. The meeting ended on an indeterminate note, with Sarraut refusing compromise.

The French demands were leaked into print, doubtless useful in Hughes's maneuver of the 16th. He pointed out to Jusserand that strict observance of the reduction formula would have granted France only 102,000 tons, and that unless she accepted the proposed figure she would find herself in the ratio of 6/1 to the combined Anglo-American tonnage. He had meantime recalled Briand's parting remark that though absent he was still head of the French delegation, and suggesting that Hughes communicate with him in case of need. Seizing this loophole, a joint Hughes-Balfour cable urged Briand to accept the proffered tonnage. He agreed to 1.75 on capital ships on the 18th, but in turn demanded not less than 330,000 tons of subsidiary craft, including cruisers and destroyers, and specifying 90,000 tons of submarines. Britain shortly used this decision to justify her own refusal to limit destroyers. Thus, through French recalcitrance,

Hughes's hope of applying limitation-by-ratio to all categories of naval craft went glimmering. Apparently a matter of less than major importance at the time, this failure would emerge into a prime source of friction as the decade wore on.

Provisional agreement among the great powers was announced on December 15, against the background of the French difficulties just described. Considerable time, however, had to be spent in negotiating further issues consequent on failure to apply the ratio principle to cruisers and submarines. Britain, with her insular location dependent upon commerce and her need to maintain contacts with her far-flung empire, was understandably reluctant to curtail her surface craft, while France and Italy persistently claimed the right to build large submarine tonnage. Britain, therefore, refused to limit her right to build what surface tonnage she considered essential to deal with the developing situation. This refusal to limit overall construction produced an American proposal of limitation by tonnage-per-unit, and eventually it was agreed, on Hughes's suggestion, that cruisers should not exceed 10,000 tons' displacement, nor should they mount guns of greater than 8-inch caliber. Since this matter of cruiser size and gun caliber was to cause considerable ill will during the remainder of our period, some explanation is in order.

British naval architects had developed during the recent war the *Hawkins* class of cruisers, displacing nearly 10,000 tons, mounting 7.5-inch guns, and capable of cruising long distances at 30 knots. Though designed to protect commerce against submarines, they were easily adaptable to destroying enemy merchantmen. Japan, too, had numbers of 6,000-ton cruisers, mounting 5.5-inch guns and still speedier than the British *Hawkins* class. Talk of war with Japan in 1920 and the distinct likelihood of an Anglo-American construction race caused American professionals to bethink themselves of a proper counter for British tonnage and of Japanese maneuverability in a theater far from American bases. Thus by 1921 the preponderance of naval opinion had settled on the 10,000-ton, 8-inch-gun cruiser as the optimum weapon for both Atlantic and Pacific operations, and Hughes's suggestion, whether reflecting Navy advice or developed on his own was cordially received and was accepted with little discussion as an immediate solution of a ticklish problem. As the subsequent story will show, an acute cruiser rivalry would shortly develop, and tonnages and gun calibers would make trouble little dreamed of by those who adopted, almost lightly, Hughes's way out of an impasse.

Later critics of the Conference would inveigh against its modest accomplishments in dealing with air power. In fairness it should be remembered that although a few (particularly Brigadier General William Mitchell) were alert to its potentialities, no one knew what to do about them. A subcommittee of the Conference, of which Mitchell was a member, worked a month on the problem of limiting the warlike uses of airplanes, and threw up its hands in despair, averring that the only feasible limitation was total abolition of the airplane! The conference succeeded in approaching the problem only obliquely, through limiting the tonnage of aircraft carriers, assigning Britain and the United States 135,000 tons each, Japan 81,000, and France and Italy 60,000 each.

Much of the cruiser problem had resulted from failure to deal successfully with the submarine. Britain, recently harried by German U-boats, preferred to outlaw the device entirely; finding no great enthusiasm for this idea, she inevitably looked askance at French demands, which crystallized on December 28 at a level of 90,000 tons. French pride was stung by the niggardly 1.75 ratio in battleships and, perhaps, by the indignity of being equated in naval power with Italy, and the French made the demand for substantial submarine tonnage the price of final acceptance of the humiliating battleship allowance. The only possible approach to French intransigence was through an attempt to humanize the use of the new and deadly weapon. American ingenuity was directed toward this knotty problem and a proposal was elaborated and embodied in a treaty designed to obviate a repetition of German tactics used between 1914 and 1918. Such an agreement did not, indeed could not in the existing climate, interdict merchantmen from carrying armament fatal to the thin-skinned undersea craft. Repetition of the tactics of 1914–1918, when British and later American vessels carried armaments and goods simultaneously, could only invite repetition of German tactics; France alone failed to ratify the treaty, which remained in effect, but ineffective, until replaced in 1930 by a still more innocuous agreement.

A draft treaty, largely the work of Theodore Roosevelt, Jr., Admiral William V. Pratt, one of the few high-ranking naval officers in sympathy with what his civilian masters were trying to do, and Professor James Grafton Wilson of Harvard, was presented to the experts of the five delegations on January 7, 1922. It carried solutions to most problems, but left one matter deliberately undetermined. Reference to the account of the Four-Power Pact will remind the reader that the three chiefs of delegation had informally agreed in December on what areas were subject to the nonfortification restrictions to be spelled out in the Five-Power Pact as payment for Japanese acceptance of the 10/10/6 ratio. The public announcement of three-power acceptance of the ratio, issued to the press on December 15, had also reported adoption of the *status quo* in "the Pacific region," which was not further defined except that the British base at Hong Kong was specifically included in the standstill agreement. Freedom to establish defense installations was accorded Canada and the United States, as well as "the islands including Japan proper." Here was a phrase which soon plagued the American technicians assigned to reduce its elastic terms to the precise language of international agreement. Sensing possible unpleasantness, the experts simply transferred the imprecise language of the press release to the draft treaty and awaited developments.

Japan promptly proposed to exclude Oshima and the Bonin Islands from the nonfortification stipulations; though they were several hundred miles from the central island group, she argued that the Bonins were not governed as colonies, but as part of "Japan proper." Britain claimed exemption from the stipulations of all islands *outside* an interesting parallelogram bounded east-and-west by the 180th and 110th meridians and north-and-south by 30° north latitude and the equator. This would permit fortification of most of her mandated islands and estop the United States and Japan from fortifying most of their possessions and mandates. Neither Japan nor Britain could see the other left free to fortify, and a deadlock ensued between January 10 and January 29. The documents supported the American contention that the December negotiations had left Oshima, the Pescadores, and Formosa subject to a nonfortification restriction; Kato agreed in January that he had also included the Bonins, which his Government was now trying to exclude. The United States, of course, could hardly condone this violation of an understanding which would advance the Japanese offensive perimeter several hundred miles toward Guam and the Philippines.

Japan, however, had a point to make. The December negotiations had not settled the status of the Aleutian Islands or of Singapore, both potentially dangerous to Japan. The Aleutians, stretching hundreds of miles west from Alaska, could house bases within striking distance of Japan's industrial complex; Singapore, hitherto a minor installation, dominated the Straits of Malacca and the trade routes upon which Japan would become dependent in case of war with the United States. And pending before the Dominions was an agreement of the Imperial Conference of 1921 to support British proposals to strengthen Singapore's defensive and offensive capabilities as part of an overall revamping of imperial defense plans. Compromise of these differences required several days of haggling, and it was only on January 29 that agreement was reached on the fortifications Article (xix) of the treaty. Here were spelled out the areas in which each of the great powers agreed to preserve the *status quo* on fortifications and naval bases. In the bargaining, the United States had included the Aleutians in the standstill category;

Britain lost her parallelogram, included Hong Kong, but succeeded in excluding Singapore; Japan applied the *status quo,* by name, to the Kurile, Bonin, Loochoo, and Pescadores Islands and to Oshima and Formosa. As presented by Hughes to a Plenary Session on February 1 and as signed on February 6, the Five-Power Pact completed the treaty signed the same day, supplementing the Four-Power Pact and adding Karafuto and the mandated islands (as well as repeating Formosa and the Pescadores) to the *status quo* area. All in all, the naval ratio, plus the standstill agreements, embodied the second stage of the global horse trade whereby Japan, in return for a self-abnegating acceptance of technical naval inferiority held her potential enemies at a distance where their armaments of the day would be ineffective against her defensive potential.

Despite the multiple efforts to establish a Far Eastern equilibrium, neither China nor the Western powers completely trusted Japan's good intentions; American interest in the Open Door, sporadic and ineffective though it had been over the years, was raised to a high pitch by Japan's war and postwar efforts to interfere with its operation, and Hughes decided early upon a vigorous attempt to elevate the doctrine from the level of a unilateral American policy to that of conventional international law. Thus it was that he asked Japan, having already surrendered her British alliance and her naval pretensions, albeit for a price, to yield yet again and permit her imperial designs, grounded on a Western pattern, to be blunted by subscribing legally to a Western doc-

124

trine to which she had never paid more than lip service. That she ultimately did so in the Nine-Power Pact has been variously explained as a triumph of Western pressure tactics, as proof of Japan's international good will, or as an empty gesture based on the conviction that other aspects of the general settlement were sufficiently valuable to warrant a paper promise of good behavior which carried no sanctions against behaving badly. At any rate, the treaty, signed on February 6, completed the major accomplishments of the conference and climaxed the global horse trade by which the Western powers, having weaned Japan from the British alliance in the Four-Power Pact and, perhaps, overcompensated her in Article XIX, now sought to discount the payment by signing her to a self-denying ordinance.

Discussion at an early session of the Committee on Pacific and Far Eastern Questions proceeded to a point where Elihu Root volunteered to draft some general principles, which he offered to the group on November 21. These "principles" underwent verbal changes but emerged essentially intact as Article I of the treaty. The first avowed the intention of the powers to "respect the sovereignty, the independence, and the territorial and administrative integrity of China"—traditional Open Door language. The second promised aid in Chinese efforts to achieve governmental stability, and the third vowed allegiance to the principle of equal commercial opportunity in China. The fourth brought a skeleton from the diplomatic closet and paraded it as a public limitation upon Japan as well as upon the other powers.

The Lansing-Ishii Agreement of 1917 was an exercise in which each party sought to persuade the other to an undesirable commitment. Under cover of pious Open Door verbiage Lansing sought, he felt successfully, to confine Japan's imperialism in China to the economic realm; Ishii sought, he felt successfully, to secure Lansing's recognition of Japan's political interests on the mainland. As if doubtful of his own success, Lansing persuaded Ishii to sign the first secret protocol in the history of American foreign relations, in which the parties agreed not to "take advantage of present conditions to seek special rights or privileges which would abridge the rights of the citizens or subjects of other friendly states." Hughes had called Root's attention to this secret document, and it went practically verbatim into Root's "principles," with the additional phrase "and from countenancing action inimical to the security of such States." This promise, because of its secrecy, had hitherto furnished no brake on Japanese imperialism. If it could be made part of a public document, subscribed to by many nations, Japan would be publicly accountable for violation of her now-public pledge. The end was laudable and the method adroit—it cancelled the protocol without public acknowledgment of its existence. Only in 1938, when the Washington Conference documents were published, did this story become public.

Presentation of the Root Principles, with later provisions designed to spell out their objective, presented Japan with a difficult problem. With Britain backing the United States in supporting principles to which she herself had repeatedly subscribed, she was almost compelled to veil any hesitancy she may have felt and to line up with the Western powers in declaring herself "against sin." She doubtless realized, as did others, particularly China, that the treaty hardly freed that

126

unhappy land from existing limits on national sovereignty. Its signature did, however, elevate the Open Door to a new status by making it part of conventional international law and went, in the late Yale President A. Whitney Griswold's phrase, "as far as pen and ink could go" toward establishing it on a multilateral base. The key to its ultimate failure is of course also patent in Dr. Griswold's phrase; as in the case of the Four-Power Pact signed earlier, a sense of national morality was the only key to its observance—no sanctions deterred any signatory from violating his own word and China's status under its provisions.

Attention, so far focused on the necessities of the Great Powers, should now turn to China, long prevented by domestic turmoil and foreign privilege from attaining many of the normal goals of nationhood, but hopeful that the present conference would, at long last, improve her lot. Torn by revolution and civil war since 1911, she had made no progress toward throwing off the "unequal treaties" giving foreigners control of her tariff (and so, to a large extent, of her economy) and exempting them (through possession of extraterritorial rights) from the jurisdiction of her laws. During World War I Japan had seized the German sphere of influence in Shantung and presented the infamous Twenty-One Demands, involving galling encroachments on Chinese sovereignty. China failed at Versailles to secure the redress she sought and welcomed the invitation to Washington as an opportunity to purge Shantung of foreign interlopers and, hopefully, to mitigate the structures of the unequal treaties.

Japan, by the same token, saw the conference as a threat to her position on the mainland as well as in the Pacific, and hedged her participation in it by proclaiming the doctrines of "sole concern" and of "accomplished fact." These antithetical hopes and fears hardly augured well for a successful negotiation.

The earlier story has recounted (p. 99) abortive moves during the summer toward direct Sino-Japanese negotiations. These ended in early September when Japan handed China (on the 7th) an unacceptable proposal. As the conference opened, then, China was demanding and Japan was hanging back, and neither was speaking to the other. Anglo-American conviction that a settlement was essential produced joint pressure on the parties and an extracurricular and time-consuming but ultimately successful procedure. Unwilling to "negotiate" directly, the two Eastern powers agreed to discuss matters in the presence of British and American representatives. Thirty-six such sessions, with Hughes and MacMurray counseling the Chinese and Balfour performing a like service for Japan, produced a Sino-Japanese agreement, signed on February 4, 1922. This was not achieved easily, however, and it became necessary to exert pressure on both parties.

With discussions getting nowhere, Hughes learned early in January that some influential senators had linked the China problem with the Five-Power Pact and were determined to defeat the one unless progress were made with the other. This emerging crisis apparently persuaded Balfour, who had announced his delegation's departure for the end of January, to remain for further discussion. Matters came to a

128

head shortly after midmonth, triggered by Senator Thomas Walsh's resolution (of the 20th) asking for a progress report on Shantung. Debate on this made it clear that only a Far Eastern political settlement would win senatorial support of a naval agreement. Balfour conveyed this fact to the Japanese, and Hughes (accompanied by Balfour) called the Chinese on the carpet at his home (on the 22d) to deliver the same message, the while instructing Jacob Gould Schurman, the American Minister at Peking, to press China to reduce her demands. All this produced a settlement which provided satisfactions for both parties and in the long run deprived Japan of the shadow and left her the substance. Political control of Shantung reverted to China, but Japan retained sufficient economic control so that China's victory was somewhat hollow.

Elsewhere, China was hardly more successful. A few token concessions failed to shake Japan's hold on Manchuria. Her formal withdrawal of some of the more extreme of the Twenty-One Demands (those in Group v) meant little more, since these had been recognized since 1915 as unenforceable. Her promise of early troop withdrawal from Siberia (made on January 23, 1922) was more important to Russian and to American prestige than to that of China. A nine-power agreement of February 6 permitted China an immediate tariff increase of 5 per cent, but postponed real tariff autonomy to an indeterminate date. Regarding extraterritoriality, she secured no more than a resolution promising future study of the entire question. On the whole, China fared badly at Washington, and her disappointments would color her relations with the West through the rest of our period.

•

The thorny problem of Yap, under serious negotiation since June, was laid to rest in a December agreement ultimately embodied in a Japanese-American treaty signed on February 11 after the conference had adjourned. The United States at last recognized Japanese mandatory rights over the former German islands north of the equator, and in return Japan granted the United States equal commercial rights in the islands, particularly the use of Yap for cable landings. Political quipsters and cartoonists were thus deprived of what had threatened to become a permanent item for use when there was a dearth of colorful grist for their mills.

Submission of the treaties to the Senate signaled a considerable propaganda battle. Press and peace agencies were in support, and Harding added his voice to those of Lodge and Underwood from the delegation. Gilbert M. Hitchcock who, as Woodrow Wilson's standard bearer in the fight over the Versailles Treaty, had faced Lodge's thrusts, now sought to embarrass the Republicans by calling for the documents basic to the Four-Power Pact. Harding's refusal, however, was based on solid grounds of precedent. Borah, Frank B. Brandegee, and Joseph T. Robinson were prominent opponents, ringing the changes on a variety of charges, chief among which was that the treaty contained secret Anglo-American commitments and that it constituted an alliance. Despite the accusations, the Committee on Foreign Relations recommended all the treaties favorably, and Lodge and

130

Underwood defended them stoutly, the former standing un-
abashed, if not unembarrassed, by claims that he had
changed camps from nonentanglement to entanglement. The
Four-Power Pact received Senate acceptance with only four
votes to spare (67/27), carrying the standard reservation to
the effect that ratification carried no connotation of alliance
and no commitment to use force in its support. The opposition shot its bolt in this debate and the remaining agreements
drew little debate and few opponents. Mark Sullivan's *Great
Adventure at Washington* was launched.

Few complicated international settlements have been subjected to sharper critical examination than that which
Hughes and his colleagues had molded. It seems to the
writer that proper appraisal of their work must proceed on
two levels, an assessment first, in terms of efficacy in solving
immediate problems and second, in terms of success in the
longer run and in light of later developments. Examination
on either level evidences clearly that the United States was
no shirker of international involvement in the area of disarmament, where she assumed her share of the initiative and
bore at least her share of the burdens.

Assessment on the first level must take account of current
conditions. Called to moderate the mounting naval rivalry
and international suspicion, the conference perforce dealt
with both technical and political problems. Its principal
members operated within domestic frameworks demanding
at least lip service to public opinion. This created an atmosphere where, though each must yield at points to secure

agreement, none could yield too much without facing unhappy political consequences. The combination of technical
and political objectives, too, subjected each to the unfavorable reaction of navy professionals when political concessions
endangered ingrained strategic concepts. Under all these
circumstances the Hughes tactics constituted an imaginative
and statesmanlike approach to both technical and political
problems. In light of existing naval rivalry, the ratio/naval-
holiday scheme went a long way toward easing an economic
burden becoming increasingly intolerable to vocal elements
in each Big Three nation. Substitution of a milder consultative pact for the Anglo-Japanese Alliance eased tensions in
this quarter. The nonfortification agreement assuaged Japanese pride, affronted at the suggestion of naval inferiority.
And the Nine-Power Pact was hopefully designed to bind
Japan to real observation of a hitherto little-respected doctrine.

Profit-and-loss elements characterized each of the principal agreements, some obvious and immediate, others proxi-
mate or even hidden from view. The Four-Power Treaty
relieved Britain of an increasingly burdensome obligation,
which she would not have honored against the United States
in a crisis. It lost Japan the exclusive partnership of Britain
and tacit British connivance at her Continental conquests. It
registered American refusal to recognize Japan's position in
Shantung and was designed to secure American possession of
the Philippines. It purchased recognition of the *status quo* in
the Western Pacific at the cost of the nonfortification agreement, considered at the time (by all but the navy professionals) as a cheap price in view of developing congressional nig-

132

gardliness with necessary dollars. It sought to establish an equilibrium whose cement was great-power good will and forbearance.

The Five-Power Pact cost the United States most in terms of actual naval strength, since the technicalities of the scrapping and nonconstruction provisions favored Britain slightly. Enhanced British good will for the moment neutralized this slight American concession, and establishment of the ratio principle was a tribute to Hughes's imagination and persistence. The 5/3 ratio (despite its unfavorable numerical connotation), plus the nonfortification agreement, left Japan in effective control of the Western Pacific. Perhaps, indeed, the most practical immediate aspect of this treaty was its effect of parcelling out sea space among the Big Three, conceding the United States dominance in the Atlantic (Britain's slight edge in combat effectiveness being neutralized by the vast area of her empire), leaving Japan in effective control of the Western Pacific, and setting Britain astride the sea lanes from the Channel to Singapore. Altogether, here was another equilibrium. The major weakness in the naval quarter was failure to extend the ratio principle to auxiliary vessels, but this became clearer with the passage of time. The Nine-Power Pact was the cement which was to preserve the total equilibrium by raising the self-denying aspects of the Open Door from an American prescription to the level of an international agreement.

Thus, many ends had been served. A naval race had apparently been averted; if Far Eastern discords had not been turned into harmony, at least some major dissonances had been softened. A start had been made, within a limiting framework, toward realization of ends desired by all. Hughes and his fellows had certainly slowed a dizzy pace, although his own judgment, that their work "absolutely ends the race in naval armament," was a trifle optimistic. Perhaps the great accomplishment was that bargaining had been substituted for unrestricted building, some international tensions had been relieved, a breathing space had been gained, and some of the hummocks in an exceedingly rough international land-scape had been lowered.

And yet many were unhappy, even at the time. Quite obvi-ously, curtailment of their specialty would please few naval officers, and there was well-nigh universal grumbling from this quarter of Hughes's roughshod treatment of the service. The spokesman for American dissatisfaction was Captain Dudley W. Knox, whose *The Eclipse of American Sea Power* (1922) and other writings voiced the professional point of view. From the scholarly standpoint, Raymond Leslie Buell's *The Washington Conference* (1922) was sharply critical of the failure of statesmanship to halt Japanese imperialism. American press comment, except for the Hearst papers, was generally favorable; the Japanese press reacted vigorously to alleged slights and losses contained in the agreement. To-kyo's militarists and imperialists found little to delight them.

Time and later developments would render a less kindly verdict on the second level, long-run results, though on re-viewing the tortuous course of the negotiations, it is hard to envision better solutions in the light of current conditions. Time would bring out the unwisdom of dependence upon promises, particularly upon Japanese promises. The record of this unreliability was yet to be written, however, and promises were the only cement available to Hughes and his fellows; no party to any of the agreements would have accepted either economic or military sanctions for their enforcement.

Inability to apply the ratio to all categories of naval shipping was doubtless, in retrospect, Hughes's major failure; its aftermath would be a cruiser rivalry which would produce severe Anglo-American friction, to which American political ineptitude and professional stubbornness would contribute as greatly as British imperial considerations. Yet the surrender on submarines and auxiliaries was the necessary price of France's acceptance of a ratio beneath her pride if not her pocketbook.

The alternative to conceding Japan virtual hegemony over the western Pacific was acceptance of the fiscal burden of a naval construction program which no amount of goading could have persuaded Americans of the early twenties to undertake. To have placed adequate bounds on Japan, indeed, would have compelled the United States to assume the task of bringing Far Eastern power commitments into balance with strategic reality—a solution never seriously contemplated since the lighthearted acquisition of Hawaii and the Philippines had launched the nation on the task of maintaining an essentially untenable strategic position with a paucity of power.

On the whole, it appears to the writer that the Washington settlements approached a viable equilibrium as closely as the temper of the time and the status of the power structure permitted. Like any composition of sharp differences by a process of give and take, they contained possibilities, perhaps the inevitability, of future disagreement; it is difficult, however, to expect greatly improved solutions from the circumstances of the day. It is unfair, too, to demand ultimate solutions from initial explorations; instead of condemning the Hughes formula as inelastic, as his later critics have done, it is more just, as well as more kindly, to credit him with the imagination to take a long step forward in an atmosphere of considerable international tension. The failure of disarmament, indeed, was not so much that of the men of Washington, who went as far as the climate of their day would permit, as of their successors, British and American as well as Japanese, who, first beset by nationalist considerations and then bedeviled by the Great Depression, failed to improve upon their vigorous but incomplete beginnings.

V

Disarmament:
Geneva, London, League of Nations

The Washington Naval Conference dampered capital-ship construction but unfortunately failed to place similar curbs on other categories. This failure spawned a new rivalry and posed a new problem involving primarily Britain, Japan, and the United States in essentially unsuccessful efforts to halt a cruiser competition that threatened to assume as ugly proportions as the earlier race to launch battleships. Though the individual tonnages involved were smaller, the cumulative effect on international comity and global strategy was hardly less—indeed, perhaps even greater, now that establishment of a ratio in capital ships had created an equilibrium of sorts in that quarter.

Here, then, was an opportunity for statesmanship to build on Hughes's beginnings and carry further the principle of limitation which he had initiated. Alas, however, somewhere between Washington, where the cruiser competition was really born, and Geneva (1927), where it was first subjected to full-scale international analysis, the statesmen had lost that control over the technicians which Hughes had so rigidly enforced, and the naval professionals, relieved of his iron-handed domination, rose to at least a par with those who put national policy ahead of naval hardware.

Neither technicians nor politicians, nor both together, could muster sufficient acumen at Geneva to reduce technical demands to the political accommodation which had been an outstanding feature of the Washington agreements. The result was to put real disarmament on a downward course during the remaining Republican years until it vanished finally in the new rearmament born of the fascism of the 1930's. Before passing on to consideration of the first lamentable failure of statesmanship at Geneva, however, the reader must be reminded that, despite the ultimate failure of the movement toward disarmament, American involvement in it was deeper, and expenditure of energy greater and longer-continued than in any other area covered in this study.

Arthur J. Balfour's response to Hughes's wholesale scuttling of battleships of November 12, 1921, had contained a seemingly mild caveat which triggered the post-Washington competition: ". . . there may be," he warned, "questions connected with cruisers which are not connected with or required for fleet operations." French refusal to include this category in the ratio limitations of the Five-Power Pact opened the door, and in the near future Japan and Britain (followed by France and Italy) began building cruisers. This caused considerable alarm among vocal Americans, many of whom had lost sight of the fact that the Washington ratio applied only to capital ships and aircraft carriers. American naval professionals were less vocal but much more concerned, having become convinced by 1922 that Japan was a potential enemy in the Pacific, though the post-Washington glow was no atmosphere in which to voice such sentiments. They took relevant action in 1921, however, deciding without fanfare (but announcing the fact only on December 6, 1922) to assign many of their best capital ships to a Pacific Battle Fleet, based on Hawaii and far superior to the Atlantic squadron. This fleet could be at least psychologically useful in supporting the Open Door or in defending the Philippines. If aggressive warfare with Japan became necessary (plans for such had been elaborated by the Joint Army-Navy Board and accepted by September, 1924), so Navy thinking went, American power must be at least twice as great as that of the defenders. This was obviously impossible under the Washington ratio. Equally obviously, multiplying Japanese cruisers would compound this disadvantage, and the Navy's fears were quite understandable.

Nor was Japan the only cause of professional alarm. The Conservatives took over the British Government in 1923 and, under Admiralty influence, promptly began fortifying Singapore and building cruisers. By mid-1925 the Navy General Board was pleading with Secretary Curtis D. Wilbur to oppose further naval limitation on the ground that the American position *vis-à-vis* Britain had already deteriorated, and was arguing that equality in tonnage was no guarantee of parity, since British bases and merchant shipping easily convertible to warlike uses conferred a considerable advantage. As with Japan, continued cruiser construction would tilt this balance still further, and make the prospect even darker.

The American naval position, contrariwise, had not improved appreciably since the Washington Naval Conference. With Congress niggardly, and with Coolidge determined to make a reputation for economy, construction lagged. Naval thinking had become committed to the 10,000-ton cruiser, mounting 8-inch guns, an expensive and not too well-designed craft whose large fuel capacity presumably adapted it to the great distances of the Pacific, where paucity of bases made its long cruising range essential. Only late in 1924 did Congress, prodded by naval and some public demands, instruct the President to start building eight of these cruisers prior to July 1, 1927. While appropriations lagged still further, the League of Nations Assembly voted in 1925 to establish a Preparatory Commission for the Disarmament Conference (pp. 182–189). Coolidge, seeing this as a possible alternative to arms expenditure, announced American participation, but by the summer of 1926 it had become apparent that it would produce no immediate results. By the end of the year, however, the European climate had moderated considerably. The Locarno Agreements augured well for French security, and the Dawes Plan's early effectiveness bade fair to ease the debts/reparations tangle. Five of the eight cruisers authorized in 1924 were under way by the autumn of 1926, when Coolidge and Kellogg began to bring into focus earlier tentative thoughts of a second conference; the President's annual message (December 7) indicated willingness to pursue the Hughes formula by applying the 5/5/3 ratio to other categories. Pressure for further construction was mounting at the same time, and Congress, refusing a presidential request to postpone work on the other three 1924 cruisers, ordered construction to begin; legislation calling for ten more was in the hopper by the end of the year. Clearly, Coolidge must build or bargain. The choice was not difficult for the economy-minded New Englander.

Thanks to the lag in construction and to poor Administration tactics for which no adequate explanation has ever been offered, the United States was less well situated for bargaining than in 1921, when Hughes had led from strength on the water, on the ways, and on the drawing board. Realizing, as has been seen, that disarmament was more a political than a technical problem, he had placed naval officers at the foot of the table, consistently subordinating their professional opinions to his political objectives.

Coolidge and Kellogg adopted an approach which minimized the political and maximized the technical side of the negotiations. Whether for reasons of economy, because they were too much concerned with other matters (this was the winter when Kellogg was under great strain over Nicaraguan affairs), or from sheer ineptitude in estimating the complexity of the problem, they failed to match Hughes's perspicacity in the choice of delegates and the balance within the delegation. Instead of choosing a group carefully for the particular occasion, they assigned the added chore of discussing naval disarmament to a delegation appointed to attend the League's Preparatory Commission on the Disarmament Conference. The Preparatory Commission was engaged in clearing underbrush for a meeting which it was known would not take place for some time; it was currently largely concerned with technical matters, for which the American delegation, composed in majority of senior naval officers with Hugh Gibson, a young and able but relatively inexperienced diplomat, and Hugh R. Wilson, Minister to Switzerland, on the political side, was well enough equipped.

The task at Geneva, however, was not clearing underbrush, but full-scale negotiation, in which the naval people participated as they had not been permitted to do at Washington. Coolidge guaranteed antagonism, moreover, by inviting the other powers to follow his example and assign their own Preparatory Commission delegations, likewise leaning heavily toward the technical side, to the Geneva discussions. The character of the conference, staffed as described, enabled the American naval people and their British opposite numbers to dominate the proceedings to a point where technical considerations remained in the foreground to the almost total exclusion of political questions of great moment. The invitation promptly raised a technical question with political overtones by suggesting American willingness to consider extending the 5/5/3 ratio to new categories; it implied that the work of the conference would be referred to the League machinery, where, presumably, political considerations could be aired. France and Italy declining to attend, the remaining powers convened on June 20, remaining in session, with a recess, until August 4.

Americans and Britons viewed the cruiser question, the rock on which the conference would founder, from widely disparate angles, each position being grounded on a conception of national interest. Britain's scattered empire, numerous bases, and long sea lanes dictated a doctrine of imperial requirements which led her, while willing to retain the ratio, to desire a smaller, cheaper type of vessel rather than that favored by the United States, and to prefer to increase rather than decrease total tonnage. She was, too, intent upon maintaining cruiser tonnage at a two-for-one ratio to that of any potential European rival. The United States, with few bases and with Japan as a potential enemy, demanded ton-for-ton parity.* The United States initially insisted on devoting her full tonnage allowance to 10,000-ton, 8-inch-gun craft with long cruising radius. She also objected to increasing overall tonnage which, under the ratio (in addition to its being unacceptable to an economy-minded Congress), would allow both Britain and Japan an undesirable increase in fire power. Japan bulked particularly large in this calculation, since the distances involved in possible naval action against her, plus recent Japanese cruiser construction, made her a bugaboo to the U. S. Navy. Permitting Japan to increase overall tonnage on the 5/5/3 ratio would, therefore, simply add obstacles to an already impossible situation. It may be pointed out, too, that mathematical parity would have amounted to practical American superiority as far as Britain was concerned, in view of the vast extent of the British Em-

---

* This the British delegation had been instructed to concede, and at a visit in the autumn of 1926 Rear Admiral Hilary P. Jones had already had the British Admiralty's assurance of willingness to extend the 5/5/3 ratio "unqualifiedly" to all categories of vessels as far as the United States was concerned.

pire; not so in the Pacific, where a-ton-for-a-ton would be favorable to Japan.

Geneva afforded no opportunity for such pyrotechnics as Hughes had exploded six years earlier. Gibson's opening statement reiterated a previously expressed American desire to extend the ratios to other classes of auxiliaries on the lowest possible tonnage level. W. C. Bridgeman, First Lord of the Admiralty, sought to include discussion of capital ships, not mentioned in the invitation and not subject to review until 1931 under the terms of the Five-Power Pact, and taboo in the absence from Geneva of France and Italy, parties to that agreement. Viscount Makato Saito contented himself with opposing new construction programs. The problem of British needs and the question of complete parity emerged early with disclosure (June 23) that British war plans demanded a minimum of seventy-two cruisers to protect their commerce and a blunt inquiry whether the United States insisted on parity in all classes, followed by a suggestion that she might not feel compelled to build as much in some categories as Britain required. It was proposed, also, that cruisers be divided into two classes, one to displace considerably under 10,000 tons. These proposals elicited no American enthusiasm, especially the move to discuss capital ships, and after some maneuvering in this quarter, deadlock loomed.

Making no headway on battleship reduction, British attention turned to cruisers and Bridgeman broached to Gibson the doctrine of "absolute need," according to which a nation's defense needs (in this instance cruisers for Mediterra-

144

nean operations) must govern its construction policy, regardless of other nations' requirements—a doctrine hardly consonant with the notion of mathematical parity. This formula presently translated itself into a bewildering succession of statistics, Britain first asserting an absolute need for 562,-500 tons of cruisers, including fifteen 10,000-tonners with 8-inch guns and fifty-five 7,500-tonners with 6-inch guns. The American counter was to demand mathematical parity at a top tonnage limit of not over 400,000 distributed among twenty-five 10,000-tonners and twenty 7,500-tonners, all carrying 8-inch guns. These figures passed through successive stages as the talks took their wearying and aggravating way into July; the fundamental point was clear enough, however —Britain wanted stabilization on a higher tonnage level, according to the doctrine of absolute need, and the United States desired parity on a lower level, with an emphasis on 10,000-tonners and 8-inch guns on cruisers of any tonnage. Saito, emphasizing Japan's supposed desire for real limitation, proposed informally to set the American cruiser figure at 450,000 to 550,000 tons, allowing Japan "somewhat above 300,000 tons," thus quietly scaling the 5/3 ratio upward on Japan's behalf.

Privately, Kellogg instructed Ambassador Alanson B. Houghton to point out to Britain the American public conviction that such a building program could only be directed against that nation. The Ambassador promptly asserted to Sir Austen Chamberlain (on July 8) that Britain, having limited capital-ship size, now sought to reestablish sea supremacy by building large numbers of auxiliaries. Strong language marked inconclusive discussions at Geneva, while

Kellogg tried to save the Conference by proposing an adjournment, after which he and Chamberlain might move the discussion up one level; Coolidge, from his Black Hills retreat, insisted that if the Conference failed the onus must be placed on the British.

An Anglo-Japanese discussion presently permitted Anglo-American tempers to cool, and several sessions were occupied in attempts to compose their differences on a base acceptable to the United States. Tonnage figures, finally arrived at, caused American trepidation because they increased the Japanese ratio from 5/3 to 5/3.25, and because a proposal to retain overage vessels in commission appeared to be a device to increase both British and Japanese tonnage without aiding the United States. Implicit in much of the discussion, though never fully spelled out, was an American desire to fix *total tonnage limits* prior to discussing *number of cruisers,* and British insistence upon settling the maximum *number of cruisers* before accepting overall *tonnage figures.* American insistence upon the right to mount 8-inch guns on small cruisers was explicitly and repeatedly expressed. While these matters were still under discussion, the British delegation was ordered home for talks with the Government, and a week's recess intervened between July 20 and 28.

The week saw positions reviewed and reaffirmed, resulting in a stiffening attitude on both sides. It is significant also to note that with two exceptions no American in a position of influence proposed any departure from already well-established demands; here the stand of the American technicians made itself paramount over political considerations to the detriment of a possible composition of differences. The

146

American demands included parity on a real limitation of cruiser strength, prime dependence on the large cruiser, and the right to mount 8-inch guns on the smaller cruiser. Gibson proposed (July 22) token recognition of Japan's desire for a higher ratio and the following day suggested a political clause permitting Japan or Britain to reopen the cruiser question if, prior to December 31, 1936, the United States built an undue number of small 8-inch-gun cruisers. With these exceptions the American attitude was increasingly hard. Backstage, too, Kellogg grew increasingly exasperated with what he suspected was a British determination to increase tonnage and evade parity.

Contemporaneous discussions and decisions in London likewise took a hard line in support of a strong cruiser force. It had become abundantly clear at Geneva that granting the promised mathematical parity to the United States would further jeopardize the British naval position, already endangered at Washington. It was decided to deny parity; moreover, Winston Churchill, Chancellor of the Exchequer, persuaded his colleagues to refuse the American request for 8-inch guns on small cruisers on the ground that such heavy artillery would be an increase in armament rather than a limitation. Technical and strategic factors thus pushed each side toward equally irreconcilable and inflexible positions, forcing into the background the political considerations which had been brought to the fore at Washington.

Informal British reports prepared the American delegation for failure in the resumed discussions, and work was started on a justificatory statement in case the Conference grounded completely. The "final" British demands, made known on the

28th, were based on the doctrine of absolute need to protect imperial sea lanes, and closely resembled the Anglo-Japanese compromise known to be unacceptable to the United States. They called for seventy-five cruisers, including a large proportion of 6,000-tonners, for promotion of numerous merchantmen to cruiser status by adding 6-inch guns, made a bow to Japan by raising her ratio to 5/3.25, and preserved several units from the scrap heap beyond the dates set at Washington. The American demand for the large gun on the small cruiser was likewise denied.

Desperate efforts to save the conference followed the confrontation, with Ishii's attempts to mediate the opposing positions encountering slight elasticity on either side. Except for repeating his proposal of a political clause ending British obligations if the United States became "too offensive" in building 8-inch-gun cruisers, Gibson remained as adamant as his technical advisers; Kellogg was sick of the whole affair, and when, under the urging of subordinates, he finally telephoned Coolidge from Washington seeking permission to propose adjournment to allow for further consideration, the President had gone fishing. Another Japanese proposal proved abortive and the conference adjourned on August 4 with a final statement by Gibson outlining the narrow area of agreement, followed by statements of national position. In his individual exposition Gibson temperately noted the impossibility of reconciling the British demand "for numbers of vessels, for the most part armed with 6-inch guns, with the desire of the American delegates for the lowest possible tonnage limitation with freedom of armament within such limitation." The British concept of absolute need had met its

148

match in the American demand for complete freedom to arm a reduced total tonnage.

Fundamentally, the conference had failed because neither of the chief antagonists would surrender previously assumed and mutually incompatible positions—the American demand for mathematical parity and the British concept of absolute need. In fact, neither was willing to yield superiority to the other. It may be argued that British refusal to make good her promise of parity was primarily responsible, but after careful study of the archival materials the writer has been unable to discover that the American delegates displayed any greater technical flexibility or political acumen than their British opposite numbers. Neither delegation was able to rise to the level of accommodation in either area which could have moderated the divergencies on which the conference foundered.

Geneva's frustrations contributed to sharply deteriorating Anglo-American relations on all levels, lasting for months and prompting the United States to seek other avenues toward security. These included further participation in the work of the ineffective Preparatory Commission and tardy and then vigorous prosecution of the tenuous approach afforded in what would go down in history as the Kellogg-Briand Pact, both of which will be treated later in the present account (pp. 182–189, 214–227). While the Preparatory Commission made few moves and less progress, British attitudes at Geneva had bred fear and anger, reaching high in American governmental circles and eventuating in legislation

149

reflecting Geneva's failure. Coolidge's annual message of December, 1927, showed his severe alarm, for this prime advocate of economy made statements which, though guarded, led naval planners to believe him willing to support legislation designed to bring their arm up to the full parity which British Admiralty and Government had refused to accord at Geneva.

Presently Congress received the General Board's recommendations, including authorization for construction of thirty-three 10,000-ton, 8-inch-gun cruisers, and increasing the range of battleships by changing the elevation of the gun turrets. Congress had previously appropriated for this when Edwin Denby, Harding's Secretary of the Navy, reported that the British were at work on such a program; but receipt of British denials, accompanied by assertions that such action was illegal under the Five-Power Pact, had ended the project. Chairman T. S. Butler introduced (December 14) an even more drastic proposal, the "71-Ship Bill," recommending this vast addition over a nine-year period. Public opinion boggled at such a great leap, and on March 17, 1928, the House passed a less explosive measure calling for fifteen cruisers and one aircraft carrier. The Senate was not yet willing to support even this relatively modest step, and it was only after the Anglo-French Naval Agreement had raised temperatures, and after a presidential nudge on Armistice Day, 1928, that it agreed to the fifteen-cruiser bill on February 13, 1929, after a vigorous debate on rearmament paralleling debate on the panacea for peace embodied in the Kellogg-Briand Pact.

Meantime the Anglo-French Naval Agreement of June, 1928, had produced one of the major irritants in this period of Anglo-American discord. At the abortive fifth session of the Preparatory Commission Lord Cushendun (Ronald John McNeill, First Baron) had handed Gibson a letter (March 24, 1928) detailing British proposals for modifying the current capital-ship arrangements, an indication that Geneva's failure had not dampened British desire for change in this quarter. A few days later Sir Austen Chamberlain discussed naval matters with Aristide Briand at a meeting of the League Council, and an Anglo-French community of interest developed, centering on British desire for numerous small cruisers and French wishes concerning certain phases of land armament not pertinent to the present narrative. Successive technical and political conversations refined the explorations into an agreement signed late in June, announced in Commons factually but not in detail on July 30, and conveyed in substance to the United States on July 31, four days after dispatch of Briand's notes inviting the powers to sign the Peace Pact. Though Chamberlain and Briand were of course entirely within their rights in discussing their own interests independently of the United States, it must have been abundantly clear to them that any alteration of the naval *status quo* might heighten existing tensions. The agreement looked to adoption of a flexible plan according to which each nation would be assigned a "global" tonnage figure which it might subdivide into four proposed categories according to its own needs. This would do away with limitation by tonnage-within-categories, which had already proved difficult for Britain in the area of battleships and cruisers, and would permit her to decrease the one and increase the other. It would also, and inevitably, offend the United States, still wedded to the tonnage-within-categories concept. And in broader terms it betokened at least the possibility of an Anglo-French rapproachement.

This agreement fluttered the Administration dovecote. Publication would underwrite the strong sentiment for twenty-five cruisers, the cost of which affronted Coolidge's economical soul, would further increase Anglo-American tensions, and would add no weight to the Kellogg-Briand Pact. Also discouraging was oral British notice of intention to remove all wraps from construction of smaller cruisers and destroyers mounting 6-inch guns or less, the type most useful to Britain and most threatening, in American naval thinking. Private assurance, however, minimized the threat of an Anglo-French bloc directed against the United States, and matters seemed to be finding their level when, on September 21, 1928, William Randolph Hearst published details of the agreement, which compelled formulation of an official statement (issued September 29) pointing out the agreement's departure from previously accepted norms, with its obvious advantages to its signers and disadvantages to the United States. This was followed by presidential denunciation in the Armistice Day address. The whole episode, unpleasant in the extreme, was probably the high-water mark of Anglo-American ill will and seems to have caused a change of heart, for by November 21, 1928, Prime Minister Stanley Baldwin was telling William R. Castle, in Europe on a postelection vacation from his departmental duties, that cordial relations must be maintained, even at the expense of offending the Navy: "We will have to consult the sailors, but when it comes to a real agreement we shall probably have to forget what the sailors have told us," a remark which may well serve to bridge the gap between the hostility bred at Geneva and the new spirit which led to London.

The London Naval Conference (January 21–April 22, 1930) marked the third Republican essay at the delicate problem of harmonizing naval armaments with political necessities in a world where heavy American practical involvement had to be kept divorced from political entanglements. At Washington, political concessions had been traded for naval considerations under careful civilian controls. At Geneva, a surrender of civilian control had resulted in deadlock and defeat at the hands of professional negotiators. At London, the civilians would again be in control, but while Anglo-American tensions would be vastly reduced, a vast amount of effort accomplished relatively little toward real solution of the problem of naval armaments, and the end of the Republican story would find a depression-ridden nation, having ironed out Atlantic differences with Great Britain, facing other and as yet hardly realized problems in the Far East.

New leadership on both sides of the Atlantic paved the way to accommodation, though British Conservatives had been groping toward the light prior to their defeat by Labor. Herbert Hoover's Quaker background predisposed him to seek solutions in terms of international goodwill. This was reinforced by his conviction of the need for Anglo-American solidarity as a means of checking an armaments race. To this end Hoover had early dispatched an unofficial emissary to spy out the land. He had developed an acqaintance with

Herbert Price Bell, long-time London representative of the *Chicago Daily News,* on a preinaugural junket to Latin America; and by the end of March, 1929, Bell was in London, where he found Stanley Baldwin reluctant to take overt steps in view of the proximity of an election which might unseat his Government. It should be pointed out, however, that several Tory moves had already forecast an effort at amelioration. Baldwin's remark to Castle in November was at least indicative of a frame of mind. On January 28, 1929, Sir Austen Chamberlain had proposed seeking an "equation" to apply to Anglo-American differences, and on May 3 a confidential feeler concerned a postelection exchange of views in case the Tories remained in power. On the strength of this tenuous approach Stimson and British Ambassador Sir Esme Howard had promptly agreed (on May 9) that Geneva's mistake of entrusting negotiation to professionals ought not be repeated. Meantime, J. Ramsay MacDonald, who would be Prime Minister if an election ousted the Tories, had tentatively extended an olive branch in a newspaper article suggesting a discussion of the explosive issue of neutral rights on the high seas in time of war. The stage had therefore been well set prior to the election which brought Labor to power on June 7, 1929.

The first real preliminaries, however, were American, centering on the so-called yardstick formula. This approach to the problem of equating the combat strength of different types of vessels was set forth on April 22, while the British election was still pending, in Hugh Gibson's address to the Preparatory Commission, then helplessly floundering in the face of the Anglo-American naval impasse. It will be remembered that Hughes had sought a "yardstick" from Denby in 1921, but the General Board had been unable or unwilling to define a "naval unit" capable of making accurate international measurements. Hughes then fell back on a more-or-less makeshift approach through displacement tonnage of capital ships, which had served the Washington negotiators reasonably well. The emerging cruiser rivalry had directed some thought to the problem of equating combat strength in this type of vessel; and in Geneva's unhappy aftermath Allen W. Dulles, reflecting on the American experience, had penned a memorandum (September 27, 1927) suggesting "a certain justice in the idea of working toward a parity of combat strength rather than insisting upon the absolute parity of naval tonnage." This he had repeated in an article in *Foreign Affairs* in January, 1929. There had been, however, no serious attempt to measure limitation in any other way than through tonnage categories.

When Gibson was readying for the Preparatory Commission convening in mid-April, Secretary Kellogg had indicated that while in his judgment limitation by tonnage categories was still the best approach, Gibson might consider a French suggestion (first made in 1927) of combining total tonnage with tonnage by categories. After Hoover entered office he conferred with Gibson on the content of the address, which was designed to stimulate discussion of naval matters rather than to offer a precise formula. In the speech as delivered, Gibson announced willingness to examine the combination of such factors as gun caliber, age, and tonnage in an effort to

155

arrive at a just balance of effectiveness among vessels in a given category but possessing varying qualifications—a yardstick designed to equate large and small cruisers to mutual satisfaction. This seemingly bold proposal received interested consideration out of proportion to its real significance, since it was more or less a trial balloon. Gibson himself had apparently devoted no hard study to its practical application, and the Navy professionals, who had been unable in 1921 to create such a unit, had not been consulted as to his formulation. But many were looking for a sign, and when Charles Gates Dawes arrived as the new American Ambassador in June he discovered Britons using the term "yardstick" more optimistically than either Gibson or the President had expected.

British developments had meantime moved apace. Ramsay MacDonald assumed the reins in the echo of Hoover's Memorial Day address—an adjuration to express faith in the new Kellogg-Briand Pact by works directed toward naval disarmament. Even before the take-over Bell had cabled word of MacDonald's willingness, if invited, to come to the United States and discuss the entire gamut of Anglo-American relations. Feeling this a trifle premature, Hoover entrusted the preliminary explorations to Dawes, then already on the high seas. Before regaining his land legs, that vigorous if seldom tactful diplomat ran the new Prime Minister to ground in his weekend retreat at Lossiemouth, ostensibly to inquire about the content of an address which Dawes was preparing for delivery to the Society of Pilgrims on June 18. MacDonald, overhopefully expecting an invitation to visit the President, swallowed his chagrin and bent himself to being a proper host. There ensued several weeks of informal Hoover-MacDonald negotiation, carried on through Dawes and the Department of State, but involving neither more than slightly, with the Ambassador's role probably less important than his voluminous *Journal* would indicate. His Pilgrim Society address made publicly clear, however, a matter on which Howard and Stimson had agreed long since, namely that any future arms conference would not be dominated by professionals; Dawes added the unpleasant intimation that these men could not be trusted to participate effectively in negotiations likely to limit their own careers.

Against the background of their lengthy correspondence, both chiefs of state made previously arranged gestures toward disarmament. MacDonald on July 24, 1929, announced stoppage of construction of two 10,000-ton cruisers and three submarines, and publicly acknowledged the principle of Anglo-American naval parity. Not to be outdone, Hoover on the same day proclaimed adherence to the Kellogg-Briand Pact and postponed laying the keels of the last three cruisers authorized in December, 1924. Up to a point, negotiation by correspondence proceeded smoothly enough on most categories. The obstacle, as usual, was cruiser strength, in which the yardstick formula was prominently involved. Sir Esme Howard's request that Stimson give specific content to Gibson's generalities left the Secretary floundering, but at a conference among Hoover, Stimson, and Dawes prior to the Ambassador's departure it was agreed to seek professional advice in establishing a naval yardstick satisfactory to civilian leadership. President, Secretary, and naval representatives continued unsatisfactory exchanges through June;

finally the Naval Board presented a formula, under pressure from Secretary Ray Lyman Wilbur, based on a denial of the yardstick principle. Meantime MacDonald, anxious to move more rapidly, reported on June 28, 1929, his willingness to extend the principle of parity (established for capital ships at Washington) to cruisers; in effect this amounted to a surrender of Britannia's long-held dominion over the waves—in Professor Raymond G. O'Connor's phrase, "probably the most important concession made by any statesman" during the London Conference preliminaries.

Stimson seems to have entered the fray in early July, and by the 11th he and the President had agreed upon and transmitted to London certain desiderata of a conference, which were strongly opposed by their professionals. The Prime Minister, crowded between the American desire to trade tonnage figures prior to a meeting and his own experts' insistence on a basis of calculation, renewed his request for a yardstick. Upon learning, to his disappointment (on July 21), that this would only be disclosed at the conference, he proceeded to frame his own proposals in the light of his experts' advice and the American desiderata. Pushed by domestic pressures, he announced publicly (on the 24th, the day of simultaneous disclosure of altered construction plans) that a conference was under consideration. Hoover's response (on July 25), to the effect that a meeting could be useful only in the light of previously established principles, hastened presentation of Britain's "asking" figures. On the 29th MacDonald transmitted his concept of parity-without-a-yardstick, according to which the United States should have eighteen 8-inch-gun and twenty 6-inch-gun cruisers to Britain's fifteen and forty-five in each category, the latter number to include 7.5-inch-gun *Hawkins* class craft until their normal replacement. The three extra 8-inchers assigned to the United States would, it was represented, offset a tonnage differential favorable to Great Britain; the proposal would enable Britain to *replace* 7,000 tons while requiring the United States, thanks to previous Congressional economy, to *build* 225,000 new tons.

Though this represented a sharp reduction of British demands since Geneva's debacle, it aroused no enthusiasm on the Potomac, where small cruisers had long been discounted by the professionals and where the 376,226 tons allotted to Britain appeared to the civilians to involve an expansion rather than a limitation of armaments. The American task from this point was to persuade the British to lower their sights to a point where parity, whether by yardstick or by tonnage, could be achieved. Numerous messages, including a sharp cable from Hoover directly to MacDonald charging that the British proposals contained neither lowered tonnage nor parity, began to be effective and, as a result of further complicated exchanges during August, total British cruiser demands were cut from sixty to fifty, and American professionals at first demanded twenty-three and later twenty-one 8-inchers to balance out (as against Britain's figure of fifteen, which stood firm throughout the discussion). With the number of light cruisers apparently negotiable, each side stood pat for some time on its large-cruiser position, making the real obstacle to agreement 30,000 tons in 8-inch-gun cruisers, estimated at about 3 per cent of the total tonnage involved.

By the end of August the American civilian leaders had

resigned themselves, in the light of British obduracy, to a higher total tonnage, and were concentrating on achieving parity at this higher level. They had abandoned hope of fashioning the international yardstick so blithely proposed in April and so hopefully sought during the early summer, though a distinctively American version had been developed and was from time to time used privately by the civilian leaders. Within a few days, indeed, Hoover was quarreling with his professionals over development of a reply to MacDonald's latest proposals; at a meeting at the White House (on September 11), the General Board at presidential insistence applied the yardstick formula, which it had created but which it did not accept as an accurate measurement of parity, to the problem at hand, coming up with a demand for twenty-one heavy cruisers, ten *Omahas,* and four 6-inch-gun light cruisers. When Hoover proposed to forward this to MacDonald as the Board's concept of parity, he was met with the flat statement that the figures reflected the formula, but not the Board's real opinion. The dispatch was altered to accord with the Board's interpretation of parity (by adding one light cruiser for a total of five), but this failure to produce a meeting of the minds hardly tended to ease the already tense relationships between Washington's civilians and professionals. The episode made it apparent, moreover, that there was no greater flexibility among the professionals in Washington than in London and that, if the essential three-cruiser differential were to be resolved, it must be done on a political level.

By mid-September, hope of a political meeting appeared dim indeed. MacDonald's private secretary, in the States to make arrangements, had gone home and Ambassador Howard was in New York preparing to entrain for a late visit to Bar Harbor's superior climatic facilities, when he was summoned back to advise the Prime Minister as to a proper course of action. Howard evidently passed the matter on to Hoover who, after taking counsel, indicated his willingness to see MacDonald, whereupon Howard was instructed to hand in the latter's self-invitation: "if the United States Government were agreeable he would start very shortly." MacDonald and his daughter Ishbel appeared presently as a prelude to a conference covering October 4–10, 1929.

The Rapidan talks, at which the two principals dealt man-to-man in well-publicized seclusion, bore few edible fruits but a large crop in the realm of the intangibles of Anglo-American good will. The cruiser difference remained unsolved, to be passed on to later expert and political discussion. Likewise, Hoover found himself unable (relying, curiously enough, on the experts whom he treated so cavalierly in other matters) to meet MacDonald's desire to reduce the maximum size of battleships from 35,000 to 25,000 tons; MacDonald (likewise depending upon his experts) objected to Hoover's desire to reduce battleship numbers. Hoover, perhaps with one eye on Borah, raised the question of neutral rights and immunities, proposing to immunize food ships from capture in time of war; MacDonald could brook no consideration of this affront to Britain's traditional attitudes. Neither could he consider a suggested abandonment of British naval bases in the Western Hemisphere. Equally bootless were Hoover's proposed amendments putting mild teeth in the Kellogg-Briand Pact and his desire to seek remedies for liquor smuggling in violation of the Volstead Act.

On a broader base, the visit was a huge success. Dawes's forebodings that a British Prime Minister's appearance would bring Anglophobes rushing from dark corners proved incorrect. MacDonald's obvious sincerity, his artfully homespun manner, his daughter's wholesomeness, and the idea of the two statesmen mulling over great matters in a sylvan glade (though none of the great problems reached solution) caught the popular fancy as few things had done in many months and served as a momentary distraction from the current downward gyrations of the Big Bull Market, which went into a tailspin later in the month. MacDonald's address to the Senate on October 7, 1929, was timed to coincide with issuance of invitations to the five Washington Conference powers to return to council in London after the turn of the year. The Prime Minister's long quest for parley had finally paid dividends.

The interim was a busy time in Washington. Stimson, who had been informed, but was relatively inactive during much of the preliminary period, now left departmental operations largely in undersecretary Joseph P. Cotton's hands and spent much of November and December at Woodley. Here, in conference with all and sundry, he devoted himself to choosing an able delegation and briefing himself thoroughly on technical matters, but less adequately on political questions. During this period, too, certain clouds, previously no larger than the proverbial handspan, began to loom larger, adding their shadow to the naval problems left unsolved by Rapi-

162

dan's amenities and forecasting some troubles the Conference would face.

Chief among these was increasing evidence that the Japanese would come prepared to seek alteration of the humiliating ratio imposed at Washington. Their curiosity aroused, they inquired in June, both in Washington and London, whether a meeting was in the wind. Fobbed off at this point, the Dawes-MacDonald conversations suggested an Anglo-American rapprochement dangerous to Japan, and by August 12 Tsuneo Matsudaira, Dawes's counterpart in London, had warned the General that Japan would confront any conference with a demand for a 10/7 ratio in any categories which might be discussed. Hoover and MacDonald, at the time when Anglo-American demands had stabilized at fifteen and twenty-one, respectively, had agreed to unite in trying to hold Japan down to 10/6 in heavy cruisers. Matsudaira tried out his proposal on MacDonald late in November, but received no encouragement. On the 12th Stimson had handed Katsuji Debuchi, Japanese Ambassador at Washington, a memorandum suggesting that continued pressure for the higher ratio would compel his Government to recanvass its attitude toward the Five-Power prohibition on further fortifications at Guam and Manila.

Undaunted, the Japanese delegation traveled to London by way of the United States and presented its demands more formally on December 29. This left Japan isolated, and faced Anglo-American negotiators with the delicate task of persuading a proud people to continue under a humiliating and smothering limitation upon what she considered both her due and essential to her prestige and security. A companion cloud appeared three days later in notice that France considered protection of long and separated coastlines and of vast colonial empires and routes of trade more important than mathematical shibboleths. With Japanese fingers pointed at an alleged Anglo-American conspiracy, and with France's general terms obviously pointing at Italy, it was evident that political acumen, as well as technical information, would be a useful commodity at London.

Two minor developments contributed to the autumn climate under which the conference assembled. William B. Shearer enlivened the public prints and stimulated presidential thinking by suits against several steel and shipbuilding corporations. That adventuresome and flamboyant promoter of armaments and of William B. Shearer had been a familiar figure at the Geneva Conference, at work for those opposing naval limitation; his alleged employers failing to reward him adequately, he sued to compel performance. Shearer's oratory exceeded the quality of his claims, but the publicity engendered by the combination encouraged the President to preach the virtues of arms limitation, buttressing his remarks by pointing out that failure to take action would cost the taxpayers $1,200,000,000 in the succeeding six years—a not inconsiderable sum in light of the current Wall Street crash. In his Armistice Day address he took occasion to reopen an issue he had posed and carefully swept under the rug at the Rapidan discussions, proposing that in time of war ships—whether belligerent or neutral—that were carrying food be granted the same immunity from capture as hospital ships. This raised the bogey of freedom of the seas, a long-time

American objective and a corresponding threat to British wartime security. The President's November return to the charge did nothing to ease the preliminary tensions under which all hands were by this time operating.

The American delegation to the London Conference was both vigorous and able. Secretary of the Navy Charles Francis Adams, though less dynamic than some of his family predecessors in public life, carried on a tradition of public service extending back to colonial times. Dwight Morrow, fresh from his successful amelioration of Mexican relations, brought his restless energy, his unfailing good humor, and his personal adviser George Rublee, who would play an important role behind the scenes. Hugh Gibson ably represented conference experience and the professional diplomats, and David A. Reed and Joseph T. Robinson continued the roles of senatorial insurance policies played by Lodge and Underwood at Washington. Each, moreover, dealt ably with particular problems, Reed working out an agreement with Japan and Robinson dealing with French aspirations. The principal naval advisers were carefully chosen to represent both sides of professional opinion, Admiral Hilary P. Jones, a chief negotiator at Geneva, was called from retirement to represent the large-navy point of view favoring retention of most of America's cruiser strength in the 8-inch-gun class, while Admiral William V. Pratt's thinking coincided with that of his civilian superiors in preferring tonnage reduction and in willingness to divide cruiser strength between large and small vessels.

London was Stimson's first great challenge as Secretary and occupied much of his time for sixteen months. He brought to it his full resources of strength plus some characteristics and attitudes less contributory to a completely successful negotiation. To satisfy his need for relaxation and, perhaps, his sense of the dramatic, he took a baronial estate outside London, working out some of the meeting's inevitable frustrations on its private golf course. Among his mental baggage was a high determination to improve Anglo-American relations, which he had observed at a low ebb upon his return from the Philippines to assume the Secretaryship. He realized that naval factors were crucial in this area, and so devoted much time to becoming letter-perfect in their technicalities. Having abandoned hope of substantial overall tonnage reduction, he concentrated on arriving at a satisfactory relationship on cruiser strength. This preoccupation with mechanics, plus, perhaps, certain native shortcomings, left him less alert to the political problems inherent in such a session, and consequently less prepared to cope with them.

Here, as Drew Pearson and Robert S. Allen point out in their lively and close-to-the-scene *Washington Merry-Go-Round,* he was for the first time no more than *primus inter pares,* instead of sitting on a high seat and dealing with such able but less powerful figures as José Moncada of Nicaragua or Manuel Quezon of the Philippines. André Tardieu and Briand were old hands at international negotiation; if MacDonald's experience was less, he had come up through a rough school of domestic politics such as had been outside Stimson's ken. Both European leaders, moreover, held power by narrow margins, subject to harsh criticism by hungry out-

166

siders, and were thus wary of making undue concessions. Stimson, likewise, was obliged to bring home a package which would satisfy the Senate that it included no dangerous international commitments. He suffered, too, from a constitutional inability to delegate authority, which kept him constantly immersed in unimportant details. His lawyer's custom of exploring all the angles of a problem drained both his time and his energies and often left him tired and peevish. This last contributed to a less-than-pleasant relationship with the press, since he tended to be less informative and more difficult than pleased the correspondents.

The conference opened on January 21, 1930, with commendable pomp and circumstance. After King George V's ceremonial words of welcome, each chief of delegation addressed the assemblage. It had been the American hope that these statements would be brief and avoid demands which might be difficult to surrender when the time for hard bargaining arrived. This hope was generally fulfilled, though evidently only by application of some pressure on MacDonald and Tardieu. Some days were occupied in organization, which followed what was becoming a routinized procession of consideration by subcommittee, committee, and plenary session, with all preliminary stages affording opportunity for consultation with technical experts on naval and political matters. By the third plenary session, on January 30, the chief delegates had agreed upon an agenda and the decks were cleared for real discussions on the lower organizational levels. As always, problems arose in parallel and were settled in series, and a narrative account must assume that while one question is to the fore others are emerging or subsiding.

Within this rhythm, the succession of major developments moved roughly from the composition of Anglo-American cruiser difficulties to Franco-Italian rivalry leading to long-drawn-out efforts to satisfy French demands for security through a consultative pact, with an offstage obbligato of Japanese-American negotiations which came to focus as the last important development of the conference.

In strictly naval matters the American bargaining position, in relation to both Britain and Japan, had deteriorated sharply since Washington and still further since Geneva. At Washington Hughes had had ships in being, ships on drawing boards, and fuller coffers (albeit closely watched) than any of his colleagues. At Geneva Britain had cruisers and the United States had plans. At London, Stimson spoke for a government far behind in its building program, headed by a Quaker President increasingly concerned with the Great Depression, and faced by nations which had been building closer to treaty limits than his own. No keels had been laid, for example, for any of the fifteen cruisers authorized in the February, 1929, reaction to Geneva's failure. Japan, having built more actively, came to London with a favorable cruiser ratio *vis-à-vis* the United States; Admiral Pratt later stated that application in 1930 of Hughes's ratio of existing power, used in the 1921 calculations, would have yielded a United States/Japanese ratio of 5/10. And in relation to Great Britain, the building program had lagged so dismally that after Anglo-American agreement was finally reached, the United States faced a billion-dollar expenditure before paper parity could be translated into equivalent tonnage on the water.

Preliminary skirmishing disclosed areas of possible friction. A MacDonald/Stimson conference on January 17 (the day the Americans landed at Plymouth) renewed Anglo-American disagreement on whether to accomplish battleship reduction by tonnage or by numbers, and agreed on united opposition to Japan's demand for the 10/7 ratio. Though he persuaded Tardieu to agree that the London meeting might come to conclusions independently of the League's disarmament machinery, Stimson soon found the canny Frenchman unwilling to talk in specific figures prior to receiving satisfaction on procedural matters. By January 26 a preliminary American plan was presented for delegation consideration. It had been formulated without previously consulting the naval advisers, who were evidently told bluntly to accept it and clothe it in the language of their guild, for purposes of discussion with Britain. It continued an implicit American surrender, objectionable from their standpoint, made when Hoover at the Rapidan talks had failed to budge MacDonald from the eighteen-heavy-cruisers figure assigned the United States by the British Admiralty. Admiral Jones objected to the surrender, continuing to demand twenty-one, and an effort was made to equate the British preference for small cruisers with this point of view—essentially a renewed search for that yardstick which Stimson had earlier abandoned. Such tension developed between Pratt, who eventually was able to reconcile himself to the British ration of eighteen, and Jones, who was not, as to make the latter ill and cause his withdrawal from the Conference; no firm diagnosis has as yet chosen between the "ulcers" to which his departure was attributed and a "diplomatic" indisposition stemming from the delegation's ultimate decision to settle for eighteen cruisers.

This *furor navalis* soon made it clear that a technical resolution of the problem was unlikely, and the delegation formally agreed to accept the eighteen, but held briefly to the larger demands for bargaining purposes. The decision was conveyed to the President, who approved it on February 5. The vigor, not to say the bitterness, of the discussion seems somewhat jejune at this distance in time, since it was conducted in what amounted to a technical vacuum; there had been, of course, no naval action in which the relative merits of the 8-inch- as against the 6-inch-gun cruiser could be put to the test. The argument, plus a conference between British and American delegates on February 3, finally demonstrated that the yardstick was undefinable, and Stimson and MacDonald agreed to end the search for that elusive unit which had been intermittently sought since Gibson's speech of April 22, 1929. Its exploration was probably not an entirely useless phenomenon, since the discussion of it created a forum from which useful decisions might emerge. The talks thus turned to a search for other, and more political, grounds of accommodation.

The proposal which the delegation presented to Hoover had set heavy cruiser totals at eighteen, fifteen, and twelve for the United States, Britain, and Japan, with total cruiser tonnages of 327,000, 339,000, and 198,655; destroyer tonnages were put at 200,000, 200,000, and 120,000, respectively, and submarines at 60,000, 60,000 and 40,000. Battleships would stand at 15, 15, and 9, with no new construction prior to 1936, except that the United States might add one to offset the more modern British complement. This would amount to Anglo-American solidarity against Japan's demand for 10/7 on cruiser tonnage. From the strictly American standpoint, it represented a decision to devote a larger share of cruiser tonnage to smaller craft, retaining superiority in heavier vessels, but abandoning the essentially large-cruiser approach supported by most American professionals, and in their view essential to upholding American policy in the Far East. Britain would receive a large tonnage of smaller craft, which she had consistently demanded, but only after lowering her sights from the total of seventy demanded at Geneva through MacDonald's total of sixty at Rapidan, to approximately fifty. Of the retreats, the American had been the most real, in shifting balance among her cruiser force, and in surrendering three large vessels.

The British response was not unsympathetic, and detailed interdelegation discussions opened on February 11. The French Government fell on the 17th, ending formal operations for the time being and facilitating the conversations by permitting Stimson and MacDonald to work quietly in the interim. Agreement was reached on the 27th, modifying the original proposal only slightly and differing but little from the final settlement. After a British contention that the American heavy cruiser tonnage be reduced to 320,000, it was agreed to split the difference at 323,500; the United States request for a new battleship was eliminated, and the entire arrangement remained a contingency pending completion of French housekeeping chores (a second Government fell on the 27th) and return to the table. The settlement had come

171

relatively easily, but brought slight comfort to those who had hoped for real arms reduction, or to those who deprecated British demands, no ton of which had been surrendered since Dawes and MacDonald opened negotiations in the summer of 1929. The military surrender (for such it was), however, had important results in the broader and less tangible but doubtless more important realm of political atmosphere, contributing substantially to ending one of those intervals of ill will which the Anglo-Saxon peoples can afford to indulge during periods of international calm and which had been deepening since the Geneva conference.

Anglo-Saxon comity did not, however, guarantee that sweetness and light would settle upon London; French and Japanese exigencies, one much to the fore and the other moved into the turbulent backwater of the Reed-Matsudaira negotiations, would hold the conference for two more months. The French position was predictable, and was made clear promptly. As Britain felt that her naval security depended upon a two-for-one ratio to any European power, so France, with two coastlines and an empire in Africa, and facing an upstart braggart who from Rome eyed her askance over the guns of a seemingly efficient fleet, demanded either naval superiority over Italy or an international guarantee of that security with which she had become almost pathologically obsessed in the interwar years. Tardieu, indeed, had told the press before the Conference opened that France would only make a naval agreement in return for a promise of consultation in case of a threat to Mediterranean peace.

172

This reflected French mistrust of the current peace machinery, since the Locarno Agreements failed to bind Britain tightly enough and the Kellogg-Briand Pact was toothless. France would seek guarantees as the price of disarmament, otherwise she would demand freedom to establish naval superiority over Italy.

By February 17 (the day his Government fell) Tardieu had given notice that France would demand an inordinately large increment of cruiser tonnage and Briand had warned Stimson of his desire to talk about a consultative pact, or an amendment to the Kellogg-Briand Treaty; Stimson, in turn, had indicated that he saw no reason why a consultative pact was beyond the realm of consideration. Japan had added to the tension by presenting her own naval demands. The fall of Tardieu's ministry plunged France into a not uncommon turmoil; the new Government fell on February 27, and it was only after Tardieu had reestablished himself that Briand returned to his assignment on March 6. Within forty-eight hours the possibility of a consultative pact loomed large, and Stimson's Diary recorded the need to avoid the "implication of material assistance if we persuaded France to reduce her fleet." Any such commitment would subject him to senatorial attack; he thus faced a political problem of great delicacy and magnitude—well beyond the cruiser-tonnage figures with which he had crammed his mental portfolio before departure.

Though his management of this political aspect of the Conference fell short of complete adroitness, it must be remembered that his area of maneuver was extremely narrow, involving as it did the unknown attitude of the President and the equally certain and inevitably hostile reaction of Borah toward anything savoring of international commitment. Thus with France pushing for promises and MacDonald, beset by a vocal parliamentary opposition, unwilling to make the commitments required to purchase reduction of French cruiser strength, Stimson's first reaction was to call in the press on March 11 and disavow American association with an agreement based on French demands. Matters reached a low point on the 12th, when Briand threatened to go home. On the 13th Stimson and Morrow saw Briand and, pulling out all the stops of Franco-American good will, the Secretary left the door open for further discussion by admitting that his Government had no objection to consultative pacts *per se,* being currently a party to several such, but could not enter one dependent on French naval reduction, since this would appear to be signing a blank check which France might try to cash in time of war. Though this was not what Briand wanted, it at least indicated Stimson's willingness to *talk* consultation—a more hopeful attitude than he had evinced two days earlier. MacDonald followed Stimson and traded threats with Briand, promising to adjourn the conference and lay the blame on the French doorstep. Briand decided to remain.

Backstage, meanwhile, the fate of a five-power agreement hung in the balance, with Italy demanding parity with France (which she could neither afford to achieve nor maintain) and the latter demanding superiority *or* a consultative pact. George Rublee, Morrow's personal assistant, became convinced that only such a pact could bring all five powers to a common ground; a series of discussions finally converted

Morrow, Stimson, and the American delegation to Rublee's view, and brought Stimson to consider consultation without guarantees. On March 25 he told MacDonald "that if the other nations [i.e., Britain] would take care of the question of mutual assistance [i.e., the guarantee] in such a way as to secure a substantial reduction of armament, I should think it possible for us to consider the question of a consultative provision, with explicit denial of military action, with an open mind." Thus over a two-week period Stimson had progressed from complete opposition to consultation to a point where he was guardedly favorable.

Here a failure to maintain communications between Secretary and President resulted in diametrically opposite statements by the two and an end of American connection with consultation. Under French pressure Stimson issued a hastily-prepared press statement at 1 A.M. London time on March 26, essentially repeating his statement of the previous day to MacDonald, to the effect that the United States would sign no consultative pact to buy a French arms cut, but that if French demands for security could be met "in some other way, then the danger of misunderstanding a consultative pact would be eliminated; and in such case the question would be approached from an entirely different standpoint." Hoover had already negated this momentarily promising approach to consultation, in a statement of March 25 refusing American commitment to such a deal, but the time differential had permitted public announcement in Britain that the United States might join. The *contretemps* was annoying and, despite Stimson's tentative approaches by other avenues, ended American connection with the episode.

Whether a more forthright attitude on Stimson's part in the early stages, or closer contacts with Hoover at the last, might have altered affairs must remain a matter of speculation. There was no great British enthusiasm for the necessary guarantees, and the blame for failure to yield to French importunities may at least be shared between Britain and the United States; indeed, British indecision as to her role in European affairs was considerable at this point, and by the end of March MacDonald found himself willing to settle for a three-power treaty.

The problem of British security now came to the fore; with France obdurately insisting upon tonnage which threatened Britain's two-power standard, and with Italy obstinately demanding parity with France, hopes of five-power agreement went glimmering. This failure was not immediately apparent, however, for Anglo-French talks continued between February 27 and March 8. They showed that British disposition to provide a Mediterranean guarantee had declined with American refusal to consult and, with Italy insisting on parity, the problem resolved itself into one of British self-preservation against possible combined Franco-Italian power. This found its solution in the escalator clause as a substitute for consultation and for the refusal of France and Italy to subscribe to cruiser-tonnage limitations. Under escalation any of the major powers could increase auxiliary tonnage whenever it considered that building by nonsubscribing powers endangered its security.

The consultative pact aspect of the negotiations could hardly be highly gratifying to any participant, though in each case attitudes reflected current realities. No amount of adroitness on Stimson's part (and he is generally conceded to have attained a considerable degree of maladroitness in this, his first major political test) could have relieved Hoover of his misgivings or Borah and his ilk of their hostility to even such a mild commitment as consultation envisioned. Mac-Donald, precariously in power and uncertain of public support of a vigorous continental policy, hesitated to risk underwriting French security. France, fearful that the shadow of insecurity might materialize into Italian sea armor, refused to divest herself of the means of protection. And Italy, last and least, refused to forego the right to build beyond her economic capacity. And so the possibility of five-power agreement vanished into escalation and another opportunity for American commitment to a mild move toward international agreement failed, due to Stimson's excessive caution and Hoover's innate distrust of even a consultative pact.

Attention has been called to Japan's pretensions, which would be more nearly realized at London than those of either Britain or the United States, leaving her in practice largely free of the humiliating inferiority imposed at Washington and placing the United States in a poor posture to interfere with her plans in Eastern Asia. Japanese demands were simple—a 10/7 ratio in all categories—and had been amply presented before the Conference opened: to Dawes by Matsudaira, and to Stimson by the Japanese delegation, which stopped over at Washington on the way to London in December, 1929. The rebuffs accorded these feelers, and similar ones extended in London, alerted Japan to an Anglo-

American solidarity which only heightened her determination to break the barrier.

As in the Anglo-American confrontation, the initial engagement centered on heavy cruisers, where Japan was asked to content herself with a 10/6 ratio of the 180,000 tons allotted to the United States by the tentative Anglo-American agreement. The discussions started in earnest with a meeting of the Big Three delegations on February 17, the day Tardieu's Government collapsed, after which they were turned over to Reed and Matsudaira, presently joined by Stimson, with the Americans assuming the unenviable task of inducing Japan to accept a continuing inferiority. Weeks of work produced a tentative agreement which Reed presented to his delegation on March 13. This was preceded by hard bargaining, accompanied by hard feelings, to a point where Stimson and MacDonald had become resigned, in case Japan refused to settle, to proceed to a bilateral treaty excluding her entirely. The Reed-Matsudaira "compromise," which went into the three-power agreement, combined token victory for the United States with practical victory for Japan.

The United States agreed to complete no more than fifteen of her allotted eighteen 8-inch-gun craft prior to December 31, 1935; Japan's retention of her twelve vessels in this category would give her an actual 10/7 ratio until that date, after which American construction could tilt the balance back toward 10/6. This was a practical victory for Japan, though the letter of the 10/6 ratio would obtain for the time being. She received her requested 10/7 ratio in light cruisers and in destroyers, each power reducing its tonnage (the Japanese cut being the lightest, that of the United States the heaviest) in the latter category. She was accorded parity in submarines. Japan, then, received concessions all along the line. There is a tendency, in view of later developments, to view this in a sinister light. In the illumination vouchsafed the negotiators of 1930, however, it may well be viewed as part of a general effort at political accommodation, essential to preserving such remnants of agreement as remained from Franco-Italian intransigence, and making possible some semblance of great-power solidarity. The Japanese Government debated three weeks before accepting it as an alternative to possible failure of the conference. American naval professionals would not, of course, subscribe to this optimistic attitude toward further surrender of Pacific capability.

The present account has omitted some phases of the negotiation, and for purposes of the record the narrative will end with a brief recapitulation of the agreements signed on April 22. The three major powers dealt with the cruiser problem, establishing ceilings on heavy craft without decreasing tonnage below previous levels. Japan resigned herself to a 10/6 legal ratio until December 31, 1935, a year from the end of the treaty period, but practically remained at a 10/7 level due to American abstention from construction of three heavy cruisers. The United States could not, under the terms of the treaty, complete more than one of her cruisers during 1936. The 10/7 ratio was established immediately in all other auxiliaries (with some decrease in tonnage) except submarines, where immediate parity was granted. The escalator clause conditioned the entire auxiliary-craft arrangement. The holiday on capital ship construction was extended to December 31, 1936, with the ratio remaining at 10/10/6, with some real

179

limitation on new construction and some scrapping of existing tonnage. All five powers signed and ratified an article designed to keep submarine warfare within bounds, similar to one signed at Washington but never effective because France failed to ratify. This was the only important five-power commitment.

The hearings held prior to ratification registered opposing views on the bargain struck at London. The disgruntled admirals, disregarded at the Conference, placed their strictures in the record, denying that the treaty achieved real parity with Britain, bemoaning the changing concept which led to surrender of the three 8-inch-gun cruisers in return for larger tonnage of light vessels, and decrying the concession of a 10/7 ratio to Japan as a further surrender of Pacific status. As on several previous occasions, a senatorial request for papers documenting the negotiation was made, and denied, and the Senate adjourned without action. Hoover recalled it on July 7, having allowed a decent interval for celebrating Independence Day, and two weeks of debate brought favorable action by a margin of 58/9. The Hoover Administration's initial first-rate international negotiation was completed.

The degree of success, as at Washington, may be measured on various levels. To contemporaries, probably the most important result was healing the Anglo-American breach; to offset this distinct accomplishment, most other relations had worsened. France was unhappy at Britain's refusal to back her demands for security, disappointed if not surprised at American refusal to consult, and left to face Italian hostility

President Harding's Cabinet, photographed on the White House lawn shortly after their appointment. Seated, left to right, Secretary of War John W. Weeks, Secretary of the Treasury Andrew W. Mellon, Secretary of State Charles Evans Hughes, President Harding, Vice-President Calvin Coolidge, and Secretary of the Navy Edwin Denby. Standing, left to right, Secretary of the Interior Albert B. Fall, Postmaster General Will H. Hays, Attorney General Harry M. Daugherty, Secretary of Agriculture Henry C. Wallace, Secretary of Commerce Herbert Hoover, and Secretary of Labor James J. Davis. *Wide World Photo*

THE DILEMMA.
—Thomas in the Detroit *News.*

Printed by George Matthew Adams

NOW, HOW ARE WE ALL GOING TO BE HAPPY TOGETHER?
—Morris for the George Matthew Adams Service.

The "Big Five" of the Arms Parley leaving one of the sessions of the conference at the
Pan American Building in Washington, November 18, 1921. Left to right, Prince Iyesato
Tekugawa of Japan, The Rt. Hon. Arthur J. Balfour of Great Britain, Secretary of State
Charles Evans Hughes, Aristide Briand of France, and His Excellency Carlo Schanzer of
Italy. *Wide World Photo*

"I SYMPATHIZE DEEPLY WITH YOU, MADAME, BUT I CANNOT
ASSOCIATE WITH YOU"

December 4, 1923

President Coolidge's Cabinet was the same as that of President Harding with one replacement. Photographed on the White House lawn, September 12, 1923, they are, seated, left to right: Postmaster General Harry Stewart New, who succeeded Will H. Hays; Secretaries Weeks and Hughes, the President, Secretary Mellon, Attorney General Daugherty, and Secretary Denby. Standing, Secretaries Hoover, Work, Wallace, and Davis. *Wide World Photo*

Senator William E. Borah of Idaho headed a subcommittee of the Senate Foreign Relations Committee which investigated the propaganda of Soviet Russia in 1924. Left to right, Senators Claude A. Swanson of Virginia, Borah, Irvine L. Lenroot of Wisconsin, and George Wharton Pepper of Pennsylvania. *Wide World Photo*

General Charles G. Dawes, who became Coolidge's Vice-President in 1925, with his famous underslung pipe. He later became Ambassador to Great Britain in the Hoover administration. *Wide World Photo*

PLAYING SECOND FIDDLE

-—Page in the Louisville *Courier-Journal.*

PREPARING ANOTHER DOSE

—Smith in the Jersey City *Journal.*

A NEW COLLEGE CURRICULUM

—Hungerford in the Pittsburgh *Sun.*

Harold (Red) Grange, University of Illinois football star, was th
national hero in the mid-twenties.

THE GREAT AMERICAN GAME SEEMS
TO HAVE BECOME INTERNATIONALIZED

Orr in the Chicago *Tribune*

UNCLE SAM, DAREDEVIL!

—Duffy in the Baltimore *Sun*.

Ambassador Dwight W. Morrow arrives in Mexico City, October 30, 1927. Left to right Mrs. Morrow, their daughter Anne (later Mrs. Charles H. Lindbergh), Arthur Schoen feld, the Ambassador, and Mexican Chief of Protocol Alfonso Rosengung Diaz. *Wide World Photo*

The U.S. Delegation to the Havana Conference (The Sixth Pan American Conference) photographed in Washington on December 29, 1927. Left to right, Morgan J. O'Brier of New York, Charles Evans Hughes, Secretary of State Frank B. Kellogg, The President U.S. Ambassador to Italy H. P. Fletcher, former Senator Oscar Underwood, James B Scott, and the Director General of the Pan American Union, Dr. L. S. Rowe. *Wide World Photo*

OIL—OR JUST MORE WATER?
—Hanny in the Philadelphia *Inquirer*.

IS IT ANY WONDER?
—Shoemaker in the Chicago *Daily News*.

GUARDING THE BASKET
—Darling in the New York *Herald Tribune*.

"BUCK UP, YOU'RE A NOBLE FELLOW"
February 27, 1928

President Coolidge signs his anti-war treaty in the East Room of the White House, January 17, 1929. *Wide World Photo*

Henry L. Stimson arrives in Washington on March 26, 1929, to take over the duties of Secretary of State. He is shown with the President and retiring Secretary Frank B. Kellogg (left). *Wide World Photo*

British Prime Minister Ramsay MacDonald at the White
House with President Hoover just before they left for the
Hoover camp on the Rapidan to discuss the question of naval
limitation. *Wide World Photo*

PEACE

"President Hoover and Premier MacDonald sat on a log—dangled
their feet—smoked, and discust the peace of the world."—*News item.*
—Johnstone in the New York *World.*

As the twenties drew to a close, organized crime resulting from Prohibition claimed national attention. Warfare between the Bugs Moran and Al Capone gangs for control of Chicago's beer business culminated in 1929 in the St. Valentine's Day Massacre, when Capone's gangsters, some disguised as policemen, invaded Moran's headquarters, lined up seven men, and shot them down. *Wide World Photo*

CRIMES
LAWS.
TO CONTROL HIS ENEMIES

NO TECHNICALITIES
NO DELAYS
NO POLITICAL PULL
NO PARDONS
NO SENTENCES COMMUTED
NO SYMPATHETIC JURORS
NO SOB SISTERS
NO BRIBING
NO BOND JUMPING
NO WEAK JUDGES

GANG RULE

SEVEN RIVAL GANGSTERS EXECUTED

HE MAKES HIS OWN LAWS

—Orr in the Chicago *Tribune*.

Photograph from United Press International Newspictures, New York City

A group of federal agents look over a haul of seized bootleg liquor. Izzy Einstein (right) and Moe Smith (left) were two of the more successful enforcement officers, employing disguises and tricks which made them famous.

JOHN BULL: "OH YES, I SEE IT NOW!"

— Doyle in the Philadelphia *Record.*

Early in 1929, as public attention was focused on Prohibition and the rising stock market, Secretary Kellogg continued his efforts toward international agreements. The stock market crash in October shocked the nation out of its complacency.

TAIL HOLT

October 5, 1929

SOLD OUT

October 25, 1929

Apple sellers on the streets of New York became a symbol of the Depression. *Wide World Photos*

In the early thirties, unemployed squatters built shacks on vacant land near many American cities. This one, called "Hooverville," grew up around the Seattle waterfront. *Wide World Photos*

without the aid she had so insistently demanded. Britain's final surrender to the principle of parity left her ahead in heavy cruisers, but gave Winston Churchill and the English admirals cause to bemoan surrender of centuries of sea supremacy. Japan's failure to secure the letter of the 10/7 ratio gave rise to charges that the national security had been jeopardized, subjected her delegation to obloquy (Admiral Takeshi Takarabe was handed a hari-kiri dagger on his return home), and her Prime Minister, Yuko Hamaguchi, to the attack of a would-be assassin for his part in pushing the agreement through the Diet. Stimson's comment in his reminiscences that "his principal hopes were realized" at London must have been an overstatement unless confined to the relatively narrow area of Anglo-American relations. Overall, the cause of real disarmament had not been particularly well served, largely because the United States had been unwilling to pay the political price of her own real desire for naval arms limitation.

Over the long pull, Japan was the gainer in that the treaty improved her chances of establishing Far Eastern dominance. This was not, however, as obvious a result as subsequent unhappy events have led many to infer; the die was not yet cast for the gambles of 1931 and later. Moreover, too few recall, on casting this unfavorable balance, that for some time Japan did no more than build to her treaty opportunities, while neither Britain nor the United States did as much. Achieving the parity vouchsafed in 1930 would have cost the United States upwards of a billion dollars in new construction. Both Anglo-Saxon powers thus entered the real rivalry of the mid-thirties with accumulated deficits. Neither short-run nor long-run results of London were more than minimal and, though the policy mistake of 1927 in leaving too much leeway to the technicians was not repeated, the combined political acumen of the able American delegation failed to match Hughes's initial move. Republican efforts at naval disarmament had started on a high level, but had failed to maintain either imagination or momentum over the long pull.

While the United States was actively seeking naval arms limitation, the League moved in a parallel direction, and even less successfully, toward general disarmament through the Preparatory Commission and the Disarmament Conference. American participation, again, was active but stopped short of real commitment, though at the end of the period proposed acceptance of a consultative arrangement marked a short step in advance of the position assumed at London in 1930; generally speaking, the United States added little to the League's effort to square the circle by reconciling disarmament and military security.

It was nearly four years after the Washington Conference before the League moved. In December, 1925, the Council implemented the Assembly's authorization of the previous September and invited representatives of nineteen nations, including the United States, to attend a Preparatory Commission for the Disarmament Conference—a preliminary meeting necessitated by French desire for prior discussion. The invitation was accepted after some delay and some private (and unsuccessful) efforts to see how far Borah would permit negotiations to proceed and how far Chamberlain would go toward divorcing land and naval armaments. At the initial session of 1926 Americans were still so fearful of association with League machinery as to insist that the Permanent Advisory Commission and the Joint Commission of Economic Experts be renamed Committees A and B, the only change being the addition of American members. The chief contribution of this session (ending in November, 1926), aside from almost four million pages of records, was the explication of variant points of view. France and most Continental nations sought security as a condition of disarmament, while Britain and the United States believed that the order might be reversed, with disarmament opening a path to security.

Moves for the ill-fated Geneva naval conference of 1927 soon pushed the Preparatory Commission into the background, and its work went on more or less unnoticed through five years and six sessions. Hugh Gibson performed yeoman service in following its tortuous and ineffective meanderings during the course of which, as he and Hoover later put it in their joint volume *Problems of Lasting Peace,* the Commission "produced a fund of valuable material and a most unedifying spectacle in the determination of many governments to avoid coming to grips with the problem." Long deliberation at its final session, lasting from November 3, 1929, to December 9, 1930, produced a draft convention for limitation of armament on land, on sea, and in the air. Despite the long period of preparation, the League decided (in January, 1931) that more time was needed, and February 2, 1932, was finally set for the opening of the conference.

183

Developments during the prolonged preliminaries assured failure before the Conference opened. At one time or another several issues had arisen, producing sharp differences and occasional compromise, but no general agreement. All contributed to an atmosphere of uncertainty, suspense, and tension. Some illustrations may be listed, without too much attempt at chronological arrangement or exploration of the issues involved. France, accustomed to a conscript army with rapid troop rotation followed by lengthy reserve status, insisted that trained reserves must not be counted in calculating military effectives. Britain, with a small professional army based on long enlistments, and the United States, with negligible land forces, disapproved this instrument of French preponderance. By 1932 Germany was demanding release from Versailles' restrictions; France would have none of this short of political reassurances of security. Britain had passed the point of willingness to grant such assurances, and the United States had never reached it. Pierre Laval had pushed the United States, in the autumn of 1931, to accept the principle of consultation, but Hoover shied off from even this half-step toward cooperation—itself a far cry from the economic or physical sanctions which alone could have sufficed. Considerable acrimony developed, too, over attempts to set up standards by which arms might be limited. One suggested avenue was to permit only "defensive" weapons. This sieve-like term reduced weaponry to semantics and outlawed nothing. Another proposal was to set budgetary limits on armaments, a solution unacceptable to the United States because of her high unit costs. It is perhaps worth noting, however, that by the sixth session the United States had made several

184

adjustments, accepting the exclusion of trained reserves and the use of budgetary restrictions on arms, and had even agreed to international supervision of agreed limitations. Over all these shifting expedients, however, hung the almost pathological, but quite understandable French demand for security; her stable population of forty millions, despite huge gold reserves and a Maginot Line, could not face a growing and industrially thriving German population of seventy millions.

Thus when the hastily recruited American delegation assembled for departure in mid-January, it faced no easy task. Stimson, nominally its head, remained in the States for some time and never played an active role, delegating the negotiating function to Hugh Gibson, by this time inured to frustration by repeated exposure to Genevan oratory. Hugh R. Wilson, a career Foreign Service man, completed the diplomatic quota. Norman H. Davis, a shrewd negotiator who had been in the Department of State in Wilson's day, Claude Swanson, a cigar-smoking senator from Virginia and long a supporter of navalism, and Dr. Mary E. Woolley, president of Mount Holyoke College, completed the devoted group.

A worse moment to discuss arms reduction could hardly have been chosen. The Hoover Moratorium had stayed but not stanched the war debt/reparations conflict. Germany was demanding arms equality with France. France, in turn, was racing Italy in naval construction, though still short of the escalation point under the London Treaty. Japan, having successfully breached the Kellogg-Briand Pact the previous autumn, was busily extending her Manchurian conquests below the Great Wall. The opening session of the Conference

185

itself had to be put off an hour to permit the League Council to discuss Japanese bombing of Shanghai's Chapei District. And at home Franklin Delano Roosevelt, hope of the Democrats, had yielded to pressure by William Randolph Hearst and repudiated the League of Nations which he had so bravely espoused hardly more than a decade earlier. The President might well have been forgiven for discontinuing such a forlorn hope but he, like Roosevelt, was seeking capital for the election, and plowed ahead in this as in domestic matters, doggedly determined to put something in the record.

Formal presentation of national proposals followed the usual ceremonial preliminaries. France tied disarmament to sanctions in a way calculated to disturb both Britain and the United States, and Gibson made a mildly conciliatory gesture by indicating American willingness to accept budgetary limitation as a partial approach, after which the Conference subsided into committee sessions lasting until an Easter adjournment from March 19 to April 11, 1932, taken to permit the League Assembly to deal with the China problem. Upon reassembling, Gibson tried a stroke designed to deal at once with security and disarmament by "qualitative" means, spelled out in a specific proposal to abolish use of tanks, gas, and mobile guns. This was in a way a gesture to Germany, since it would abolish weapons forbidden that nation. Britain supported the scheme. France, while objecting, agreed to discuss the mystical question of the distinction between defensive and offensive weapons. At this point Stimson attempted to stimulate action by a personal appearance during the latter half of April. After a token attendance at the Conference he retired to a nearby villa, where he saw many leaders but exerted no appreciable influence. The debate over offensive and defensive weapons dragged on for weeks and ended in deadlock, and it was clear by June that only drastic action could move the gathering from impasse to achievement.

Here Hoover, who had been cogitating the matter for some time, made a drastic proposal (a mild version of the Hughes shock technique at Washington a decade earlier), possibly intended to improve his domestic political fortunes, perhaps to neutralize a threatened Borah blast, and certainly an expression of his own strong convictions and an attempt to galvanize the conference into action. The plan was hatched with Stimson's technical assistance, but over his objection; it appeared to him at one stage to be "just a proposition from Alice in Wonderland," though he finally concluded that the gesture must be made. Its formulation also marked one of the high points in their personal disagreement, as his *Diary* records that in one of their drafting sessions the President "looked at me with one of his rare smiles and rather shy hesitation and said he had been much troubled because he was afraid that I did not approve of what he was doing . . . ," in reply to which Stimson admitted that he "had been a good deal troubled because of my fear that I was losing his confidence."

As announced on June 22, the Hoover plan would abolish entirely tanks, heavy guns, and aerial bombardment. At Versailles Germany had been allowed a police-force army of 100,000 per 65,000,000 of population; taking this minimal figure as a fair one, Hoover proposed to cut by one-third all national armies currently larger than this ratio. Extending his scalpel to the fleets, he suggested a similar excision in certain naval categories, and one of 25 per cent in others. This rearrangement would obviously alter the Continental balance of power to French disadvantage, and so received initial German and Italian support and, predictably, alarmed France, faced with a possible combination of Italo-German land forces against her. Sir John Simon's reaction was outwardly mildly favorable, but was full of escape hatches inspired by the proposed naval cuts, which would further jeopardize the British position established at London two years earlier over Admiralty protests. France, intent on military domination of the Continent, dubbed the plan, in Edouard Herriot's words, "totally unacceptable" and promptly demanded compensatory security pledges. In the ensuing weeks of discussion most nations except the really important ones followed the Hoover lead but when, having raised the security issue, the Americans could make no implementing commitments, even to the extent of promising to consult in case of a threat to the peace, the talks degenerated rapidly.

On July 23, 1932, the conference adopted Simon's resolution collecting the few matters on which agreement had been reached as a prelude to a summer recess. On the 31st Germany, which had meantime withdrawn as a result of the July 23 resolution, elected a government in which the Nazi membership of 230 constituted the largest single component. At home, Stimson made occasion, in addressing the Council on Foreign Relations on August 8, to state that in case of threatened violation of the Kellogg-Briand Pact "consultation becomes inevitable"—apparently a long step ahead until he pointed out that consultation would be directed toward

188

"invocation of the power of world opinion" rather than a preliminary to effective action. Though five-power talks in December lured Germany back to Geneva, the Conference reassembled in January, 1933, only to watch the appointment of Adolf Hitler (on January 30) as Chancellor of Germany and his subsequent assumption of dictatorial powers. This moved agreement further than ever into limbo, and Roosevelt's offer (in May) to consult in return for *prior* agreement to reduce arms, though representing a reversal of the American refusal at London to consult under any circumstances, was of no avail in the temper of the time. Further frustrations under the Democrats shortly faded into the rearmament madness of the mid-thirties. The Hoover negotiations, at London and at Geneva, contributed evidence, perhaps clearer to later students than to contemporary negotiators, that disarmament, on even the mildest scale, was a hopeless cause until military security was guaranteed by a viable international organization including all the first-rate powers. No contemporary political genius was able to achieve this miracle.

This exposition of disarmament matters, opening with Washington's temporary success and following a descending curve ending in the League's utter failure at Geneva, has shown the United States as a prisoner of her own self-imposed limitations. Always anxious for arms reduction and fertile in ingenious but seldom effective expedients looking in particular directions, American impulses always and finally terminated against the impenetrable obstacle of refusal to equate commitment with involvement. Her statesmen were

189

unable, since they believed, correctly, that her people were unwilling, to pay the required price of political guarantees for the desired objective of arms reduction. Nor, in the last analysis, were her leaders either disposed or able to stir their people to the necessary action. Europe's leaders, closer to the alternatives of security or chaos, were equally unsuccessful in using the instrument ready to hand—the League—to achieve disarmament; nor were they willing to follow American half-measures to dubious conclusions. The result was failure of European, of League, and of American efforts to use arms limitation as the foundation of a peace structure—a structure which, before the Disarmament Conference ended had already, in effect, succumbed to Japanese activities in Manchuria.

VI

European Miscellany: *War Debts, Reparations, Kellogg-Briand*

The war debts/reparations complex impinged upon several aspects of affairs during the Republican years. The narrative has dealt (in Chapter II) with the strains attendant upon the transition from debtor to creditor status. Debts due from Europe constituted an important element in this transition, and their payment played a correspondingly significant role in relations between impoverished new debtors and their new creditors, comfortably off and not yet adjusted to their altered status. Debtors, seeking a means of meeting their obligations, found American tariff policy stupidly blocking the normal channels through which trade might be used to pay international balances. The debtors saw an obvious alternative source of funds in the income from the heavy reparations levied on Germany for wartime damages; to them the relationship of debts to reparations was crystal clear, and the necessity of collecting the one for payment of the other quickly became axiomatic. To American official and public opinion, however, a debt was a debt, due and payable regardless of whether reparations were collected or uncollectable, and a myopic refusal to admit any connection between the two, maintained almost uniformly throughout the Republican years, became and remained a source of sharp disagreement, considerable ill will, and ultimate failure to solve this crucial politico-economic problem.

At the same time American private investors and public figures became heavily involved in both sides of the question. Europe shortly accepted the formula that debts due the United States could be paid only by, and to the extent of, German reparations payments. Only a prosperous Germany could make such payments, and only in the United States was money available to shore up the German economy; American private investors became heavily, and gleefully, involved, to the extent of several billions, in buying bonds of public and private German enterprise. Individual Americans (S. Parker Gilbert, Agent General of Reparations, and Charles G. Dawes and Owen D. Young through the "Plans" bearing their names), moreover, lent their personal expertise and prestige to management and attempted solution of reparations problems. Here, then, as in several other areas, Americans and American interests were heavily involved in European affairs, but official policy remained largely insensitive to the problems and refused commitment to their solution.

.

American loans, the source of the debts, began early in the war when Woodrow Wilson yielded to bankers' pressure and permitted the hard-pressed Allies to finance the conduct of their operations through borrowing from American private investors. Entry into the war in 1917 shifted the burden of these loans to the American Government, which, through taxation and the sale of Liberty Bonds, carried on to the end of hostilities. Relief and rehabilitation succor continued into the postwar period, granted alike to wartime associates and to new states freed from enemy domination. Loans to twenty nations (sixteen in Europe, plus Armenia, Liberia, Cuba, and Nicaragua) totalled, when funding operations finally began, $12,036,376,000. Obviously, to American investors, taxpayers, and subscribers to Liberty Bonds, here were straightforward commercial transactions, evidence of willing aid to friends in need, but evidence, too, of obligations due. Calvin Coolidge's probably apocryphal reply to suggestions of lenient treatment of these debtors— "They hired the money, didn't they?" —is more than an expression of hereditary Vermont thrift; it undoubtedly represented the attitude of most of his fellow citizens.

Payment of the debts would also disturb the American economy, adjusting uneasily and inefficiently to a new creditor status. Normally, although superficially expressed in fiscal symbols, debts clothe themselves eventually in goods and services. The average European debtor saw little or none of the high explosives, the ships at sea, the factories, or the railroads into which so many billions had been poured. He, or at least his more sophisticated political leaders, could see, however, that either gold (which was not available) or other goods and services would have to be "traded," preferably with the United States, in payment of the debts. The war-ravaged European economy could not provide enough of these to meet the needs; nor, because of American tariff policy, could the available goods find their way to the American market according to the pattern by which international balances were normally settled. The debtor, to pay, had to sell to the creditor, who in turn must be willing to buy. By her tariff policy the United States interfered with this normal economic pattern.

Other aspects than the purely economic, however, agitated the European debtors. Prominent among these was a radically different concept of the whole debt problem, stemming, perhaps, from the day when victorious Britain had written off the post-Napoleonic debts of her Continental supporters. Early in 1915 she and her contemporary allies had pooled their financial as well as physical potential, and in underwriting their war effort she had loaned them upwards of ten billions of dollars (her debt to the United States eventually amounted to about four billions). These loans she regarded as uncollectable at the close of hostilities. She and her Allies (it will be recalled that the United States was an "Associated" rather than an "Allied" power) believed that their debts to the United States should be subject to negotiated adjustment, which in its extreme form would amount to cancellation. An added point, seldom mentioned but never far from mind, was the fact that while Europeans had been dying, Americans had been profiting. What more reasonable, then, than the British intimation, made to Wilson at Versailles in December, 1918, of willingness to cancel debts due

194

her if Wilson would cancel British obligations to the United States?

Woodrow Wilson, whether from Calvinistic scruples similar to Coolidge's later attitude, or from a conviction that he could never gain domestic support for such an extreme solution, promptly rejected the idea, looking at the debts as valid obligations, to be settled in due course. Here was one Democratic precedent which Wilson's Republican successors could follow without qualms of conscience, particularly since it had broad popular support. The European idea of downward adjustment died hard, however, and persisted well into the postwar period.

At this distance of time it may be seen that some weight of justice lay on each side. Americans of the day viewed the debts, honestly enough, as due and payable on the basis of most historical precedents; understandably less percipient than a later generation, they failed to realize that their loans to the belligerents had been as much political as fiscal in character, and that the question of their ultimate liquidation must be considered in political as well as monetary terms. When European desire for downward adjustments, derived alike from wartime experience and current conditions, evoked American resistance based on traditional economic grounds, a spontaneous eruption of political ill will ensued. American tariff policy soon moved what might possibly have remained a fiscal question, to be settled by normal economic processes, further into the political realm, where the pressures remained and increased through the Republican years.

•

195

European debtors soon linked their obligations to the United States with reparations, a connection which succeeding American Presidents denied with a stubborn tenacity incomprehensible east of the Atlantic and productive of major problems throughout the period under review. The question, born of desire to hurt a fallen foe, to prevent him from returning to his evil way, and to assuage the victor's suffering and repair the damage to his estate, was too thorny for settlement among Versailles' multiple pressures. Eventually a Reparations Commission dominated by France presented a bill of $32 billion, plus interest, in April, 1921. Less than France had wished, it was still far more than the economists at Versailles had deemed just, and its amount, and the devices surrounding its payment and adjustment, contributed to more than a decade of European turmoil. Germany accepted only under duress, and took up the hopeless burden of a schedule of payments which failed even to meet the interest, leaving final liquidation of the principal a matter of the indefinite future.

Assuming, as did the United States, that the debts were valid obligations, the first problem was to establish their amounts and the conditions of payment. Congress, ever jealous of its control of fiscal policy, established the World War Foreign Debt Commission by an Act of February 9, 1922 (the Washington Conference had adjourned five days earlier). Its membership included the Secretary of State, the Secretary of the Treasury, the Secretary of Commerce, and representatives of each House of Congrsss. It was charged with negotiating individual refunding agreements with each debtor nation, providing (the original terms were drastically altered over the years) payment over a relatively short period (twenty-five years, provided arrangements were completed by the end of the current calendar year) at interest not lower than 4.25 per cent. Delicate and prolonged parleys conducted between May 1, 1923, and May 3, 1926, completed arrangements with thirteen nations. Additional negotiations extending into 1930 resulted in acceptance of total obligations in the amount of $11.5 billion, to be paid over sixty-two years with interest averaging 2.135 per cent; accruing interest raised the total amount due to over $22 billion. Along the way the principle of "capacity to pay" was adopted (first in the French agreement of 1925), resulting in wide discrepancies among the amounts required of various nations; the British debt, for example, was reduced by about 20 per cent, that of France by 50 per cent and that of Italy by almost 75 per cent. Despite the generosity of individual settlements, there was no departure from the position that the debts were due; nor was there any deviation from the assumption that debts and reparations occupied distinctly separate compartments.

Reacting tardily to the legislation of February 9, 1922, Britain attempted once more to interest the United States in cancellation and, if unsuccessful, to enlighten Americans as to the connection between debts and reparations. With Germany at the moment in full default, the so-called Balfour Notes went out to six of Britain's debtors on August 1, 1922, offering to cancel both debts and reparations payable to Britain "as part of a satisfactory international settlement," which of course implied American willingness in turn to cancel debts due herself. It being reasonably certain that this was a vain hope, the Notes went on to state a British policy so aptly suited to the circumstances as to appeal universally to debtors to the United States: debt payments must be equated with reparations receipts: "In no circumstances do we propose to ask more from our debtors than is necessary to pay to our creditors, and while we do not ask for more, all will admit that we can hardly be content with less." Thus was established a dichotomous approach to an identical problem in which each side would persist to the end of the Republican chapter.

The reparations question agitated American official thinking long before the debt-payment pattern was fully established. However, Germany reluctantly took up the burden, paying in full through August, 1921, and continuing partial payments into the early months of 1922. By this time it was obvious that domestic political turmoil and the accompanying inflation (in December, 1922, a dollar would buy 6,865 marks) would interrupt the flow of reparations, with consequent danger of political and military reprisals. The possibility that such a sequence of events might involve the United States exercised Hughes as early as September, 1922, and he began quiet operations designed to shift reparations from the political to the economic realm as an insurance policy against entangling the United States in Europe's troubles. Between September and December, 1922, he approached both Germany and France (the latter on at least four separate occasions) concerning the "desirability of utilizing nonpolitical fiscal aid" in resolving the French-German impasse. With Raymond Poincaré uninterested, nothing happened.

By November 7 Hughes was thinking that knowledgeable financiers should be assembled *qua* financiers, rather than as government representatives, and charged with developing a plan for German payment in accordance with the national ability. The notion incubated slowly until December 27, two days before he was to address the American Historical Association at New Haven. Waking early, the idea of turning experts loose on the reparations problem recurred; clearing with the President on the way to his own office, he incorporated it in his address, advance copies of which had already been distributed. "The crux of the European situation," he wrote, "lies in the settlement of reparations. . . . There will be no adjustment of other needs, however pressing, until a definite and accepted basis for the discharge of reparations claims has been fixed. It is futile to attempt to erect any economic structure in Europe until the foundation is laid."

Hughes expressed his fear of a resort to force in case a forthcoming Allied conference failed to break the deadlock, and suggested as an alternative calling in experts able to chart an economic course out of the morass. American talent could be enlisted in such an operation, he said, provided Germany's creditors would face the reparations problem frankly, *and* would exclude interallied debts from their discussion. At another point in his address, however, he himself skirted perilously close to recognizing the forbidden connection of debts and reparations: ". . . So far as the debtors to the United States are concerned, they have unsettled credit balances, and their condition and capacity to pay cannot be properly determined until the amount that can be realized on these credits for reparations has been determined." *

Hughes's suggestion bore no immediate fruit; though it was later reported that France and Germany were favorably disposed, France had proceeded too far toward the use of force, and the Ruhr invasion followed in early January, 1923, only thirteen days after his New Haven address. Months of international ill will and diminishing economic returns finally convinced France that her approach was ineffective, but though Germany proposed adoption of the Hughes avenue to settlement in June, 1923, it was only in the autumn that it was explored in earnest. A British feeler of October 13 sought to ensure American cooperation even though France might be unready. Early in November Britain proposed formally that France, Italy, and Belgium join her in inviting the United States to study the reparations problem. French reluctance was eventually overcome, resulting in the appointment (on November 20) of a committee of experts chaired by Charles G. Dawes and including Owen D. Young and Henry Morton Robinson as American members. This group, working from January 14 to April 9, 1924, evolved the so-called Dawes Plan.

* On October 15, 1923, Hughes handsomely redeemed his near-slip in a statement to Great Britain which may serve as a sample of the oft-repeated official line: "The government of the United States has consistently maintained the essential difference between the questions of Germany's capacity to pay and of the practical methods to secure reparations from Germany, and payment by the Allies of their debts to the United States, which constitute distinct obligations."

The Plan, which became operative on August 30, 1924, was admittedly an interim scheme, dependent upon restoration of a viable German economy. The experts attacked the problem from the angle of enabling Germany to pay a reasonable amount. They concluded that properly rehabilitated, she could begin to pay an annual levy of one billion gold marks, to be increased to a maximum of 2.5 billions over a four-year period in an open-ended arrangement which contained no terminal date. To ensure compliance, outsiders were to control the sources of funds sufficiently to guarantee payment. A loan of 800,000,000 gold marks ($200 million) was designed to begin restoration of German industry to a productive level. This was promptly underwritten, Coolidge personally soliciting J. P. Morgan and Company to handle $110 million of the total.

Thus arose an interesting and, as events would demonstrate, vicious cycle. Germany, resigned to the yoke of reparations, was forced to borrow to ease her burdens. The urge to borrow increased with returning prosperity and the easy availability of funds, and applications for loans poured forth in ever-greater volume. American willingness to lend matched German desire to borrow. Indeed, American bankers, it can be argued, were at least as culpable in pushing German bonds as were Germans in promoting an increasingly shaky expansion. And the American investor, with money in his pocket, contributed to the ensuing near-madness by buying avidly. The revived flow of reparations payments coincided roughly with completion of the debt settlements, and it became increasingly apparent that one would help to balance the other; in fact, a rough approximation of the situation posited in the Balfour Notes presently emerged, and by the end of the fourth Dawes-Plan year Germany had paid $1.25 billion in reparations and had borrowed $1.5 billion. A routine was thus established: American investment dollars were transmuted into gold marks in the German industrial and commercial complex; these were funneled through the reparations hopper to Western Europe, emerging thence as pounds, francs, and lira in satisfaction of war-debt obligations. That a cyclical element characterized these successive transactions probably occurred to few American investors; no American statesman could afford to admit the elementary economic fact so apparent to later critics of the policy.

Germany presently became restive under the Dawes Plan. The machinery of collection placed foreigners on her soil in derogation of her sovereignty. Failure to establish a date for termination of payments inflicted a burden of unknown duration. The reparations total of $32 billion assigned in 1921 reminded her alike of French vindictiveness and Allied lack of realism. All these factors prompted S. Parker Gilbert, the American Agent General for Reparations, to suggest (as early as October 27, 1927) the importance of negotiating a permanent settlement. This time, France, which had originally opposed the Dawes Plan talks, supported the proposal; she currently had capital in surplus and hoped for an arrangement which might be capitalized into income-producing securities. It took months, however, to bring the nations to take action, and it was only on September 16, 1928, that talks ancillary to the League Assembly brought France, Britain, Japan, Italy, and Belgium to the point of discussions looking to evacuation of the Rhineland and revision of the Dawes Plan arrangements on a finally definitive and realistic base.

Again long-drawn-out proceedings ensued. After five months a committee of experts convened in Paris on February 11, 1929. Its sessions continued until June 7, eventuating in an agreement bearing the name of Owen D. Young, its American chairman. The Young Plan scaled the reparations total from $32 billion to something over $8 billion, and set up a schedule designed to complete payments in fifty-eight and one-half years. At the proposed interest rate of 5.5 per cent, Germany's total payments on interest and principal would have amounted to over $26 billion, substantially short of the original exaction. She accepted, though grumbling that the amount was excessive, and the plan became effective in the spring of 1930. The experts, including the Americans, were more percipient than American statesmen in that they established an exact correspondence between the number of reparations payments and the still-unpaid installments on the European war debts. Thus, after nearly a decade, the reparations problem seemed on the way to a reasonably satisfactory solution—one sufficiently extended to permit Germany to pay without undue hardship and at the same time geared to Europe's necessities in meeting transatlantic balances, while allowing the United States to preserve the fiction that reparations and balances bore no relation to each other.

Neither Young Plan economists nor American statesmen, however, could discount successfully the one factor essential to successful operation of the whole nicely balanced scheme —namely, a continuance of economic prosperity. Attention has been called to the enthusiasm with which Americans, egged on by their bankers, poured funds into the German economy. The result was that in the seven years ending June 30, 1931, American investors furnished 55 per cent of approximately \$2.25 billion placed in German long-term bonds. Late in 1927 Prentiss Gilbert began warning the Department of State that German political units were engaging in dubious fiscal practices. This made it more difficult to secure departmental clearance for the flotation of bond issues, and the bankers resorted more and more to short-term loans, which required no clearance. An estimated \$925 million went into this form of investment. Americans thus held evidences of over \$2 billion of German foreign obligations which, overall, totalled approximately \$6 billion. The flow of funds dwindled, beginning in 1928, when suspicion of German financial stability encouraged Americans to empty their wallets into the maw of the Big Bull Market. The heavy residue of investment remained, however, subject to any interruption of the current upward spiral.

This interruption, in the Depression of 1929, was both sudden and dramatic, and was a well-established if unpleasant fact by the time Young Plan payments were inaugurated. Herbert Hoover first viewed it as a temporary phenomenon, but its persistence convinced him by the end of 1930 that it was an international problem and required treatment accordingly. Discussion of the world economic situation reached cabinet level on April 7, 1931, after Montagu Norman, Governor of the Bank of England, had reported the flight of gold from Britain and Germany. The situation revealed sharp differences in attitude between Hoover and his Secretary of

State. As Secretary of Commerce and a member of the World War Foreign Debt Commission, Hoover had, so he asserts in his *Memoirs*, favored cancellation of the pre-Armistice debts of the major powers and collection of those incurred after the Armistice. Balked in this, he had proposed to cancel the interest and spread the principal over a considerable period. His colleagues had again overridden him, insisting that Congress would not approve. As President, he shared his predecessors' insistence upon compartmentalizing debts and reparations, and was convinced that, the Depression aside, Europe was able to pay the scaled-down Young Plan obligations. Stimson, on the other hand, argued that there was a connection between the two and that, since the debts themselves were uncollectable, they should be cancelled. These differences, though probably having little bearing upon policy formulation, contributed to the deteriorating climate of Hoover-Stimson relations toward the end of the Administration.

The Hoover Moratorium linked the European Depression to that in the States, forced the President to skirt perilously close to the debts/reparations complex, and showed him the possessor of considerable ability and no little courage. Austrian fiscal difficulties matched those of Germany, and, in an effort to solve their joint problems, the two proposed a customs union on March 22, 1931. France opposed this as the possible precursor of a Danubian political consolidation dangerous to her security. Her objections created a diplomatic impasse during which, on May 11, the Kredit Anstalt, one of the bulwarks of Central European finance, was forced to close. By the third week in June the German Reichsbank had lost over 40 per cent of its reserves through gold transfers and liquidation of short-term loans. Clearly, unless something were done, the private American stake in Germany would be jeopardized, and with it the whole structure of reparations and debt payments.

Hoover's concern had been enlisted prior to the Kredit Anstalt failure when Ambassador Frederic M. Sackett, Jr., reported personally on May 6, 1931, that German matters were in a serious state. The ensuing month brought disturbing rumors that Germany might seek relief from reparations payments, and on Sackett's departure (he sailed on June 2) Hoover had instructed him to assure Germany that "we would endeavor to be helpful"; he stated his view, for repetition to the German authorities, that "the whole reparations and debt complex could well be temporarily reviewed in the light of capacity to pay under depression conditions." Supplementary talks with Dawes and with Hugh Gibson prepared him for a session with Stimson, Mellon, and Ogden L. Mills, Undersecretary of the Treasury, on June 5.

At this interview Hoover stated his conviction that matters had passed the point where mere "review" could suffice. Action being necessary, he suggested the proposal of a one-year postponement of payments on Allied debts, conditioned on a corresponding suspension of reparations collections. Stimson "felt more glad than I can say" at this prospect; Mellon was flatly opposed and Mills, who looked longingly toward a balanced budget, raised doubts as to presidential authority to act under existing legislation. The following day, June 6, Germany announced her inability to pay further reparations. Several hectic days ensued. Hoover's counselors remained divided, and he himself became alarmed lest the proposal link debts and reparations in a fashion threatening unpleasant political repercussions. Mellon felt that France should be approached early; others did not. All feared a leak to the press, and conferees came to the White House by separate entrances to avoid detection. The mercury hung high in the capillary tubes, and tempers shortened accordingly. Stimson undertook to talk with Ramsay MacDonald over the trans-Atlantic telephone; this irritated the President, as did an apparently unauthorized and disturbing statement by Castle. The German situation deteriorated further in the face of presidential inaction and continued maneuvering. At this crucial stage Hoover departed on a swing into the Midwest, where he performed the embarrassing and long-overdue ritual of dedicating a memorial to Warren G. Harding.

Returning to Washington on June 18, Hoover ended his considerable period of indecision, to which many factors had contributed. Added to his own uncertainties was the fact that Congress, rather than the President, controlled debt policy, and by the further fact that, in making proposals on reparations he was dealing with a matter in which the United States had no legal concern and which he himself had often professed to believe was divorced from the debts. Congress not being in session, he was legally bound under the funding agreements to demand payment of a few installments due on June 15 (most were payable on December 15), after which he was free to make proposals, subject to subsequent congressional ratification. Having taken the plunge, he told the press somewhat cryptically on the 19th that he had been in touch with party leaders concerning "certain steps we might take to assist in economic recovery both here and abroad. . . . No definite plans or conclusions have yet been arrived at, but the response I have met from the leaders of both parties is most gratifying." Official announcement came on the 20th, accompanied by the formal hedge that the President did not "approve in any sense of the cancellation of the debts to us."

Once the President had been brought to the point of action, Stimson's principal task was to win French approval and in this he received the initial support of Ambassador Paul Claudel, who approved the plan, though he was probably not overjoyed at being kept in the dark until so close to the event. French leaders were still less happy, since they had learned of the proposal from news reports leaked by those with whom Hoover had talked on June 18, prior to Stimson's briefing of Claudel; very practically, too, they stood to lose $79 million of expected reparations payments during the moratorium year. Their indignation, according to Stimson, was at least partly for public consumption; though privately approving, they wrangled for three weeks over details and postponed acceptance until July 6. Hoover's work with individual members of Congress contributed vitally to general public approval and ultimate congressional enactment (on December 23, 1931) of a one-year moratorium on payments of reparations or intergovernmental debts, made effective retroactively to July 1, and so, in effect, postponing reparations payments to December 15, 1932. This timetable, in practice, removed the problem from active negotiation until after the election of 1932.

The President's action had been taken courageously in the face of inevitable domestic opposition and possibly unfavorable political consequences. Though it helped save Germany from internal political crisis, it came too late to prevent wholesale bank failures in Eastern and Central Europe and thus failed to have the mitigating effect for which Hoover had hoped. Its influence was at best temporary and palliative, and it could have succeeded fully only as part of an overall political stabilization for which Europe was in no mood and to which the United States was in no position to contribute.

The Administration, however, was not out of the woods. The moratorium stabilized long-term credits, but did not cover hundreds of millions in short-term credits, which were equally endangered. It seems clear that American bankers, put to it to find productive outlets at home, had been vigorously pushing their depositors' money into the German market for short-term loans. Ambassador Sackett had reported in January that the Chase Bank and the Guaranty Trust Co. had, respectively, $190 million and $90 million (nearly half of their total capital) in such loans. During the summer Hoover secured from the Comptroller of the Currency statistics indicating that American banks held over $1.7 billion in short-term obligations based on poor collateral or none at all, subject to quick call, and difficult to renew. If forced to default on these, both European banks and American investors would be in dire straits.

Attempting to fend off this new threat, Hoover instructed Stimson, then in Europe, to undertake conversations in London designed to effect a "standstill" agreement which would do for these private debts held in Germany and Central Europe what the moratorium had done for intergovernmental obligations. At the London talks France renewed an earlier alternative proposal for a joint governmental loan of $500 million to help Germany weather the storm. Stimson and Mellon, who was also present at the talks, urged Hoover to travel this path, but he refused to do so. With France still unhappy over the moratorium, Stimson attempted to present the standstill as a joint Anglo-American move, hoping thus to moderate French hostility. Hoover, however, gave its content to the press as his own, just as Stimson in London was linking Ramsay MacDonald to its sponsorship. This episode did little to improve the deteriorating relations between President and Secretary of State. The American bankers, naturally enough, preferred the loan scheme to one freezing their own assets. They protested vigorously and accepted the standstill only when Hoover, indignant at their overextended loans, threatened to publish a full account of their irresponsible conduct. The agreement, negotiated between July 20 and 22, 1931, placed bank acceptances on a standstill basis until September 1, 1931, and was later extended to March 1, 1933.

This agreement concludes the development of formal American policy toward the debts/reparations complex. The persistent refusal of official leadership to consider cancellation of the debts or to accord political recognition of a connection between factors patently inseparable economically will remain a monument to the power of American public opinion and the necessary subservience of political leaders

210

to its dictates. Their private subservience to the economic myth of compartmentalization is hardly a monument to their courage or acumen.

The effects of the moratorium and the standstill were no more than palliative and in at least one instance harmful, the combined freeze on reparations and private debts contributing to abandonment of the gold standard in numerous nations, climaxed by British action in September, 1931. One particular aftermath was the visit of French Prime Minister Pierre Laval to Washington in October. In their discussions Laval and Hoover agreed that the moratorium period should be utilized to seek long-run agreement on the postponed question of intergovernmental debts, not merely for the moratorium year, but "covering the period of business depression." It was agreed that the takeoff point in approaching the *debt* question should be found in European initiative in solving the *reparations* problem. This, Hoover's closest approach to admitting a connection between the two, inspired European effort to arrive at a solution.

The Lausanne Conference (opening on June 16, 1932) brought Germany and her European creditors together. Three weeks' discussion produced agreement to cut the Young Plan reparations figures to $714,600,000 in 5 per cent bonds, which Germany would contribute to a fund dedicated to the reconstruction of Europe. This gracious gesture proposed forgiveness of about 90 per cent of the Young Plan total, but its magnanimity depended upon a large "if," the whole scheme being predicated upon the success of Germany's creditors in reaching satisfactory arrangements with their own creditors—i.e., the United States. Reduction of reparations, then, hinged upon reduction of debts, and the forbidden connection was in the open again.

It had come into the open, too, at a peculiarly inopportune moment, as the American election campaign was getting under way. The debts became a campaign issue and, domestic exigencies constraining both candidates to demand full payment, the Lausanne proposal perforce went into the discard. The postelection period brought requests for postponement which Hoover felt compelled to deny, though he tried to ease the burden by offering to receive the December installments in foreign currency, to be held abroad and forwarded when conditions warranted. Britain in turn rejected this proposal, paid her December 15 installment in full, and was joined by five other debtors. France, "deferred" payment and, with four others, went into default. Clearly, debt revision would be a live issue for the incoming Roosevelt Administration.

Several factors frustrated Hoover's honest attempts to make constructive use of the interregnum. His developing personal antagonism toward Roosevelt, his continuing lack of rapport with Stimson, and the President-elect's unwillingness to assume responsibility until clothed with authority all played their part in adding to Hoover's woes. The postelection month saw Hoover, Stimson, and Mills (who had succeeded Mellon at the Treasury in January, 1932) in almost daily consultation; Europe meantime was alert for the slightest indication of Rooseveltian complaisance. Roosevelt, moreover, was wrapped up in preinaugural plans and never more than mildly interested in the debt problem anyway; he delegated it almost completely to Raymond Moley, one of his Brain Trusters, who irritated the Republican leaders. Matters, therefore, moved unpleasantly from Roosevelt's initial (and mistaken) conviction that Hoover was trying to do him wrong on the debt question. Hoover, at the end of his physical and psychological tether, had become convinced that Roosevelt intended to let the country sink into the depths, to be rescued by the knight in shining armor. Their debt conference of November 22 was probably doomed before Roosevelt, accompanied by Moley, arrived at the White House to confer with Hoover, Mills, and Stimson. The meeting itself was awkward, the three Republicans disliking Moley on sight, and its results largely negative. Hoover attempted to commit Roosevelt to a joint meeting with congressional leaders at which the two would urge reactivation of the World War Foreign Debt Commission to renegotiate the whole question. Though unwilling to attend such a meeting, Roosevelt agreed to give it his blessing; he declined, however, to subscribe to an agreed statement on the debts and, after some further aggravations, informed the press that the debts were "not his baby," and the defaults ensued.

The debts would not down, of course, and eventually, at Roosevelt's suggestion, Felix Frankfurter opened negotiations which led to a Roosevelt-Stimson conference on January 9, 1933, at Hyde Park; Hoover consented only on condition that the formal invitation go across the presidential desk. The two American aristocrats found common personal ground at once, though the clutter with which Roosevelt delighted to

213

surround himself gave the Squire of Highhold and Woodley a feeling of confusion. Their five-hour discussion ranged widely; as reported by Stimson, Roosevelt placed heaviest emphasis on Far Eastern matters, and nothing startling emerged on the debt question. A second session in mid-January, 1933, with Moley present, was likewise unproductive, though Roosevelt and Moley indicated that they too would put debts into a compartment by themselves, separating them from other aspects of economic cooperation. This ended inter-Administration debt discussions and left the question, after all was said and done, not so far from where it had been when the Republicans took over in 1921, still a ground of international friction and ill will. When Roosevelt took power in his own hands he refused to commit himself to negotiation of general revision, and excluded the subject from the London Economic Conference agenda in 1933. Eventually the debtor nations, except Finland, settled the matter by defaulting. The whole debt story singularly exemplified the unwisdom of measuring wartime cooperation in fiscal terms and encouraged Roosevelt to use another and better, if still hardly perfect, approach in 1941–1945; meantime, debts and reparations eventually disappeared into a common limbo.

The Kellogg-Briand Pact of August 27, 1928, brought fifteen nations (and later almost the entire world) into covenant to renounce war "as an instrument of national policy." Realistic contemporaries would call attention to its failure to establish penalties for noncompliance. Later observers, ridiculin its sole reliance on moral sanctions, the qualifications with which its framers hedged it about, and its failure to ful-fill its supposed promises, would cite it as a supreme example of the ineffectiveness of words without deeds and of posing ends without willingness to provide means. Viewed, as it should fairly be, through the eyes of its earnest promoters, it established a focal point around which, hopefully, principle could rally moral force to counter evil intent. Like other pol-icy formulations of the period, it would draw strength, or display weakness, from the current temper at the time of its testing. As signed, it was a harbinger of hope and a consid-erable advance upon previous American involvement; look-ing back, one can only grieve that a sense of national and international responsibility had not developed between its signature and its testing by Japanese aggression.

The vision of a warless world which has long intrigued mankind attracted an odd assortment of Americans in the 1920's, and the forces which finally came to focus in the Pact of Paris drew upon many sources. Charles Clayton Morrison had for years inveighed against the evils of war in the col-umns of *The Christian Century*. Salmon O. Levinson, a Chi-cago lawyer with a sense of mission, picked up the slogan "outlawry of war" and pushed the notion that international fiat could end international strife. He sought to recruit Borah to sponsor outlawry in the Senate. Borah found the idea at-tractive and introduced a resolution on February 13, 1923, making war a public crime under international law. Opposed to forcible sanctions, he hesitated for months to speak out on the floor. Others supported the Geneva Protocol for the Pa-cific Settlement of International Disputes (1924), relying upon the elimination of war through compulsory arbitration and ultimate disciplinary action under League auspices. Professor James T. Shotwell of Columbia University and David Hunter Miller were active in its support. The Protocol, which Borah opposed, was defeated in 1925. Borah became interested in a number of other issues—Prohibition, the World Court, recognition of Russia—and Levinson, who pursued outlawry single-mindedly, was driven to distraction. He succeeded in pushing Borah to reintroduce his resolution in December, 1926, but no ringing speech in support was forthcoming. The winter of 1926–1927 found Borah having a field day attacking the Administration's Nicaraguan policy, and still no speech on outlawry.

Here matters stood in the spring of 1927, when Shotwell played, momentarily, an important role. Returning from lecturing in Berlin, in March, he was invited to call on Aristide Briand. He improved the occasion to urge the Foreign Minister to lend French influence to a proposal for the outlawry of war, a term which Levinson had already been using for months. He presently permitted himself to be persuaded to furnish Briand with a draft address on the subject. On April 6, tenth anniversary of American entry into the war, Briand spoke to a French audience, basing his remarks on the Shotwell paper. In this highly unorthodox fashion he told the French people, the American people, and last but most important the Washington authorities, that his government was prepared to enter a Franco-American pact "tending, as between those two countries, to 'outlaw war,' to use an American expression."

Briand's move was both undiplomatic, in its disregard of

216

normal channels, and badly timed in that a number of unpleasant problems occupied Kellogg's energies, only recently restored after a winter of recurrent annoyances which had driven him to the verge of exhaustion. Mexican relations were simmering down after difficulties extending over many months, but Dwight Morrow's light touch had not yet been applied to their still volatile elements. Henry L. Stimson was about to turn his sterner but equally effective hand to a reduction of Nicaraguan domestic and international tensions, which at the moment remained vexing (see Chapter VII). The Nanking Incident had muddied Far Eastern waters (see Chapter IX). France had refused to attend the Geneva Naval Conference, and demands for war-debt payments did nothing to improve Franco-American relations. All in all, Kellogg might be excused for not receiving Briand's oblique invitation with open arms, particularly when it could be interpreted (as Kellogg did view it) as a veiled move to create a bilateral political alliance contrary to long-standing American policy.

Nor was he overjoyed at continued academic sallies into the world of affairs. When Briand's move went largely unnoticed, President Nicholas Murray Butler of Columbia wrote a letter to *The New York Times* (April 25) which elicited considerable comment and even threatened to unite the normally dissident elements of the peace movement. The indefatigable Shotwell and his fellow Columbian Joseph P. Chamberlain produced a draft treaty embodying the Briand scheme and published it late in May with the comment, addressed to the Department of State, that it would serve as a trial balloon to sound out public sentiment. Kellogg, in no mood for balloons, trial or otherwise, sharply resented this academic persistence, classed Butler *et al.* as "———fools," in company certain to relay the remark to Morningside Heights, and publicly ignored the Shotwell-Briand-Butler *démarche*.

With the Department carefully refraining from public comment, interest shifted to Borah, who as early as May 6 indicated a wish that Briand had made his proposal in treaty form. On May 9, at Cleveland, he made an important statement, linking his still-pending resolution on outlawry with the current Briand proposal, and suggesting that both be broadened into an *international* treaty "branding war as criminal." Although he was at the moment most interested in preventing the powers from using force on troubled China, this remains the first public suggestion of the multilateral base upon which the Kellogg-Briand Pact ultimately rested. Within a few days (on May 25) Morrison was editorializing in favor of multilateralism in the *Christian Century*. Privately, Castle cannily doubted to his diary (on May 11) that Briand would take kindly to adding further signatories, which would dilute the Franco-American flavor of his proposal to French disadvantage. After Borah's mild display of interest in May he turned to other matters through the summer and only reverted to outlawry in the autumn when public sentiment for a Franco-American agreement was brought to his attention.

Meantime, Charles A. Lindbergh and the *Spirit of St. Louis* proved excellent ambassadors to France (the solo flight occurred on May 20–21), and a few days later Briand returned to the charge, inquiring (on June 2) via Ambassador Myron T. Herrick as to the possibility of opening conversations on the subject of his April remarks. After a week of departmental hesitation, Herrick was instructed to inform Briand of American willingness to conduct exploratory talks —a clearly dilatory tactic, as evidenced by the suggestion that the French Ambassador to Washington (who was on home leave until late in August) should act on behalf of France. Undeterred, Briand handed Herrick (about to depart for the States) on June 21, 1927, a draft bilateral agreement condemning war as between the parties and renouncing it "as an instrument of their national policy towards each other." This forced departmental cogitation, if not action. In a long memorandum of the 24th, J. Theodore Marriner marshaled a number of negative factors for the Secretary's consideration, concluding with the first official mention of a possible multilateral approach which has come to the writer's attention, suggesting that "if any step further than this were required, it should be in the form of a universal undertaking not to resort to war, to which the United States would at any time be most happy to become a party." This postdates Borah's suggestion by over a month and antedates Kellogg's first hint of a similar point of view, recorded on July 6 when he told Howard that his country would "not desire to make any treaty with France which we would not be willing to make with Great Britain, Japan, *or any other country.*" (Emphasis supplied.)

Kellogg reacted negatively to the Briand bilaterial treaty draft of June 21. He opposed Briand's proposal to speak publicly of the matter on July 4, and told Coolidge (on June 27) that he felt the longest step the government could take would be to renew a series of expiring arbitration treaties negotiated by Elihu Root with Great Britain, France, and Japan, and to bring the latter into an open-ended series of Bryan conciliation treaties already including France and Britain. After giving vent to his pique at the efforts of "high French officials and certain individuals in private life, apparently in touch with these officials," to stampede him into action by outside pressure, he left the matter alone for some months and resisted French efforts to revive it in September.

The Geneva disarmament failure of the summer, contributing to a revived move for naval construction, furnished little incentive for talk of peace; Borah, however, revived his interest and, recurring to multilateralism, suggested to the Reverend Sidney Gulick (on November 1) that, since Briand had made an initial move, it would be well for the United States to enlarge the framework to include Britain, Italy, Germany, and Japan. Senator Arthur Capper of Kansas sponsored a Columbia-bred resolution (December 9) which would record senatorial willingness to have the United States join France and other nations in a war-renunciation treaty. And in December interviews between Castle and Claudel made it clear that there was departmental thinking in multilateral terms.

Borah introduced his antiwar resolution on December 12, and an exchange of letters with Kellogg (December 14, 15) and interviews during the ensuing week clarified the Senator's interest in a multilateral approach to outlawry and contributed to Kellogg's increasing appreciation of that approach. Matters came to a head at Kellogg's session with the Committee on Foreign Relations on December 22. Called ostensibly to consider renewal of the Root arbitration treaty with France, the discussion veered to multilateralism as a means of outlawry. Here the record becomes complicated and a bit obscure. Kellogg later claimed that the suggestion of multilateralism was his own. Enough evidence has been marshaled by Robert H. Ferrell and John Chalmers Vinson to make it clear that others, particularly Borah, had preceded him along that line of thinking and had educated him to that point of view sufficiently to entitle Borah to a claim of joint authorshop.

At any rate, multilateralism soon became the American line. After cautiously submitting the idea for Elihu Root's scrutiny, Kellogg directed two notes to France on December 28. One proposed to renew the expiring Root treaty, a routine opening gambit. The other addressed itself to Briand's objective of ending war, as embodied in the June proposal, so long held in careful abeyance. Kellogg now shrewdly proposed a vastly different vehicle of outlawry (a word, incidentally, which he never employed in the lengthy correspondence), one which must have been vastly disconcerting to the Frenchman. Instead of accepting the cozy Franco-American deal offered in June, Kellogg proposed to bring all nations into the act; if Briand had hoped to involve the United States in the complex guarantees by which France had sought security, that hope dissolved into the mist of a proposed Franco-American invitation to all the world to unite in renouncing war. Kellogg, the tardy convert, had seized the initiative, and it was now Briand's turn to plan maneuvers and calculate consequences.

Briand clung to bilateralism and Kellogg contented himself with countering the Frenchman's quibbles over terms and his suggestion of tempting but dangerous bypaths designed to safeguard French interests. Matters hung fire for some weeks, during which Borah entered the lists with an article in *The New York Times* (February 5, 1928) arguing that the Kellogg proposal would serve as a reinsurance of the League Covenant and the Locarno treaties. The article was an interesting example of a cooperative spirit rare in Borah's career: Kellogg sought his help in countering some of Briand's arguments; Borah, relying on material furnished by Levinson, replied to Briand's (privately) expressed fears of disharmony between the Kellogg scheme and France's prior obligations under the League/Locarno paraphernalia. This reasoned argument, a far cry from Borah's sometime bellicosity, showed him *en rapport* with the Secretary, who used the article in his official reply to Briand (of February 27).

It was Briand's turn to ponder again, and during the month which preceded his repy (of March 30) Kellogg changed from a lukewarm supporter of a mild peace gesture into an ardent advocate of his own gloss on Briand's idea and began to press the Foreign Minister to take favorable action. Moving gradually and reluctantly toward the Kellogg position, Briand yielded to the point of expressing willingness to explore multilateralism. This was merely a prelude to posing conditions. He took the American attitude, said his note, to include willingness to absolve signatories from their obligation in case of aggression by one member against another, to include a reservation of the right of self-defense, and to recognize previous League/Locarno promises. The treaty, he suggested, must become effective only after universal acceptance, or upon agreement among its signatories to bring it into force despite abstentions. Acceptance of these conditions would induce France to join the United States in proposing "a draft agreement essentially corresponding in purpose to the original proposal of M. Briand, in the multipartite form desired by the United States with the changes of wording made necessary by the new concept. . . ."

Briand proposed that, if Kellogg accepted his stipulations, the two nations join in submitting the previous correspondence to Britain, Germany, Italy, and Japan. Kellogg inquired bluntly (on April 5) whether Briand was willing to act on his own suggestion. Optimistically construing a partly decoded reply (of the 7th) as favorable, and determined to retain the initiative, he drafted notes to the four without further ado and without including France in the communication; he enclosed a treaty draft and asked each to measure its terms against the yardstick of League and Locarno obligations, and to inform him whether it would be possible to join the United States in "an unqualified renunciation of war." The note was singularly reticent on French contributions to the proposal, though such would of course be obvious to careful readers of the correspondence. Short of a French roadblock, however, a "Kellogg Plan" might soon emerge.

Final decoding of the French reply disclosed that later pragraphs qualified its initial acceptance of the American proposal of joint approach. Kellogg, undaunted, decided to have his notes presented (they were delivered on April 13) with addenda indicating that France was not bound by American action and might, if desired, submit clarifications of her own. Briand had agreed to this procedure (on April 11), promising to add a Franch draft treaty to the imposing documentation already in the record. Kellogg found this (it arrived on the 20th) "entirely unacceptable" on several grounds, most objectionable of which was a too-specific reservation of the right of self-defense; more generally, he asserted, it shifted the emphasis from peace to war, seeming "in effect to be a justification rather than a renunciation of the use of armed force."

His growing conviction of the importance of agreement, however, led him to move toward the French position, as evidenced in a hastily arranged address to the American Society of International Law on April 28. By May 5 he was writing Mrs. Kellogg that a successful treaty would be "the greatest accomplishment of my administration or of any administration lately," and visions of a Nobel Peace Prize were floating before his eyes on the strength of newspaper nominations for that honor. His indignant silence of June, 1927, was now swallowed up in a desire for accomplishment.

France presently endured an election and Briand sustained an illness, affording opportunity for recovery from the shock of Kellogg's seizure of the initiative. Britain moved into the role of objector, proposing a reservation intended to safeguard her position in the sensitive Suez-Egyptian sector. Kellogg continued to press for elimination of reservations, and a Briand-Chamberlain interview produced guarded optimism in Paris; Claudel presently (June 7) reported that France would not insist on treaty safeguards of the right of self-defense, nor would she demand unanimous acceptance before the treaty became effective. She still desired treaty stipulation of the binding force of existing commitments and recognition that violation of the treaty absolved other parties from obligation to the offender. A spirit of accommodation began to animate both parties to the long dialogue.

Kellogg completed the *rapprochment* in a note to France and thirteen other governments (delivered on June 23), clothing in diplomatic verbiage his capitulation to the French demands. Reference to his April 28 address to the international lawyers included the positions there assumed as interpretations of the original draft treaty. He submitted a revised draft treaty including the Locarno powers among the original signatories; this made any violator of Locarno's promises *ipso facto* a trespasser upon his multilateral engagement. To satisfy French insistence upon absolution from obligations to a treaty violator, he buried in the preamble a statement which, the covering note asserted, gave "express recognition to the principle that if a state resorts to war in violation of the treaty, the other contracting parties are released from their obligations under the treaty to that state. . . ." India and the British Dominions were invited to become initial participants, giving the agreement a broadened territorial and political base. To disarm any final French reluctance, and to dispel any lingering French ill feeling, he offered to suggest that the signing exercises take place in Paris.

Some Anglo-French maneuvering failed to materialize into formal criticism, and an August ceremony was put in train. A few minor irritations intervened but made no real difference. Kellogg's willingness to go to Paris for the signing ceremony was predicated upon the presence of his opposite numbers

225

(except the Japanese Foreign Minister, whom he excused from the expensive trip), and when neither Benito Mussolini nor his second-in-command found attendance convenient, the Secretary's choler was momentarily aroused. A Spanish request to be an original signer threatened to open the way to similar Russian overtures, but the problem was handled safely and diplomatically. These minor matters left Kellogg free time to devote to the groundwork of ratification, and mollifying gestures went out to possible opponents, particularly crafty assurances to the New York *Herald-Tribune* and to William Randolph Hearst, big-navy advocates, that there was nothing in his pact incompatible with naval strength.

As he prepared to leave for Paris to sign the final document, Kellogg could discount his early indifference and look with satisfaction at his conduct of the episode which would make the heaviest immediate impress of any during his tenure. He had shifted a dangerous French proposal into safer channels of multilateralism; he had avoided formal insertion of dangerous reservations and insulated them successfully; he had completed a document which in awesome simplicity committed the nations to "condemn recourse to war for the solution of international controversies, and renounce it as an instrument of national policy in their relations with one another." The aura of "renunciation" shadowed the total absence of sanctions; no one was bound to lift a finger, much less fire a gun, in defense of the promises so solemnly given on August 27, 1928. Had this thought occurred to Kellogg as his shaking hand signed on behalf of the United States, he might have taken comfort in the fact that no treaty containing sanctions could have gone so far as the signing table. Its tentative and ultimately worthless promises were well within the temper of his time in avoiding a commitment which could command performance. They were, too, within the framework which was increasingly demonstrating, as the decade proceeded, that isolationism was a matter of degree, which, though it signified an unreadiness to yield to commitment, was ready enough to commit involvement.

Announcement of the Anglo-French Naval Agreement (late in July) punctuated, unpleasantly, Kellogg's preparations to visit Paris, and he departed under presidential injunction to comment on nothing but his immediate mission, and to snub the British partner to the agreement by refusing to visit London, where he had spent happy days as Ambassador; a stop in Ireland underscored this deliberate insult to Britain. The treaty's course through the Senate found it in competition with the cruiser bill, born of Geneva's disarmament frustrations. Executive pressure was vigorously applied, Borah's support was enlisted, and senatorial fears were calmed by adoption of a committee report spelling out the right of self-defense and eliminating sanctions from measures available for enforcement, and the Senate consented to ratification on January 15, 1929, by a vote of 85/1. Kellogg's great achievement was in the hands of his successors.

The foregoing chapter has portrayed a series of curious episodes, illustrating well the hesitant and tentative character of policy during the Republican years. Debts were debts and reparations were Europe's problem, and never the twain must meet. Thus was affirmed American aloofness from Europe's complications, the while individual Americans contributed to their solution, and an American President sought their amelioration. The Peace Pact story, with its sequence of initial reluctance, enthusiastic involvement, and ultimate avoidance of commitment, truly reflects the temper of the time—a time when lack of positive accomplishment stemmed alike from a dearth of strong leadership and from a national climate averse to experiment and satisfied with the *status quo.*

VII

Latin America:
Mexico and Nicaragua

The new Republican regime of 1921 faced many Latin-American problems. These had been inherited about equally from Woodrow Wilson and from more remote presidential ancestors of their own political faith. Indeed, Caribbean intervention, well established prior to the Republican take-over in 1921, was distinctly a bipartisan operation. It will be the task of this and the succeeding chapter, in part, to show that the moderation of Caribbean imperialism, sometimes associated primarily with Roosevelt's Good Neighbor Policy in the 1930's, owes a good deal to Republican beginnings. Though these beginnings were sometimes reluctant and seldom completely successful, the record will show that they were so substantial as to warrant application of the bipartisan label to the retreat from, as well as the advance into, Caribbean affairs.

Theodore Roosevelt's gloss on the Monroe Doctrine had arrogated to the United States, quite unjustifiably, the right to intervene in the affairs of American states when European interests in areas close to the Panama Canal were so jeopardized as to make European action likely. He himself had applied his "Police Power" theory to Dominican finances in 1904–1905. William Howard Taft set marines in Nicaragua in 1912, and Woodrow Wilson, an avowed anti-imperialist, had intervened forcibly in Haiti in 1915 and in Santo Domingo in 1916.

Wilson moved a step beyond forcible interposition, too, in 1913, proclaiming his doctrine of "constitutional legitimacy," denying recognition to governments gaining power by other than constitutional means. This at once reversed a policy of *de facto* recognition of successful revolutions going back to Thomas Jefferson, frustrated a congenital Latin-American tendency to revolution, and, if forthrightly maintained, might be used to impose a *Pax Americana* on the uneasy environs of the Panama Canal.

Developments early in the century, focusing on a transIsthmian channel, generated the "Panama Policy" of extreme sensitivity to political instability within a considerable radius of any potential canal. In the same period arose the specter (probably never more than such) of German interference in Caribbean affairs; the specter took some form in German antics in the Zimmermann Note to Mexico just prior to World War I, and in the early postwar years when considerable currency was given to the alleged pro-German activities of Mexico's wartime President, Venustiano Carranza. These prewar and wartime pressures had conduced to the establishment of a thoroughgoing United States hegemony over the Caribbean and had produced sharp anti-American reactions in Mexico, herself in the throes of violent revolution since 1910. Together, they had amply earned for the United States the opprobrious title of "Colossus of the North," and had created a situation calling for a high degree of diplomatic acumen.

Though the problems were not all of Republican manufacture, their solution would depend largely upon successive Republican Administrations. Germany was no longer a menace, if she had ever been one. War-weary Europe, in both political and economic areas, was well content to let the Roosevelt Corollary insure peace and dividends. Isolationism, whatever its weight in European relations, had never hampered United States policy toward nations to the south. Briefly, the Republican problem of 1921 was one of dealing with weak, unstable, barely solvent or insolvent states, dependent upon raw-material economy, permeated with antipathy, and resentful of actual or threatened intervention. The Republican response was generally slow, at first niggardly to the point of churlishness, and aimed at particular sore spots rather than general therapeutics.

As the period wore on, however, more general considerations emerged, and by March, 1933, the foundation and some of the superstructure of the Good Neighbor Policy were in place. Some observers trace the start of this construction back to the Hughes regime, though this requires a somewhat optimistic outlook; Coolidge and Kellogg built reluctantly but definitely, and Hoover moved forward along a more cal- culated course. This effort at improving relations was both highly desirable and long overdue. United States policy was almost universally condemned south of the Rio Grande, and was increasingly distasteful to many north of that river. The actions to be described, halting and hesitant though some of them were, combined to ease Franklin D. Roosevelt's way to a greater success than the Republicans were able to achieve in their day.

As the Republican years opened, the situation was not a happy one. Cuba had been vulnerable to intervention since her acceptance of the Platt Amendment of 1901 had granted this right, subject only to United States discretion. Taft had scolded Cuba periodically to refresh her memory and fore- stall the irregularities which might necessitate repetition of the formal intervention of 1906, and Wilson had continued the custom. Collapse of the sugar economy in the postwar period had compounded the danger of political interference. United States influence in Nicaragua had been consolidated, after the intervention of 1912, behind a reasonably docile succession of Conservative presidents, supported by a token Legation Guard and supplied with funds under fiscal ar- rangements satisfactory to northern bankers; the Bryan- Chamorro Treaty of 1916 provided for the construction of a second Panama Canal should such become desirable. In Haiti, occupied in 1915 after generations of political unrest and economic stagnation, self-government was a mockery and actual control was in the hands of a marine officer who reported to the naval officer who acted as President of Santo Domingo. Haiti had begun, not too happily, to exchange this

232

political abnegation for economic and social betterment. Santo Domingo, occupied in 1916, had been only less disturbed and backward than Haiti. Her subjection was equally complete, with officers of the United States Navy controlling both domestic and foreign relations and supervising the autocratic, but not unsympathetic, improvement of internal conditions. Mexico, to be noted first in detail, was not under the United States yoke, but was headed by a regime as yet unrecognized.

Here, then, were conditions to inspire complacency or criticism, depending upon one's attitude toward the imperialism which they represented—an imperialism adopted in the aftermath of turn-of-the-century exuberance and grounded in a natural desire to protect the site, and then the reality, of the Panama Canal. In the temper of the twenties, expressions of complacency were less popular than critical attacks, which were launched as early as January, 1922, when Hiram Johnson proposed a senatorial investigation of the Nicaraguan intervention, and was joined by William H. King of Utah, Thomas J. Walsh of Montana, and George W. Norris of Nebraska. Criticism of other policies followed, with Borah not infrequently involved. Outright supporters of the Panama Policy went increasingly on the defensive under congressional and public criticism, and it became the task of succeeding Administrations to mediate between the necessities of existing interventions and rising pressures for their liquidation. This attempt to adjust past policy to changing attitudes was registered in numerous episodes and, before the period ended, had wrought considerable change without avowed reversal.

Harding and Hughes, like Wilson and Bryan before them, faced a question of recognizing a revolutionary regime in Mexico. The comparison, however, stops at this point, since Mexico had advanced far along the road to revolutionary nationalism by 1921. At Wilson's advent in 1913 the long-pent forces opposed to Porfirio Díaz' dictatorship (in power since the 1870's) were still contending for the preferment of an ignorant and bewildered populace. Victoriano Huerta had just seized power by the simple expedient of murdering Francisco I. Madero; his bloody hands were soon fending off the attacks of others equally willing to take power by similar means. Such antics revolted Wilson's orderly soul, and he attempted, by refusing to recognize Huerta, to impose constitutional processes upon those whose knowledge of constitutionalism was less than rudimentary. Venustiano Carranza finally emerged sufficiently from the Mexican maelstrom to earn Wilson's reluctant recognition in 1917.

Once in power, Carranza proceeded to commit Mexico, by the Constitution of 1917, to attacks on the forces which had held Mexico, and Mexicans, in virtual bondage. These were the Church, whose largely foreign clergy had rendered the peasants poor service while allying themselves with the aristocracy; the landlord, whether foreign or domestic (the Church also held much land); and the foreign capitalist, who had poured hundreds of millions into mineral, oil, and grazing enterprises. Carranza's constitution furnished the doctrinal and legal foundation for a fundamental economic, social, and political reorientation. Through it he proposed to subordinate the Church to the State and to minimize clerical influence in education; to strip the landlord (whether lay or

234

clerical) of his holdings for return to the peasant in the presumably idyllic *ejido* system of communal tenure; and to restore national control of national wealth, which Díaz had
adroitly alienated to the foreigner.

This alienation had been accomplished by repealing the
Spanish-Roman rule that subsoil minerals belonged to the
State and substituting the English common law principle
that ownership of the soil carried possession of what lay beneath. Acting on this overt invitation, foreigners had made
huge purchases of land known to contain metals and, it was
hoped, oil. These lands, removed from domestic control and
exploited by outsiders, decimated Mexico's patrimony to the
profit of foreigners. Carranza's constitution restored state
control of subsoil minerals, and the anguished cries of the
dispossessed rose to Heaven, and to Washington. The latter
was involved in a war. Little was accomplished save ill will
and near-intervention, but with peace came mutterings that
Carranza had sympathized with Germany; these soon
mingled with appeals for a stronger Mexican policy contained in the report of a Senate Committee headed by Albert
B. Fall of New Mexico, spokesman of powerful oil interests.
Here was marshaled impressive evidence, appealing to wide
segments of American opinion, much of it far removed from
petroleum, to prove that Carranza's policies were too dangerous to foreign interests to be tolerated further.

While the pressure for action mounted, Carranza in his
turn was overthrown and killed in 1920, and Wilson passed
on to Hughes and Harding the problem of recognizing General Alvaro Obregón, who succeeded after the brief tenure of
Adolfo de la Huerta. Meantime, however, the objectives of

the Constitution of 1917 looked forward to the creation of a vastly different state of affairs. Through attacks on the Church, the landlord, and the foreign capitalist, this document, and its implementive legislation, were designed to end Mexican subservience to essentially alien influences and to start the Republic along a path to real national independence. This was a momentous development, the course of which would outlast the Republican years, and one with the facts and consequences of which any United States Administration would have to reckon. The story as it unfolds becomes one of increasing adjustment of United States policy to Mexican realities—an accommodation often slow, seldom willing, but always an accommodation—which steadily subordinated the desires of American capital to the demands of Mexican nationalism. All this operated to the not inconsiderable advantage of Mexico herself and the relief of her neighbor nations, watching the United States anxiously for any sign of a more relaxed Latin American policy.

The year of the Republican take-over was important for both Mexico and the United States. Like all revolutionaries, Obregón needed funds, as well as recognition, and a call for loan negotiations went north in February, 1921, to be side-stepped until after March 4. Mexican oil wells pumped 193 million barrels in 1921, as events would prove, a peak of production, just as geologists were warning United States consumers of prospective domestic shortages. The land expropriation policy was well under way. Hughes attempted a joint solution of several of these problems—one hardly notable as a tactful approach to a sensitive neighbor. It was contained in a draft treaty of amity and commerce (presented

236

on May 27), designed, among other things, to protect United States nationals from losses under decrees implementing the land clauses of the Constitution of 1917. Obregón could earn recognition only by signing the treaty. When he delayed, feeling quite correctly that the proposal savored strongly of coercion, Hughes brusquely announced that "when it appears that there is a Government in Mexico willing to bind itself to the discharge of primary international obligations, concurrently with that act its recognition will take place." This further trespass on Obregón's revolutionary pride forced him to defend himself, and his unsatisfactory counter-proposals (of November 19) initiated months of notewriting before a face-to-face discussion could be arranged.*

Obregón, meantime, made a gesture of good will which failed to satisfy Hughes's demands. The Mexican Supreme Court, more amenable to executive pressure than its northern counterpart, had before it in the summer of 1921 several cases involving Article 27 of the Constitution, designed to regain national control over land and subsoil minerals. Subservient to executive wishes, the Court over a period of several months rendered five decisions in the so-called Texas cases, declaring that foreigners who had acquired lands prior to May 1, 1917, for purposes of exploiting oil resources, and

---

* Obregón sent an emissary to Washington in June to report that the commercial provisions of the treaty were acceptable, and that the Mexican Supreme Court had prepared, but was holding up, decisions that the land clause of the Constitution was nonconfiscatory (a point in contention), fearful that such would be considered an attempt to purchase recognition. He insisted that acceptance of Hughes's terms prior to recognition was equivalent to political suicide.

237

who had implemented their intentions by "positive acts," would be secure against retroactive interference with the rights acquired under the Díaz regime. Executive practice followed the Court's line, but Hughes feared lest another President, or procedural vagaries, might negate the gains registered in the decisions; he still demanded a treaty, which Obregón could not in good conscience sign. Both statesmen, however, presently found themselves increasingly embarrassed. Obregón was firmly in power, and continued refusal to deal with him brought Hughes under attack, not only by holders of Mexican rights, but by the powerful Borah. The calendar, by 1923, began to obtrude itself—both Administrations faced elections in 1924 and began to consider concessions as a means of favorably compromising the subsoil minerals problem.

These considerations produced a negotiation (May 14–August 15, 1923) and an agreement named after Mexico City's Callé Bucareli, where the sessions took place. Hughes might salve his pride by reflecting that accord was reached prior to recognition of Obregón, which took place only on August 31. On the other hand, Obregón obtained recognition without signing a treaty; the Bucareli arrangement was an executive agreement, later held not to be binding on succeeding Mexican Administrations. By and large, the Mexican negotiators held their own fairly well. They accepted an obligation to negotiate claims arising since 1868, but only after formal recognition. The Americans eased conditions of payment for lands taken over for the *ejido* system, agreeing to accept bonds in lieu of cash for tracts up to 1,755 hectares seized for *ejidos,* the price to be determined by value at

238

the time of expropriation; cash would be paid for larger properties. Of prime importance, the Americans accepted Mexican control of subsoil minerals, contending only that regulatory action not be made retroactive beyond May 1, 1917. Spelling out this aspect, the doctrine of positive acts, generously defined, was written into the agreement, confirming the tenure of foreigners who had performed such acts, and giving those who had not performed them preferred status in relation to third parties.

Several factors rendered the position of American oilmen less than ideal under the Bucareli Agreement. As mentioned above, Mexico could, and later did, interpret it as a temporary arrangement. Practical application of the seemingly liberal positive acts doctrine enabled her to recover considerable territory suspected to contain oil. By 1924, furthermore, the northern oil fields began to yield salt water, a phenomenon apparent in the south since 1921. After some encouragement under Kellogg and Coolidge, to be noted presently, the oilmen never received the stout government support to which they believed themselves entitled. With resources dwindling and Washington rendering inadequate backing, they tended, in the later decade, to slow production in established fields and to forego extensive prospecting operations in post-1917 lands.

The lull following the Bucareli Agreement lasted through Hughes's incumbency. Elections in 1924 chose new Administrations in both nations; in Mexico City Plutarco Elías Calles (who would virtually control Mexican affairs until 1936) continued Obregón's firm insistence upon Mexico's rights; in Washington, Coolidge's indifference and Kellogg's ineptitude created severe tensions, lasting for months but eventually emerging into one of the important turning points in Mexican-American relations and a real recognition of the signifiance of the Mexican revolution.

Kellogg was probably unduly influenced at first by James Rockwell Sheffield, who became American Ambassador to Mexico in 1924. Sheffield was never more than peripherally aware of what was transpiring there; his contacts were with the "Old Mexicans" who were being dispossessed of power and property along with the foreign capitalists, and he shared their hostility to the new possessors of power, referring disparagingly to Calles' "Indian or Oriental-Latin-Indian nature." He likewise listened favorably to the arguments of American oilmen leveled against Mexican restrictive regulations. These attitudes were not lost upon Calles, who had come to power through a school combining armed force and revolutionary chicane, and who faced (successfully) the task of reorganizing national finances and maintaining his own power and continued harmony with the United States.

This last objective soon encountered dire strains, due to Sheffield's activity and Kellogg's impulsiveness in dealing with a possible change in Mexican policy in the spring of 1925. Hitherto the Constitution of 1917 had normally been implemented by executive decrees, but as Mexican dissatisfaction with the Bucareli arrangement mounted, rumors arose that legislation might replace decrees—an approach likely to be more drastic, if less capricious, than executive enforcement. Sheffield replied to Kellogg's request for advice on procedure with unfavorable reports on Calles, his judiciary, and his regime in general. He followed his own advice to Wash-

240

ington while on home leave and undoubtedly influenced the spirit, if not the language, of Kellogg's incendiary pronouncement of June 12, insultingly conveyed through the press rather than normal diplomatic channels. The Secretary pointed out that he had

> seen the statements published in the press that another revolution may be impending in Mexico. I very much hope this is not true . . . it is now the policy of this Government to use its influence and lend its support in behalf of stability and orderly constitutional procedure, but it should be made clear that this Government will continue to support the Government in Mexico only so long as it protects American lives and American rights and complies with its international engagements and obligations. The Government of Mexico is now on trial before the world. . . .

Calles replied, likewise through the newspapers, attempting, as he said, to reorient the record toward "truth and justice." A brief period of diplomatic sparring and of press excitement ensued. Significantly, criticism about balanced support, and press interest was short-lived; Kellogg was seldom defended warmly and many stressed the statement's obvious threat to inter-American relations.

Two Mexican laws presently fulfilled the earlier premonitions. Scheduled to become operative on January 1, 1927, each entrenched upon foreign property rights. The Petroleum Law of December 18, 1925, enforced and extended the presidential decrees implementing the subsoil minerals clauses of Article 27. It violated the Bucareli Agreement, which Calles held did not bind him as it had bound Obregón, by increasing the Bucareli limits on foreigners' property rights. The Agreement had exempted owners who had performed positive acts prior to May 1, 1917, from the restrictions of Article 27; the law extended Mexican control over *all* oil lands, and defined a positive act more narrowly than the Agreement. It required performers of positive acts to seek, during 1926, new concessions which must be exploited within fifty years. The Alien Land Law of December 23, directed to other portions of Article 27, likewise contravened the Bucareli Agreement, and both laws contained "Calvo clauses" denying foreigners the right to seek governmental support in adjusting differences with Mexico under their provisions.

American investors promptly brought this threat of retroactive and confiscatory action to the attention of Secretary and Ambassador. A series of exchanges ensued while the laws moved toward passage. Sheffield, aligned with the oilmen and ill disposed toward Calles and the legislation, counseled more vigor than Kellogg, responsible to Congress and the public, was willing to display. The latter's threats, accordingly, were veiled and mild, and he confined his action to assembling proof that Calles was personally responsible for the Mexican enactments. Most significant, overall, was the decision to make haste slowly. The wisdom of this is obvious today; at the time it earned Kellogg the ill will of the oilmen, sharply threatened by the pending legislation.

Their impatience, understandable under the circumstances, emerged strongly during 1926, to the accompaniment of long and involved exchanges between Kellogg and Aarón Sáenz, Calles' Minister of Foreign Affairs. The companies desired to protect their preferred position, menaced by the legal requirement of obtaining, prior to January 1, 1927, confirmatory concessions of limited scope and duration. Having been denied departmental support, they concertedly refused compliance with the law and initiated injunction (*amparo*) proceedngs to prevent its application. Against this background of action the Kellogg-Sáenz correspondence gained in volume as it approached an impasse. Basic factors emerged on each side: Calles' determination to control Mexican affairs and resources, even at the cost of much-needed oil revenue; and Kellogg's aim to preserve the peace, even at considerable cost to domestic petroleum producers.

As 1927 approached, several new factors emerged. One American oil company (Transcontinental Petroleum, a subsidiary of Standard of New Jersey) had given notice (in mid-October, 1926) of application for the confirmatory concessions required under the law. Kellogg, alarmed at alleged Communist activity in Mexico, aimed at stirring disaffection in Central America and the Canal Zone, countenanced, if he did not engineer, an inflammatory news report airing such charges in mid-November. These appeared just as the Department was under attack for recognizing Adolfo Díaz as a sort of trained-seal chief executive in Nicaragua. Kellogg's health suffered under these and other pressures, rendering him ill fitted for the stresses of early 1927.

After a disturbing start Mexican relations moved, during 1927, into a new and conciliatory phase which would characterize the remaining Republican years. Kellogg, still under the Communist spell, submitted to the Senate Foreign Relations Committee (on January 12) a memorandum on "Bolshevik Aims and Policies in Mexico and Central America," which furnished congressional critics of both parties a club with which to belabor the Administration and facilitated passage of a Senate Resolution (on January 25) proposing submission of Mexican-American differences to the Hague Tribunal. Mexico, meantime, was also unhappy at the course of events. Oil revenue, needed to bolster the shaky fiscal structure, would be scanty until political relations improved. Arbitration found Mexican favor only briefly, and for some weeks there were few important developments when suddenly, on April 25, the President made one of his few sallies into Latin-American affairs.

Addressing the United Press on April 25, Coolidge fired a double-barreled salvo, first asserting stoutly that "The person and property of a citizen are a part of the general domain of the Nation, even when abroad. On the other hand, there is a distinct and binding obligation on the part of self-respecting governments to afford protection to the persons and property of their citizens, wherever they may be." Sheffield and the oilmen, reading this passage, could take heart, and most commentators have followed their rising spirits and interpreted the address as a sort of sequel to Kellogg's fulminations of 1926. Less attention has been paid to another and more significant conciliatory passage in which the President asserted that

> we do not want any controversy with Mexico. We feel every sympathy with her people in their distress and have every desire to assist them. . . . Instead of desiring to pursue any aggression or to take part in any oppression, we are endeavoring through the most friendly offices to demonstrate to their Government that their attitude in relation to property will not only

result in the economic disadvantage of their own people, by preventing the investment of outside capital so necessary for their development, but will greatly impair their friendly relations with other interested nations. . . .

In Mexico, meantime, the oil companies engaged, briefly, in illegal drilling operations, but soon desisted when it became apparent that, despite Coolidge's stout assertions of April 25, no real government support was in sight. Several ceased drilling in the face of Administration indifference, but remained dissatisfied when the Department of State declined (in August and September) to support their repeated requests for assistance against what they contended were confiscatory Mexican policies. With the Department cautious about applying pressure, several factors moved Mexico to consider negotiation. Overproduction in other areas curtailed the demand for Mexican petroleum, and the onset of the seasonal rains put a natural damper on production. The temporary inactivity of the American producers heightened the current financial crisis; the Mexican government was constrained to ask the companies, which it was allegedly persecuting, to prepay their July 31 tax installments, and in September word reached the Embassy that the Penn-Mex Fuel Company had advanced two million pesos which could only be recovered by remission of taxes on oil to be processed in a still unfinished refinery. Clearly, by mid-1927, both sides sought moderation; this is indicated further by Kellogg's progressive disengagement from Mexican affairs, management of which passed first into the hands of Robert E. Olds and eventually was delegated almost completely to Dwight W. Morrow, whose ambassadorship marks the overt transition from hostility to conciliation in Mexican-American relations, though Coolidge's April gesture should be remembered as at least a harbinger of the "new" policy.

Conciliation well became both parties. The Sheffield-Kellogg *brusquerie* had profited nothing and Mexico was increasingly hard pressed to meet her foreign obligations, payments on which would be suspended in 1928. The Morrow appointment moved American policy from a tentative to a positive phase, permitting both Governments to abandon positions of increasing difficulty. Morrow came to formal diplomacy after a successful career in the House of Morgan, where he had sharpened his innate talents as a negotiator. Coolidge's willingness to bring his Amherst classmate into government coincided with Morrow's own desire to devote himself more fully to public service than his banking connections would permit. He agreed to accept the post in June, 1927. Sheffield's resignation took effect in July, Morrow's appointment was formalized in August, and he traveled to Mexico in his private railroad car in October to create a new atmosphere and make real if temporary progress toward alleviation of some outstanding problems.

Speaking enthusiastically to all sorts of people in a version of Spanish peculiar to himself, he endeared himself to the commoner by haunting the market places, to the wealthy by building a house at Cuernavaca, and to Calles by trusting the President's own interpreter to moderate their early discussions. The writer has found no record of Embassy reaction to his introduction of a private roster of advisers (J.

Reuben Clark, George Rublee, and Captain Lewis McBride, who doubled as Naval Attaché), upon whom he depended more fully than upon the professionals. Given *carte blanche* by his superiors, he flouted most of the rules, negotiating orally instead of relying on notes, using the telephone instead of the telegraph (sublimely indifferent to the knowledge that his wires were tapped), and trotting directly to any official, including the President, whom he thought might be able to satisfy his insatiable curiosity.

Olds had supplied him with a policy memorandum prior to his departure listing oil, claims, the agrarian question, and an arms embargo as problems which might demand attention, and advising him to deal first with oil in order to furnish Mexico with revenue to apply on her indebtedness. The wisdom of this approach is evidenced by the fact that Mexico borrowed almost three million dollars during the year to maintain her debt service, and by the additional fact that an International Committee of Bankers, of which Morrow's former Morgan partner Thomas W. Lamont was a prominent member, would be expecting to receive interest and principal payments in the amount of $59 million in 1928.

He entered his assignment convinced that threats would not divert Mexico from her revolutionary course, already a decade old under the Constitution of 1917. Less apt to rely upon legal arguments than those more experienced in the Foreign Service, he sought by less formal means to balance Mexican exigencies and capitalist American desires. His personal charm thawed the somewhat suspicious Calles to a point where the President, on their second breakfast engagement, asked him point-blank for a lead into the thorny oil question. The Ambassador had a ready answer in the Texas Oil Company cases of 1921, in which the Mexican Supreme Court had held that later government action aimed at recovery of subsoil oil violated a prohibition on retroactive legislation contained in Article 14 of the Constitution. Cases attacking the Petroleum Law of 1925 on similar grounds were before the courts, and Morrow blandly suggested that he was "expecting" confirmation of the Texas Company precedent.

Offered this easy solution, Calles gave the judges their orders, and decisions emerged in less than a fortnight voiding those sections of the Petroleum Law requiring exploitation of preconstitutional lands within fifty years. Calles was pleased; Morrow was pleased; Washington was pleased. Kellogg, indeed, suddenly discovered that "it is best for Mexico if possible to deal with these matters on her own initiative without any pressure from the United States," a far cry from his "The Government of Mexico is now on trial before the world" of 1925. Not so happy were the oil producers. The decision protected their interest in lands on which positive acts had been performed, but left indeterminate the status of "untagged" lands—preconstitutional holdings where no positive act had taken place. The producers demanded a further ruling safeguarding these lands against interference—important not only as a permanent assurance of access to their Mexican holdings, but as a precedent which might be transferred wherever their roving prospectors might find oil.

While the companies quibbled over the verdict, Calles sponsored proposals designed to harmonize law and decision, and the result fully protected the lands where positive acts had been performed. Next followed drafting and promulga-

248

tion of regulations putting the law into practical operation; again the companies attempted unsuccessfully to derive some advantage, but Morrow held aloof. At this point (March 27, 1928) a statement was issued in Washington declaring that law and regulations "would appear to bring to a practical conclusion the discussions which began ten years ago. . . ." The status of the untagged lands plagued the companies, as did a regulation requiring them to obtain a "confirmatory concession" for exercising their rights on pre-constitutional lands on which positive acts had been performed. With one eye on the future, they sought clarification, but without departmental or Embassy support; Morrow, indeed, was not convinced that their position was in any jeopardy. The companies, in fact, were seeking complete and permanent guarantee of their rights, uncluttered by any "concession" requirement, but the Department rested on its March 27 statement and advised them that their rights were subject to Mexican establishment and interpretation.

The business of securing the confirmatory concessions moved smoothly, and the oil question passed offstage after months of ill will. Kellogg had blustered and Coolidge had mollified; Morrow had won a settlement, not too pleasing to the producers, which contained something of victory for both governments. Mexico recognized the binding validity of property rights conferred by the Díaz regime, but essentially enforced her own concept of the conditions under which such rights might be exercised. The United States recognized Mexican sovereignty over Mexican oil, subject to guarantees that such sovereignty would not be exercised in reactionary or confiscatory fashion. Mexico fared best, and the oilmen worst, for their untagged lands were left without guarantee and their future operations without protection.

Mexico won the oil controversy, but it was something of a Pyrrhic victory, since oil revenue followed a declining curve of production. The years of diplomatic controversy (1925–1927) saw the producers desperately trying to outrun a salt-water invasion of the fields; 1,355 new wells were sunk, but 64 per cent were dry holes and many of the others suffered a briny dilution. Production dropped from 115 million barrels in 1925 to approximately 40 million in 1930, and the producers rapidly transferred their major activities to less chancy Venezuelan fields.

Two other activities occupied Morrow. The Alien Land Law of 1925 was designed to regularize the take-over of privately held lands for peasant occupancy. United States policy was directed toward securing adequate compensation for the injury suffered by its nationals through the exercise of this recognized sovereign right. Morrow's action here was largely a holding operation which occupied him only occasionally and which he never brought to the top of his agenda. The central government had found it difficult to control local officials, who conducted many of the actual confiscations; it was Morrow's policy, acting under Olds's instruction, to recognize Mexican authority in the premises, to seek redress in individual cases, and to moderate the unpleasantness of both central and local administration of the policy. He actually accomplished very little, and devoted slight attention to the matter. Its relative unimportance may well have resulted from Mexican difficulties in initiating the peasants into the *ejido* system and rising second thoughts on the part of leadership as to its intrinsic merits.

His final and, in the writer's opinion, his most important activity concerned the touchy domestic problem of Church-State relations, which obviously lay outside his formal diplomatic assignment; indeed, there is practically no notice of this phase of his work in the published correspondence. He involved himself heavily in the matter on the theory that domestic stability was essential to international comity. He promoted secret meetings and open negotiation between high political and religious figures designed to reopen Mexico's churches, closed in 1926 in protest against government efforts to subject the Church to state control. He labored indefatigably for eighteen months, eventually contributing heavily to an agreement which reopened the churches and temporarily healed the worst of the wounds. Here, as in his more publicized negotiations, the Government maintained its dignity and authority; the Church made the major concessions. Morrow himself shuttled between the proud and suspicious protagonists, cajoling each to moderate extreme positions toward an agreement which, if it did not turn out to be permanent, stood for some time as a monument to his tact and persistence.

No further important policy developments occurred during the Republican years. Kellogg and Coolidge had moved slowly but definitely from asperity to accommodation under Dwight Morrow's persuasive touch. It should be kept in mind, moreover, that aside from Kellogg's initial unfortunate accusation, the American intention had never gone beyond legal and verbal support of American rights. And in the face of Mexican vigor, this support, although voluble, was never threatening. It is likely that the aggressive attitude of domestic oil producers irked Department and Morrow alike, and, perhaps, contributed to the *rapprochement* which Morrow was able to achieve. The period marks a sharp turn for the better, and the chief credit should be awarded to Morrow, to whom the Administration virtually surrendered control of Mexican policy, though not everyone would subscribe to Arthur Bliss Lane's statement that he "was in fact the real author of the Good Neighbor Policy." Nor should it be forgotten that Mexico had progressed into a new phase of her own revolution, in which consolidation was replacing violence (though the latter was never far beneath the surface) and in which she held her own quite creditably with the erstwhile Colossus of the North, now moving reluctantly, but moving, toward recognition of greater maturity south of the Rio Grande.

Nicaragua, strategically important as a canal site and for its proximity to Panama, had been the scene of the earliest formal and continued United States intervention. When Hughes and Harding entered office she had been under light Marine Corps occupation since August, 1912; this would continue, with a brief interruption, until Hoover's last days. The rein was generally a light one, though domestic disturbance would bring a heavier curb in the Coolidge period. The forms of democracy were generally preserved, with due regard to maintenance of administrations conscious of their duties to the United States, and the intervention was much less burdensome than some; indeed, Washington was occasionally compelled to self-denial in resisting repeated local invitations to proceed to full control. Nevertheless, Nicaraguans, like Haitians, Dominicans, and Latin American observers generally, must have found Hughes's protestations somewhat hollow when at Rio de Janeiro in 1922 he denied that imperialism animated his country.

By March, 1921, a good working relationship had been set up. The Bryan-Chamorro Treaty of 1916 authorized United States construction of a canal and provided for establishment of a naval base to guard its approaches. American bankers had worked out fiscal arrangements refunding the national debt and supervising collection of the customs which provided for its service and amortization. A token Marine Corps contingent of one hundred at the Legation prompted Nicaraguan good manners and discouraged revolution. United States capital investment in Nicaraguan enterprise was not and had never been large.

Under these circumstances Washington decided that it was time to liquidate the intervention. An insurance policy designed to contribute to Central American stability had been negotiated in 1923 when the Republics signed (on February 7) a remarkable self-denying ordinance agreeing to deny recognition to any chief of state (or relative of such by blood or marriage) who secured power by revolutionary *coup d'etat*. Emiliano Chamorro, formerly President and currently Ambassador to Washington, had signed this undertaking on behalf of Nicaragua. The United States, though not a signatory, had formally accepted its principles in June.

Taking advantage of existing tranquility, Hughes informed Nicaragua (on November 14, 1923) that the occupation would be terminated following installation of the next President, due to occur in 1925. A political Donnybrook ensued during which a coalition ticket headed by Carlos Solórzano (Conservative) and Dr. Juan Sacasa (Liberal) defeated Emiliano Chamorro amid the latter's loud (and doubtless justified) cries of fraud. Precariously in power, President Solórzano begged Hughes not to withdraw the Marines until a native constabulary could be trained under American leadership, but he lagged badly in establishing it. Nevertheless, the Marines sailed from Corinto on August 4, 1925, leaving Nicaragua to her own devices.

The Marine-policed calm soon vanished. Chamorro, leader of the normally pro-American Conservative Party, engineered a series of dramatic moves, individually constitutional, which ousted Solórzano, put Sacasa in flight to Guatemala, and placed Chamorro himself in the presidency in obvious contempt of the 1923 treaty. These political and military acrobatics raised acute alarm in Washington, endangering as they did the sanctity of the treaty, the security of minor American investments in Nicaragua, and the posture of the United States *vis-à-vis* Latin America. Suspicion that Mexican influence was behind the Chamorristas complicated Kellogg's problem, for 1925 to 1927 were his years of trial in Mexican relations and undue pressure on Nicaragua would further complicate an already unpleasant situation.

Chamorro promptly began a long, and losing, quest for recognition. Under the the astute advice of Chandler P. Anderson, an American lawyer, the Nicaraguan Legation tried

254

to persuade the Department of State that unconstitutional procedures in the election of the Solórzano-Sacasa ticket voided the nonrecognition obligations of the 1923 treaty. The Department, however, refused to recognize any regime headed by Chamorro, though Kellogg let it be known that he would not object if Chamorro could maintain himself without recognition. This he continued to do for some time, the American fiscal officials in the Republic having complaisantly allowed him access to funds.

As 1926 wore on, anti-Chamorro sentiment developed in the United States, and revolution, allegedly supported by arms arriving from Mexico, broke out on the east coast, cut off from the more prosperous and politically important west by a well-nigh impenetrable wall of mountains. Responding to mounting pressures, Kellogg expressed "grave apprehension" over the military dictatorship, and Chamorro, seeing the handwriting on the wall, requested American assistance in choosing a successor. A conference held at Corinto under American auspices in mid-October came to naught, but late in the month Chamorro transferred power to another Conservative equally unacceptable to Washington. Kellogg presently opined (on November 2) that he would look with favor on the choice of Adolfo Díaz, whose previous presidency had been pro-United States, and who according to the Secretary was eligible under the 1923 treaty. A reconstituted Congress formalized his election on November 11, and his Government received recognition on the 17th.

Kellogg's troubles continued, since revolution still plagued the east coast. Sacasa appeared on home soil on December 1, proclaiming himself constitutional President, and was inaugurated by his followers. Díaz, moreover, was nearly bankrupt and was asking point-blank for aid against his enemies. American business interests urged intervention on his behalf; Borah upheld Sacasa's claims, and Kellogg became well-nigh distracted. He persuaded Coolidge and the Cabinet to renew intervention by restoring the Legation Guard, which arrived at Managua on January 6, 1927. Coolidge rescinded an arms embargo imposed in 1926, to the advantage of the Díaz regime, and on January 10 expressed "deep concern" over the threat to Nicaraguan stability posed by "outside influences." On the 12th Kellogg presented his semi-hysterical memorandum on "Bolshevik Aims and Policies in Latin America" to the Senate Committee on Foreign Relations, and a small public furore ensued.

Hostilities shortly leaped the mountains, breaking out on the west coast in February, while Sacasa's forces fought their way inland from the east despite a warning that military success would not win him a departmental blessing. By mid-February Minister Charles Eberhardt was deluging the Department with recommendations for "positive, complete and immediate intervention"; this was implemented on the 20th by landing a force sufficient to constitute factual if not full-scale interposition, and within a month 2,000 troops were on Nicaraguan soil. The Administration, however, hesitated to court domestic censure and universal Latin-American condemnation by engaging in all-out military support of Díaz, and decided to mask (but thinly) the iron hand in the velvet glove of the Stimson mission.

Here for the first time Kellogg abdicated control of policy to a proconsul (he would place Morrow in a similar position later in the same year), and here Henry L. Stimson received his initiation as a high-level negotiator, though the earlier story has indicated that he brought to his task some practice in policy-making. Neither was this his first chore for Kellogg, who had already asked his counsel concerning the Tacna-Arica question. (See p. 282). He departed under a presidential injunction to "straighten the matter out" if possible, with presidential agreement that Díaz must be kept in power, that a Liberal victory in 1928 must be risked, and that forcible subjection of Sacasa was to be avoided if at all feasible. Interviewing leaders of both parties at Managua in mid-April enabled him to hammer home the twin aspects of the policy which he had come to deem essential—retention of Díaz in office and American supervision of the election of 1928. He persuaded Díaz to accept his proposals of general amnesty and disarmament as a condition of American supervision of the election, a contingency which he had not cleared with Washington before presenting it to Díaz.

Sacasa would be harder to persuade, since retention of Díaz would place him in the ranks of the unemployed. Moreover, he was out of touch with his army, led by General José Maria Moncada, who was far in the interior and much closer to the realities than Sacasa himself. Fighting vigorously, he was closer to Managua after each engagement, which the Conservative press loudly proclaimed as Liberal defeats. He, his lieutenants, and his troops would likewise suffer humiliation if Díaz remained in office. In a series of meetings with Moncada and delegates representing Sacasa, held on May 4, 5, and 11, Stimson acted on his own conviction that the Liberal leadership would yield to threats rather than fight the United States, and on departmental permission to invoke such threats. Moncada persuaded most of his fellow officers, and ultimately his troops, to accept Stimson's terms, and on May 12 the Tipitapa Agreement ratified Díaz' continuance in office and accepted American supervision of the election; general amnesty and immediate peace followed; a cash bounty was offered for surrender of weapons, and the soldiers returned home in time to plant the spring crops. Stimson's pressure on both sides, under Coolidge's injunction to "straighten the matter out," had resolved a threatening situation, with more immediate success than Morrow would achieve in Mexico, but with a residue of imperialism which Morrow would avoid.

For in Nicaragua, Sacasa's pretensions had been denied, and one of his leaders, General Augusto C. Sandino, had refused to accept the Stimson-Moncada agreement and retired to the north, whence no available number of American troops sufficed to dislodge him. Practical occupation, moreover, remained a fact, which supervision of the election of 1928 could only serve to emphasize. This event, however, went off peaceably thanks to the stationing of a Marine at each polling place and the closing of the *cantinas* on election day, and with unprecedented honesty, since each voter on approaching the polls was requested to dip a digit in a mercurochrome solution designed to discourage repetitive voting. General Moncada defeated a wealthy Conservative who returned from Spain to undertake the campaign, and entered office peacefully; few commented that, as the leader of an unsuccessful revolution, his legal status was hardly better

258

than that of Chamorro, who had revolted successfully, only to be denied recognition.

The Kellogg-Coolidge policy toward Nicaragua, while less liberal than their Mexican policy, produced similarly calming results. Withdrawal in 1925 was ill advised even if generously intended. When the inevitable disturbances followed, there seemed no recourse except to renewed intervention, which occurred, as will be noted later, at a time when Latin-American resentment at this policy was rapidly growing; the result was a sharp increase in inter-American tensions. The action itself seems to have generated less local ill will than any similar United States activity, despite the obviously imperialistic connotations involved in use of force and continued intervention.

Hoover and Stimson inherited the fact of intervention, the obligation to supervise elections, a continuing Latin-American and domestic resentment of United States pretensions, and the Sandino guerrillas. Hoover approached Latin America with greater interest and more knowledge than his predecessors, having informed himself widely if not deeply on its problems during a post-election junket to the south. His first annual message (of December 3, 1929) let it be known that he took no pride in the Nicaraguan and Haitian interventions. After giving the statistics of Marine occupation forces, he asserted that "in the large sense we do not wish to be represented abroad in such manner."

He was not able, however, to suit action to words immediately. Sandino, who had withdrawn to Mexico for a time after Hoover's inauguration, renewed his harrying tactics in the north early in 1930. Marine forces were meantime being reduced and by June of that year numbered no more than 1,000; this number was not increased during Hoover's term. In April, 1931, a Sandino sally resulted in loss of American lives near Puerto Cabezas on the east coast. Warships were dispatched to the scene, but the episode offered an occasion to announce a new policy relative to the protection of American citizens abroad. Coolidge had said, in admonishing Mexico in 1927, that the United States would protect the persons and property of Americans "wherever they may be." Now, at least as far as Central America was concerned, the Administration served notice that citizens feeling unsafe in the interior must go home, come down to country where protection could be provided, or stand by and take whatever consequences might develop. As for Sandino, he was neither defeated nor apprehended during the Republican years, and continued to be a problem for both Moncada and the Marines.

The last act of importance developed when President Moncada sent a bipartisan group to Washington to urge that American authority over elections be used in 1932 to provide for choosing delegates to a constitutional convention instead of electing a Congress charged with the normal function of picking a president. He argued that the Constitution was out of harmony with current electoral laws, the Bryan-Chamorro Treaty, and the agreement providing for a native constabulary. Some were so unkind as to suggest that the proposal was a diversionary tactic designed to lengthen his own hold on power by converting the electoral machinery to unusual uses. He abandoned the scheme in the face of Stimson's threat to withhold supervision of the election.

The day of interventionism was passing as Hoover left the White House, and he was able to make good on repeated Republican promises of withdrawal from Nicaragua. The election of 1932 saw the old warhorses, Díaz and Chamorro, teaming on the Conservative ticket, with Sacasa standing for the Liberals. Thus three figures important in Nicaraguan affairs contended for preferment as the Republican day drew to a close. Sacasa was elected and inaugurated on January 1, 1933. The next day the last Marines left Managua, bringing full circle the most durable of Republican interventions, the further tale of which will be surveyed in the following chapter.

VIII

Latin-American Miscellany:
Intervention, Recognition, Boundary Controversies

The story of Republican relations with Latin America is one of transition and amelioration, though neither change nor improvement had reached full fruition by 1933. Thus, wide scope remained for Franklin D. Roosevelt's talent for Good Neighborliness. What needs emphasis, however, is the difference between the American stance of 1921 and that of 1933. The Republicans inherited an imperialism which Wilson and his Republican predecessors had created and which found the United States exercising hegemony, established by force or treaty, over Panama, Cuba, Santo Domingo, Haiti, and Nicaragua. This hegemony had been so thoroughly and in some cases so recently established that the winds of protest were only starting to blow from the south. Nor had the forces of domestic disapproval found many spokesmen.

The Republican years would witness rising condemnation, from those under bondage and from American objectors to the master-servant relationship. The condemnation had, by 1933, begun to bring results, and considerable advance had been made toward the improvement of intrahemispheric relations. The recognition, however, had been slow and grudging, and a real *rapprochement* was still in the future. If both the theory and practice of hegemony and intervention had been moderated, the possibility of their reassertion had not been exorcised. Despite particular evidences of good will, most Latin Americans would keep a weather eye cocked northward. Even such a wary attitude, however, was a far cry from the well-nigh universal fear and suspicion characteristic of 1921.

The Republican period opened with imperialism firmly in the saddle but soon to face attack. Both parties had contributed to the establishment of the Panama Policy, which had made virtual satrapies of Haiti and Santo Domingo, had put Panama, Cuba, and Nicaragua under bond, and had embittered relations with Mexico. A public reaction had set in, both at home and to the south, against the domination established under the Roosevelt Corollary; this tide soon began to run heavily against the party in power, which had fallen heir to Wilsonian interventionism, and Hughes's early efforts were divided between fending off new troubles, justifying the *status quo,* and liquidating the intervention where a restored independence seemed most likely to succeed.

General instability made Central America an area where

political disturbance might at any time raise problems of further intervention. Hopefully, Hughes sponsored a meeting of the five Republics at Washington in December, 1922, encouraging them to draft a number of peace-keeping treaties, including one signed on February 7, 1923, denying recognition to a government gaining power by revolution; this essentially applied to Central America the theory of recognition under which Woodrow Wilson had justified his rejection of the Huerta regime in Mexico. The United States did not join the agreement, but was understood to sympathize with its objective and was expected to observe it. Nicaraguan developments, noted in the preceding chapter, put a strain on adherence to its principles both in the United States and Central America; it was observed in the case of revolutions in Guatemala in 1930 and El Salvador in 1931, but was abandoned by its signatories in 1934. Meantime, it had stood as a barrier, however uncertain, to revolution, and so served as a minor preventive of trouble.

At the Fifth International Conference of American States (these were popularly known as the Pan-American Conferences), opening at Santiago, Chile, on March 25, 1923, a Colombian delegate vigorously attacked American interventionism and the Monroe Doctrine, asking treaty definition of the latter. This prompted Hughes to defend the *status quo*, while attempting, vigorously but without much success, to reassure Latin America. In speeches to the American Bar Association (August 30, 1923) and the American Academy of Political and Social Science (November 30) he undertook to explain the Doctrine as one of self-defense rather than of aggression, stoutly denying the observations which occasionally have been made implying a claim on our part to superintend the affairs of our sister republics, to assert an overlordship, to consider the spread of our authority beyond our own domain as the aim of our policy, and to make our power the test of right in this hemisphere.

His country had, he argued, policies and obligations other than those included in the Doctrine, and in the Caribbean "it has been necessary to assert these rights and obligations as well as the limited principles of the Monroe Doctrine." Claiming the right to interpret the Doctrine unilaterally, he sought to divorce it from the right of intervention. Significantly, however, he did not then or at any other time renounce the latter, though seeking to localize it in the Caribbean. The exegesis was magnificent, but it had little effect on Latin-American tempers, and attacks on interventionism continued, producing, finally, considerable results.

Hughes himself contributed significantly to modifying the practice, if not the theory, of intervention in engineering withdrawal from Santo Domingo in 1924, marking his last important act as Secretary in the area of Latin-American policy. The Republic, occupied since 1916, was the scene of the last and most thorough of United States interventions, involving complete subordination of local authority and control by the United States Navy. Under wartime pressures the Department of State had paid little attention to the Military Government since 1917. Hughes moved early to implement Harding's campaign promises of improvement and Wilson's lame-duck (December, 1920) recommendation of withdrawal. Within months a more sympathetic local administration was installed, and on June 14, 1921, a full-blown plan of evacuation was proposed. The terms proved unpalatable to the local leadership, providing as they did for retention of American armed forces during the election, which would restore local control of affairs, ratification of the acts of a severe occupation, establishment of a constabulary officered by Americans, and acceptance of drastic fiscal controls after physical withdrawal.

Months of deadlock ensued, punctuated by lengthy senatorial hearings around the turn of the year 1921–1922 which produced two volumes of testimony, much of it derogatory of the occupation. Presently Francisco J. Peynado, a man without political prominence, opened discussions in Washington with Hughes and Sumner Welles, Chief of the Division of Latin-American affairs, in a calmer atmosphere than the surcharged air of Santo Domingo. The conferences produced sufficient agreement to warrant summoning leaders of the Republic's political parties in June of 1922, and a Memorandum of the Agreement of Evacuation was signed on the 30th. Welles, sent to ascertain Dominican opinion on the Agreement, found it more favorable than that of Military Government officials who sought unavailingly to tighten its provisions. A provisional President was chosen and inaugurated under the plan in October, 1922, and after an interim period a full-fledged successor was elected and took over in July, 1924. Evacuation proceeded apace, being completed on September 18. Other negotiations produced a milder and more acceptable control of Dominican customs, designed to service and safeguard the bonded indebtedness (signed December 27, 1924). This remained the sole legal reminder of a galling interlude, and a first step in retreat had been taken.

Latin-American pressure continued during the Kellogg-Coolidge period and, though it produced no overt results, a leaven was beginning to work. Between the Santiago meeting and the sixth Pan-American Conference at Havana (January 16–February 20, 1928) United States prestige suffered and American policy was under severe attack. The Mexican and Nicaraguan episodes, already recounted, furnished fresh fuel for anti-imperialist fires; Haiti and Tacna-Arica, to be noted presently, fanned the flames, and as a result Kellogg faced the meeting with some misgivings, as indicated by his remark that it would be "the most important to this country that has ever been held."

He evidenced his concern by refraining from attending the Conference (he was heavily involved in the Kellogg-Briand business at the time), by persuading Charles E. Hughes to head, and Dwight Morrow to join, a distinguished delegation, and by persuading the President himself to journey to Havana to address the opening session. As early as midsummer, 1927, he was concerned lest "political" questions rise to trouble the waters, and was carefully trying to arrange the agenda to avoid such unpleasantness, hoping to keep the Conference away from the explosive Monroe Doctrine/intervention complex. Hughes took the bull by the horns, however, in addressing the Havana Chamber of Commerce (January 21, 1928). He commented frankly but not apologetically on the long-standing Nicaraguan and Haitian interventions, indicating that though the interpositions were based on "an imperative but temporary emergency," they would be terminated with maximum speed, a statement hardly likely to soothe his Latin-American hearers.

The skeleton of intervention, once dragged from the closet, dogged the Conference, and it was only with difficulty that it was presumably postponed, to be discussed at the Seventh Conference five years later. At the concluding ceremonies, however, a parliamentary maneuver brought an unequivocal nonintervention resolution to the floor. A lull in the proceedings enabled its supporters to rally their forces, and presented Hughes with the delicate forensic dilemma of defeating the motion without yielding the principle. This he did, in a powerful half-hour extempore address, winning postponement and a personal ovation, but leaving Haiti and Nicaragua still under occupation, the problem of intervention still unsolved, and Latin-American feelings still outraged.

This was the last high-level defense of interventionism. Within a few weeks Hughes himself was deprecating the Monroe Doctrine as a "cover for extravagant utterances and pretensions," and in January, 1929, the Senate condemned the Roosevelt Corollary. Backstage, too, a retreat from extreme Monroeism was under way. With at least one eye on the upcoming senatorial debate on the Kellogg-Briand Pact, which might bring the Doctrine into discussion, Kellogg instructed Undersecretary J. Reuben Clark to compile a full dossier of official statements. The result was a *Memorandum on the Monroe Doctrine*, submitted December 17, 1928. This "Clark Memorandum" was put together under pressure and, according to its compiler, expressed merely his personal views and was confined in its application to the relations between the United States and Europe, being inapplicable to "purely inter-American relations." It has, of course, become known for its renunciation of the right of intervention under the Doctrine—a formal repudiation of the Roosevelt Corollary. It was published in 1930 and received official approbation in statements by Stimson and Undersecretary Castle, but created only mild interest in Latin America, where the prime concern was whether the United States would intervene, not the grounds upon which intervention might be justified. Though the *Memorandum* became a landmark in the history of the Doctrine, three observations should be made: (a) that it was elaborated during the Kellogg-Coolidge period, thus entitling these worthies to share in whatever mild improvement it worked in inter-American good will; (b) that, whatever atmospheric clarification it produced, it retained the right of intervention, merely depriving it of Monrovian support; and (c) that even during the Hoover Administration the Department of State busied itself in minimizing the memorandum's importance, and the Roosevelt Administration disclaimed all responsibility for it.

Whatever noninterventionist kudos the Hoover Administration might earn would, therefore, have to be sought elsewhere. The withdrawal from Nicaragua was the high point in this story, but Haitian-American relations furnished another significant chapter. As in Santo Domingo, the Haitian occupation was inherited from Wilson. Since its inception in 1915 it had reduced the Negro Republic to political subjugation and to an enforced reorientation of its life, designed to benefit the ignorant and poverty-stricken masses by programs deeply offensive to the elite groups which had hitherto battened on the nation's marginal economy. As a candidate, Harding had deprecated Wilsonian Policy, and the Haitians hoped for better things. Dr. Carl Kelsey conducted an investigation early in 1921 on behalf of the Department of State, and subsequently gave influential testimony before a Senate committee created in response to pressure for improvement in Haiti's lot. This committee, headed by Medill McCormick, reported formally in June, 1922, criticizing specific aspects of the occupation, but advocating a cleanup and centralized control rather than withdrawal.

Since many of the proven excesses had occurred under military authority, it was hoped in Haiti, and expected in the United States, that the new High Commissioner, recommended by the McCormick Committee, would be a civilian. However, before the committee's final report was issued, the position was tendered (in February, 1922) to John H. Russell who, as a colonel, had been in charge during much of the period of military activity and was now rewarded by promotion to the rank of general. This promotion of a Georgian, who, though well intentioned and completely honest, was a tyro in business and political operations, was justified on the ground that only military influence could effectively carry out the treaty services.

Louis Borno's election in 1922 to succeed President Sudre Dartiguenave reflected Department of State wishes and the responsiveness to Washington's pressure of the electoral machinery established under the occupation. Borno was convinced of the necessity of cooperation; Dartiguenave had been less so. With Russell's thorough backing, he controlled the machinery of legislation; with Russell in turn receiving orders from the Department, the fiscal and political machinery moved smoothly, if not democratically. When the machinery developed crotchets, a popular plebiscite underwrote constitutional changes designed to ease the operation of the "joint dictatorship" of Russell and Borno—a vote registering the sovereign will of an electorate deemed too ignorant to choose legislators intelligently.

The foregoing somewhat cynical analysis should not obscure the fact that both parties to the dictatorship were dedicated men, who labored earnestly for their conception of what was best for Haitian welfare, if not for Haitian democracy and autonomy. The same applied to the three Americans who successively occupied the combined post of financial adviser and receiver general of customs for a decade after 1924. The national finances were in excellent order, the debt services were ahead of schedule, and the debt was being rapidly reduced—too rapidly, in the view of those who saw needed services going unfilled. This, again, is not to say that the occupation was inactive, but that from the viewpoint of influential Haitians, the wrong kind of activity was going on.

The educational system was a major area of friction between the native leadership and the American authorities. Convinced that sound agriculture and craftsmanship were essential to national stability, occupation officials had created, without treaty authority, the Service Technique de l'Agriculture et de l'Enseignement Professionel. A major portion of educational funds was allotted to this branch, serving roughly one-eighth of the school population in about four score agricultural and industrial schools, while the other seven-eights, attending about a thousand schools whose literary/classical curricula were geared to the wishes of the elite, got along on the remainder. This "misuse" of occupa-

272

tion authority more than outweighed, in Haitian eyes, solid contemporary achievements in health, medicine, and public works.

Political conditions, too, left much to be desired by the elite, deprived by occupation machinery of the practice and profits of politics. The President, chosen by a Council of State, in turn chose the Council. This arrangement, quite satisfactory to President, Council, and Occupation, returned Borno regularly, except in 1928, when he dispensed with the formality and remained in office; it was to remain in effect until the President, at his own discretion, should decide to call an election to the Chambers (which constitutionally chose the chief executive) in January of an even year. Borno had promised in April, 1928, that constitutional government would be reestablished by mid-May of 1930. However, early in October, 1929, he rescinded his promise of an election the following January.

These events faced Haiti with the prospect of at least two more years of dictatorship, and served to catalyze a number of influences which had been gathering for some months. As early as 1926 the Women's International League for Peace and Justice had dispatched a team of investigators, one result of which was publication, in Emily Greene Balch's *Occupied Haiti* (1927), of a moderate and soundly reasoned critique of existing conditions. A. C. Millspaugh had resigned as financial adviser in 1929, announcing that the objectives of the occupation could not be realized by 1936, the expiration date of the treaty governing Haitian-American political relations. The Council on Foreign Relations and the Foreign Policy Association had also published critical surveys in 1929.

273

Much of this activity had developed, without positive results, during the Kellogg-Coolidge incumbency. Its cumulative effect was heightened by events of 1929, which included
a student strike at the Central School of Agriculture (October 31), resulting in minor bloodshed and Marine police action; strikes in various branches of the occupation machinery
ensued and, on December 4, General Russell proclaimed
martial law. Hoover had included Haiti in his new approach
to Latin America and in September, prior to the forcible
demonstrations, had suggested to Stimson that an investigation be mounted. The autumn's incidents reenforced this
conviction, and his first Annual Message (delivered the day
before martial law went into operation) deprecated the Haitian and Nicaraguan occupations. The accumulation of
events led him to ask Congress (on December 7) for funds
and authority to appoint the commission which he had proposed to Stimson nearly three months earlier.

Assuming that withdrawal was in the cards, Hoover
charged the commission, headed by W. Cameron Forbes,
with deciding when and how to accomplish it, and with devising a policy to manage the interim. It investigated
promptly, returned, and reported its plan for the temporary
government which would precede withdrawal. This was as
ingenious as it was extraconstitutional, providing that the
Council of State should elect a President proposed by the opposition but acceptable to Borno. He would serve until regularly chosen Chambers could elect his successor, thus marking a return to full constitutional procedures. Eugene Roy
assumed office under this scheme on May 15, 1930, and five
months later Stenio Vincent was elected, in mid-November,

274

to serve until 1936. The Commission recommended abolition of the High Commissionership and appointment of a civilian Minister who would supervise the American treaty officials. Russell resigned on November 1, 1930, to be succeeded by Dana G. Munro as Minister. The services, except for the Garde National, were rapidly Haitianized and effectively administered under Munro's watchful eye.

On October 1, 1931, Haiti resumed control of most domestic functions except fiscal and military operations. A year's experience with these increased responsibilities preceded negotiation of the Munro-Blanchet Treaty, signed on September 6, 1932, and designed to complete the separation. Under it Haitian control of the Garde was to be completed by December 31, 1934, and the Marines (except for a training mission) were to be away within thirty days thereafter. The fiscal aspects were less favorable, providing for replacement (on December 31, 1934) of the financial adviser-receiver of customs by a "fiscal representative" who would collect customs, inspect the internal revenue service, and audit outgoing payments pending liquidation of a loan of 1922. The fiscal and military strings, particularly the former, galled Haitian public opinion as an attempt to perpetuate fiscal control after loosing the political bonds. The National Assembly rejected it unanimously on September 20, despite Vincent's intimation that he had accepted its unfavorable terms in order to have relations regularized, even though on unfavorable terms, because of the possibility that American policy might pass into the control of Franklin D. Roosevelt, who had claimed paternity of the Constitution of 1918, source of many of Haiti's woes.

275

Thus, ironically, Hoover was deprived of the honor justly due him, and the final settlement, delayed for some months, was credited to his successor. Hoover continued to relax controls, despite defeat of the treaty, and his Haitian policy stands alongside the Nicaraguan story as an example of calculated effort to relinquish obligations assumed under a theory of empire outmoded but not yet formally abandoned. His period was one of intelligent retreat, under pressures internal and external, from a decade and a half of interventionism which had suited early-century thinking but was being pushed aside for nonintervention formulas more compatible with hemispheric good will. His contribution to this shift was deliberate and positive, whereas his predecessors' steps had been halting and reluctant. It was registered formally at the end of his Administration when Francis White, acting on behalf of the Department, agreed (in January, 1933) to place the draft of an antiwar treaty prepared by Dr. Carlos Saavedra Lamas of Argentina on the agenda of the Seventh Pan-American Conference scheduled for Montevideo in 1933. Since the Kellogg-Briand Pact already covered the antiwar aspects of the Lamas draft, it appears that the Argentine move was a maneuver to open the subject of intervention to inter-American discussion, and cooperation in the move may be taken as an earnest of willingness to face the issue squarely.

Close kinship exists between intervention and recognition, since granting or denying the latter may become an instrument of accomplishing the former. Here, too, the Hoover Administration marks a period of transition. It will be recalled that Woodrow Wilson had modified the traditional policy of *de facto* recognition by his doctrine of "constitutional legitimacy" developed originally as a device to avoid recognizing the Huerta regime in Mexico. His Republican successors maintained the doctrine, and looked favorably upon the Central American treaty of 1923 which applied the policy specifically to that area. Hoover himself withheld recognition from revolutionary regimes in Guatemala (1930) and El Salvador (1931) in accordance with its principles, thus perpetuating on behalf of his government a policy confined to a particular area which would be abandoned only when the treaty became inoperative among its signatories in 1934.

Hoover and Stimson seem to have deprecated the Wilsonian approach as ineffective, despite its moral impressiveness, though Stimson had bordered closely upon it in dealing with Nicaragua in 1927. Conditions, moreover, called loudly for consideration and possible modification of the policy regarding the areas not covered by the Central American treaty. Before he had been two years in office revolution or severe domestic disturbance had visited nineteen of the twenty-one American republics, and in South America only Colombia, Uruguay, and Venezuela had escaped the contagion of actual revolution. Clearly, continued adherence to Wilsonian non-recognition would soon find the United States in a ridiculous position. Undersecretary Cotton stirred Stimson to action in mid-September, 1930, upon the Secretary's return from an extended vacation following his intensive labors at the London Naval Conference. Within forty-eight hours a circular instruction informed American diplomats in Argentina, Bolivia, and Peru, currently operating under postrevolutionary governments as yet unrecognized, that the Wilson policy was no more and instructing them to enter normal diplomatic relations with the succession regimes. Thus, except for Central America, Hoover brought the United States back to the more flexible historic policy which made recognition depend upon *de facto* physical control, manifestation of intent to honor international obligations, and leanings, at least, in the direction of democratic political procedures. While Hoover thus made a virtue of virtual necessity, he also seems to have acted upon a conviction that the Wilson policy was a mistaken one and a real desire to improve relations in the American family of nations.

The foregoing account of the Hoover-Stimson attitude toward the problems of recognition and intervention makes it clear that a new sentiment pervaded White House and Department of State between 1929 and 1933, since important modifications of both policies emerged during their incumbency. Scholars have for years been busily engaged in researches tending to force Franklin D. Roosevelt to share the architecture of Good Neighborhood with earlier practitioners (witness the works of Alexander DeConde, Robert H. Ferrell, Dexter Perkins, and the present writer). The fact remains, however, that the actual steps which Hughes and Kellogg took were relatively short and tentative as compared with those of Hoover and Stimson, whose Latin American policy, despite its modest achievements, remains their most successful.

•

The preceding story has perhaps indicated that the way of the interventionist, like that of the Biblical transgressor, is hard. The role of the mediator, likewise, is not apt to be easy, since it must be played in the full sight of parties to the dispute, of observers anxious to use established precedents to their own advantage or the disadvantage of prospective opponents, and of domestic critics keen to pounce on mistakes of political judgment to which mediators, like all mankind, are prone. United States mediation of Latin-American disputes occurred, too, in the special climate of ill will toward the Colossus of the North which animated much of that area during the Republican years. Thus American action attempting to forward settlement of the Tacna-Arica, Chaco, and Leticia disputes is one of considerable delicacy mingled with occasional firmness. All three episodes illustrate aptly the fact that small matters may stir international interest entirely unrelated to their intrinsic significance.

The Tacna-Arica question, dating back to the nineteenth century, concerned an area left in dispute after Chile's defeat of Peru and Bolivia in the War of the Pacific. The Treaty of Ancón (1883) left Chile occupying the two territories until a plebiscite could decide their ultimate allocation. Continued Chilean control bred Peruvian discontent but, so isolated and poor was the land that it was only in 1922 that President Harding was asked, as arbitrator, to determine whether a plebiscite was in order; if he answered affirmatively, he was to announce its conditions. The day before Kellogg took office Coolidge, who had fallen heir to the duty, rendered a favorable judgment, leaving it to the new Secretary to implement his decision. The problem thus posed plagued Kellogg throughout his term, and was finally solved only after he left office.

Chilean domination had caused many Peruvians to depart the area, leaving the populations so unbalanced, and the Peruvians so intimidated, as to jeopardize the fairness of any election. The three-man Plebiscitary Commission, headed by General John J. Pershing, found itself in hot water from the start of its labors in the summer of 1925. Driven to conclude that Chilean preponderance made a plebiscite impracticable, the Commission was bound by its mandate to try to conduct one. Shortly, and privately, its members decided to explore the possibility of a diplomatic approach. The episode thus moved turbulently on two levels characterized by charge and countercharge between the parties to the dispute, and Chilean allegations that the United States favored Peru.

Pershing became convinced that the Commission must be given physical control if a plebiscite were to be meaningful. Kellogg, distracted by the problem's ramifications, sought Hughes's advice and was told that, in default of agreement between the parties, the Arbitrator (the United States) was entitled to "complete control" of the voting. This was hardly pleasing to Chile, and a threatened deadlock brought further suggestion of a diplomatic approach. Kellogg continued to press for a plebiscite but hinted (October 31) at willingness to tender good offices (i.e., to use diplomacy) if the parties could agree on such a request. Matters teetered for some time between the two approaches, with preparations for the election paralleling diplomatic maneuvers. Chile chose this moment to present the problem to the League of Nations, creating embarrassing implications as to United States ability to deal with it.

Doggedly persisting, Pershing and the Peruvian member set the plebiscite for April 15, 1926, only to have Chile file notice (on December 14, 1925) of intention to appeal the decision to President Coolidge. At this point Pershing gave up the struggle, resigned (January 19, 1926), and returned to the States, presumably in search of dental care. Coolidge upheld the Commission's decision on the election date but Pershing, on his arrival in Washington, urged recourse to diplomacy and was seconded by his successor, Major General William Lassiter. Further months of discussion ensued, with a definite tender of good offices being made on February 16. Chile accepted, but Peru hedged her approval with a veiled demand that the United States guarantee any diplomatic settlement that might emerge—sufficient to discourage the cautious Kellogg from further moves in this direction.

Negotiations attained a level of complexity bordering on the ridiculous, but in April both parties agreed to permit Kellogg to explore a diplomatic solution in Washington, and if such could be arrived at, to suspend the plebiscite pending final agreement. Meetings between Kellogg and the Ambassadors of the two powers extended from April 6 to mid-June, 1926, when they collapsed. Kellogg offered various solutions, including division of the territory between Chile and Peru, its neutralization, either as independent or under general South American protection, and, finally, its transfer to landlocked Bolivia.

As good offices evaporated, the plebiscite again emerged,

with Kellogg increasingly dubious as to the possibility of a fair election. He took advice from Elihu Root and in personal interviews with Hughes and Stimson, having engaged the latter as a paid consultant, leaning heavily on Hughes's advice in a series of conferences in April. Stimson's final report (May 27) held the local authorities and the Chilean Government responsible for making a fair plebiscite in Tacna impossible. The Commission accepted this conclusion, Peru joining the United States in voting (June 14) to abandon it. A year of constant and often frantic negotiation left matters at a dead end, and Kellogg wrote his wife (June 17): "It is the first big job I have ever undertaken and made a failure of."

After a public proposal of cession to Bolivia (November 20, 1926), which failed to gain acceptance, Kellogg left matters alone for some months but returned to the charge in 1928, when he took a long step forward by bringing the two parties to resume diplomatic relations in October, and to engage in direct conversations under his watchful eye. He was now casting worried glances at the calendar, hopeful of concluding matters prior to leaving office. This proved impossible, though he remained in charge of the Department through most of March, 1929, awaiting Stimson's return from an assignment in the Philippines.

The direct negotiations had bogged down over port facilities, and Hoover was shortly able to present his own revision of a tentative agreement between the parties, acceptable to each. This they embodied in a treaty signed on June 6, 1929, assigning Tacna to Peru and Arica to Chile. Peru was to receive from Chile all public works and government buildings in Tacna, $6 million in cash, free port privileges, and a customs house and railroad station in the Bay of Arica. Only Bolivia, disappointed in her hope of gaining a seaport as a by-product of neighboring tensions, bemoaned the settlement. Thus closed a long and tangled controversy to the solution of which both Kellogg and Hoover contributed, the former by his dogged if somewhat harried determination and his persistence if not his patience under early strains, the latter by his understanding of the problem, gained on his post-election travels to South America, and by his ability to adjust finally the differences which the two powers had themselves reduced to reasonable scope.

Though South Americans devoted much energy to revolution, they seldom went to war; two resorts to international force in Herbert Hoover's day accounted for half of the total to that date. One war, between Bolivia and Paraguay, revolved about ownership of the Chaco Boreal, a region some seven hundred by three hundred miles in area, described with feeling and some verisimilitude by Julian Duguid in a book entitled *Green Hell* (1931). Two colorful Americans had tried, unsuccessfully, to exploit its vast savannas. George L. "Tex" Rickard's talents as a boxing promoter earned him more laurels, and cash, than his cattle-raising adventure there. All that William H. Murray, later Governor of Oklahoma, earned in the Chaco was a nickname, "Alfalfa Bill," which clung to him after his agricultural adventure there came to naught.

Bolivia's interest in this enormous but unexploited area

stemmed, as had her concern over Tacna-Arica, from the landlocked condition imposed upon her by the War of the Pacific. Possession of the territory would afford her access to the Pacific via the Pilcomayo and Paraguay Rivers. Though Bolivia's title was the better, Paraguay had the advantage of possession. Argentine support of Paraguay and Chilean backing of Bolivia bred no improvement in relations, and hostilities broke out in December, 1928, to be halted temporarily to permit study of the question by a commission established through the good offices of the International Conference of American States on Conciliation and Arbitration, which happened to be in session at the moment.

The Commission of Conciliation included delegates from the United States, Colombia, Cuba, Mexico, and Uruguay, all but the last remote from the area of friction. Its charge was to determine responsibility for destruction of "Fort Vanguardia," a jungle outpost built by Bolivia on allegedly Paraguayan territory—the act which had precipitated hostilities —and, if possible, to settle the dispute. By September, 1929, it had proposed a settlement, but a revolution in Bolivia and renewal of hostilities delayed its acceptance. The Commission persevered, however, and in May, 1932, it presented a nonaggression pact proposing a neutral zone five kilometers wide between the facing armies, a resumption of diplomatic relations, and resort to diplomatic negotiation. Bolivia, however, preferred further hostilities and in mid-June seized a Paraguayan fort.

With matters likely to mushroom into a threat to the general treaty structure, Stimson began working through a Commission of Neutrals representing the Pan-American Union

284

and chaired by Francis White of the Department to focus united American pressure on the combatants. After several days of negotiation, nineteen of the American republics adopted a suggestion of José M. Puig Casauranc, Mexican Ambassador to the United States, to address the contestants jointly, and on August 3, 1932, they urged the parties to suspend hostilities and present their respective cases to the Commission of Neutrals. The Declaration, moreover, proposed to refuse recognition of territorial changes accomplished by other than peaceful means. To all intents and purposes, this applied the Stimson Nonrecognition Doctrine (see pp. 325–346) to the Americas. For good measure, the Nineteen also wrote into the Declaration the war-renunciatory doctrine of the Kellogg-Briand Pact. Paraguay, behind in the fighting, accepted the Declaration; Bolivia announced that, since the territory involved was Bolivian, the proposal of the Nineteen was inapplicable.

The Declaration of August 3 gave comfort to the legalists, but the fighting continued, developing into open warfare in the autumn. In mid-December the League of Nations and the Commission of Neutrals joined in representations; these Paraguay refused to accept. The final step of the Hoover period was a League proposal to send a new commission to the area. The Department demurred, on the ground that a new agency would complicate existing efforts through the Commission of Neutrals, which was still working valiantly but unsuccessfully. On this note Hoover, who had been too occupied with the Depression to play an active role, and Stimson, whose Diary indicates that he was informed by White but not particularly active, handed the torch to the new Administration, which witnessed a formal Paraguayan declaration of war, to be followed by hostilities lasting until 1938. Republican efforts, though devoted, had availed neither to prevent war nor to make peace.

Another long-standing controversy, this time involving Colombia, Peru, and, peripherally, Brazil, centered on the remote and minuscule but strategically important village of Leticia, consisting, according to Professor Robert H. Ferrell, of sixty-five huts, two of which were roofed. Possession would give Colombia a foothold on the Amazon; to Peru it would mean monopoly of such commercial advantages as might accrue. A treaty between the two presumably settled its complexities in 1922, but contained provisions disturbing to Brazil. Acting at Colombia's request, Hughes involved himself in the matter, helping to construct a three-power agreement signed just before he left office. Dissatisfied with the situation thus established, Peru seized the village, on Colombian soil, on September 1, 1932. Colombia retaliated by sending a naval expedition 2,500 miles up the Amazon, which was attacked by Peruvian air power, touching off minor but provocative hostilities which resulted in a rupture of relations (February 15, 1933) just as the Republicans were readying to leave the scene.

All this had alarmed Stimson mightily and since mid-September, 1932, he had been casting about, formally and informally, for means of dampening the conflict. On October 14, after officiating at the opening of telephone communication with Peru, he took the Peruvian Ambassador to one side and lectured him sharply, warning that "if I were to convey my real sentiments to his honorable chief . . . I should have told him that if he didn't get his damned scoundrels out of Leticia without delay I'd string him up." Early in October Peru called upon the Permanent Commission on Inter-American Conciliation to undertake a full investigation. Colombia refused to countenance such procedure, but indicated willingness to discuss the entire question after regaining Leticia. All this grieved Stimson, as indicated in a diary entry (of November 11) after a conference with White:

> I am getting quite blue over the bad way in which all Latin America is showing up. It seems as if there is nothing we could count on so far as their having any courage and independence is concerned, and yet if we try to take the lead for them, at once there is a cry against American domination and imperialism.

Four days later he looked favorably on White's proposal to use the conciliation treaties in an effort to bring the parties together; failing success in this approach, Stimson forecast a later line of action: "I may have to invoke the old Kellogg Pact again and try to put some new back teeth in it," an interesting comment in view of the already demonstrated toothlessness of the Pact in the Manchurian episode (see p. 323 ff.).

Brazil offered mediation in late December; Colombia agreed but Peru refused, and in early January, 1933 (on the 10th), the Department implemented Stimson's November thought, without "back teeth," by warning Peru that her actions violated the Kellogg-Briand agreement. The League soon entered the picture, reminding both parties of their obligations under the Covenant. On January 23 Peru requested the League Council to order hostilities suspended; on the same day Colombia asked signers of the Kellogg-Briand Pact to remind her enemies of their promises under it. On the 24th Stimson tried to bring these multiple approaches into some sort of harmony. Calling a conference of representatives of Kellogg-Briand signatories at Woodley, he announced formal United States invocation of the Pact against Peru and urged her to accept the earlier Brazilian offer of mediation. He suggested that his hearers follow his example, and indicated greater sympathy with League action than in the Chaco dispute by sending Geneva a copy of his note to Peru, thus setting the United States on a course parallel to that of the League.

This cognizance of the League was continued in the Administration's last important action. At Colombia's instance, the Council proposed (on February 21) establishment of a League Commission charged with managing the controverted area while working out a solution of the basic issues. Acting on the Council's request, Stimson counseled both parties (on the 27th) to accept the League suggestion. The settlement, like that of the Chaco problem, postdated the Republican period, but the decision not to object to League involvement in an American problem was not without significance, particularly in the light of almost contemporary reluctance to permit League entry into the Chaco dispute.

·

United States connection with the three boundary problems just recounted illustrates a willingness to become concerned in the problems of sister republics and to undertake considerable activity in efforts to solve them. Care should be taken not to equate the degree of success with the amount of effort expended; though only one of the three problems was brought to solution during the Republican years, all three received careful attention and enlisted serious effort—all together, another evidence of greater, and more intelligent, concern for Latin-American welfare than had obtained in earlier years.

The preceding chapters chronicling the Republican years have described a period of transition in Latin-American relations. In 1921 the United States had amply earned the opprobrious title "Colossus of the North." Marines policed Nicaragua, Haiti, and Santo Domingo, and Cuba and Panama remained under long-established tutelage. By 1933, however, the winds of change were blowing strongly both from the south and from within the United States. Interventionism, originally assumed as an uncomfortably necessary attribute of power, used to protect Canal and hemisphere from possible foreign aggression, had ceased to possess either necessity or justification. It remained, however, an irritating and continuing obstacle to inter-American comity and understanding.

Republican leadership had finally, and tardily, recognized these facts of hemispheric life and had begun to cope with them, but the recognition had been slow and grudging and the action was at first reluctant and at the end remained short of final effectiveness. In justice it must be said, however, that very considerable steps had been taken. One may in retrospect wish that the steps had been longer, and taken with greater initiative and alacrity, but they were taken, and they carried the United States a fair distance along the path toward the Good Neighborhood of the 1930's.

IX

The Far East:
China

F_{ar} Eastern policy patterns in the Republican years stemmed in considerable measure from developments coming to a focus around the turn of the century. The exuberant imperialists who planted the flag in Hawaii and the Philippines took little account of the long-run political and military costs which might ensue. If there was concern over the creation of a vast strategic salient in the Pacific, it was lost in dreams of profits in trading with the new possessions, in exploiting their resources, and in access to a huge Chinese market which somehow never enlisted great activity on the part of American capital or returned great profits on the modest amounts invested. However, the new possessions, and the China prospects, embarked the nation willy-nilly upon relations with others already interested in the same area.

Prominent among these was Japan, just emerged as a first-rate power and a rival of European powers already entrenched on Chinese soil through the establishment of "spheres of influence" over which they sought to maintain primary if not exclusive commercial control. Japan had been rebuffed, in the mid-nineties, in her effort to block out her own sphere of influence in pursuance of the European example; the rebuff still rankled, and her desire to share in the Chinese bonanza continued. American tradition forbade entry into the scramble for spheres, but like Japan she sought a share in the China trade, with which continuance or expansion of the spheres would interfere. Here then was the problem: How could the United States safeguard her new Asiatic position and prospects? Military support of commercial policy was out of the question. The economic stakes were never large enough to generate a public opinion favorable to military backing of an economic or political position. Further, providing the necessary military sinews had never been part of the calculations of those who had launched the Far Eastern adventure or of their normally nonmilitaristic countrymen.

The answer, it was hoped, had been found in the Open Door policy of 1899–1900, an American exhortation to all hands to share the Chinese market equally while maintaining that shaky domain as a going concern. This received lip service from all, including Japan, but when the latter wrung concessions from China which contravened its somewhat flimsy terms, the United States felt bound to pose objections to her pretensions. Though these were no more than weak and temporizing, they were objections, and generated Japanese antagonism. Paralleling this source of friction was the American desire to apply to Japanese immigrants restrictions as stringent as those already in effect against Chinese workers. This aim had been accomplished by a face-saving device (the Gentlemen's Agreement) under which Japanese continued to enjoy the treaty right of free entry, but were prevented from leaving the homeland by domestic regulations. This attained the desired result, but hardly improved the climate of opinion. Finally, a naval rivalry developing after the War of 1914–1918 convinced many sensitive Japanese that the United States intended to extend her Far Eastern influence in ways which could only threaten their national interest.

Thus by 1921 a nexus of problems had developed out of the great leap Far Eastward so lightly undertaken two decades earlier. Relatively few Americans, in 1921, would have subscribed to Professor Samuel Flagg Bemis' dictum that the turn-of-the-century projection of American interests into the Pacific was "The Great Aberration" of American foreign policy. By 1933, however, a great deal of Republican energy had been devoted to Far Eastern matters, and affairs in that quarter had taken so unfavorable a turn as to render almost equally embarrassing the choice between continued involvement and progressive disengagement, as embodied in prospective withdrawal from the Philippines.

China, meantime, was passing through deep waters, whose transit would outlast the Republican period. Unlike Japan, she had been unable to extricate herself from the so-called unequal treaties, which hampered her economy by limiting her right to levy tariffs and which subjected her to the humiliation of having foreigners tried on her soil in courts of their own jurisdiction. With these tariff and extraterritorial limitations still in effect, the anachronistic Chinese Empire succumbed in 1911 to a revolution whose years of internal turmoil and international impotence seemed to prove the wisdom of Western strictures on her sovereignty and subjected her, too, to external aggression and the influence of radical ideology. Japan furnished the aggression in the Twenty-One Demands of 1915 and in wartime seizure of the German sphere of influence in Shantung Province. Neither China's token participation in the War nor Wilson's efforts at Versailles sufficed to remove these burdens, and she entered the Republican period still under their yoke.

Domestically China was prey to fractionation of political control and to invasion by Russian Communism, intent as always on using ideology as an instrument of political domination. The "government" which spoke for China at the Washington Conference was one largely by courtesy, and she received more sympathy than real action in response to her urgent pleas for relief from the unequal treaties. Early post-Washington developments failed to brighten the picture. In 1923 Sun Yat-sen, head of a southern government based on Canton and one of the most vigorous contenders for power, accepted Russian aid in rebuilding his Kuomintang or Nationalist Party on a Communist base. This failed to endear him to the West, most of which continued to accord recognition to a northern government based on Peking. On the fringes, powerful war lords continued to jeer at both "cen-

tral" governments, as border war lords had done for generations.

Two major developments emerged from this chaos during
the remainder of the decade, political diversity yielding to a
semblance of order, and foreign infringements of sovereignty
suffering sharp attack and some diminution. Bitter conflict
improved the fortunes of the Cantonese faction after it came
under the control of the young and energetic Chiang Kai-
shek, who by 1927 had shed the Muscovite trappings under
which he had originally operated. His arms secured control
of more and more territory and gained corresponding respect, if not affection, from the Western powers, which by
1929 had deserted Peking and recognized Chiang and the
Kuomintang as at least the putative masters of China; the
war lords continued to jeer, but less loudly. As his power increased it became apparent that his shift away from Communism did not connote adoption of Western political ideas.
Doubtless the strong hand was the only way to manage current Chinese turbulence; at any rate, Chiang's rule came
more and more to approximate the Fascist norms already familiar in Italy and presently coming to characterize Germany and Japan.

Insistence upon recognition of Chinese nationhood advanced at least as rapidly as Chiang's legions marched to
power. The moribund Peking government, indeed, had made
some minor gains before succumbing to the Nationalist onslaught. These took the form of "equal" treaties in which
several weak nations agreed to surrender all or part of the
special privileges retained by the great powers. Chiang's negotiators noted the gains and profited by the example to urge

similar concessions on the major powers. This pressure was symptomatic of a burgeoning nationalist spirit which took various forms, most of them out of proportion to the degree of unity that Chiang had been able to achieve.

To Japan, and to the West generally, this nationalist spirit was important, and dangerous—dangerous because its growth and realization would endanger entrenched positions. Elimination of tariff and extraterritorial privileges would deprive westerners of long-standing preferment in their relations with China. Among Chiang's objectives was restoration of control over Manchuria, where Japan had long possessed treaty-guaranteed rights, and where Russia had expansionist designs which a strong China would thwart. Chinese moves northward, insistent and increasingly powerful, promptly produced Russian and Japanese countermoves. These contravened Western interests and the Open Door and threatened the peace machinery so laboriously created in the postwar period.

The Chinese story in the post-Washington years centers in general on the factors indicated just above. In the case of the unequal treaties it is one of repeated insistence upon their removal, backed by adroit maneuver on China's part, the maneuver being partly bluff and partly shrewd exploitation of Western friendship for China and Western inability to agree on continued repression. In this area China won half her battle in removal of tariff restrictions; here she found the United States well disposed toward her aspirations and playing an important role in their realization. The American attitude toward abolition of extraterritoriality was similarly sympathetic, but here China's efforts were less successful, and the Republican years ended without removal of this burden. It is to these aspects of Chinese affairs that the present chapter will be directed, leaving the Manchurian story, which soon advanced from diplomacy to force, for later treatment.

Reference to the earlier narrative will recall that at the Washington Conference Chinese progress toward relief from the unequal treaties had been limited to permission to increase tariff rates by a mere 5 per cent *ad valorem*. It was also agreed that within three months of adjournment commissions should be assembled to consider further tariff increases and the abolition of extraterritoriality; the powers might individually accept or reject the recommendations of the latter. These commissions could meet only after all the Washington Conference powers had ratified all the Conference agreements. Since France failed to act on the tariff arrangement until August, 1925, a considerable hiatus ensued, and the matter became pressing only after Kellogg had taken office. He was not allowed to remain long unconcerned for, whatever its internal difficulties, the Peking Government (it will be remembered that the factional strife was still boiling briskly and that Chiang's rise would develop only in 1927) was determined to keep the issue of the unequal treaties alive. Hardly a month after assuming office Kellogg had decided that, as soon as French action cleared the way, China should call a tariff conference, which the United States would be prepared to attend by September 1, 1925; by the end of May Silas H. Strawn, a wealthy Chicagoan, had agreed to head the American delegation and was in Washington for briefing.

Renewed hostilities between Chiang and his enemies, developing around Shanghai in mid-March, also forced China upon the Secretary's attention. The policy resulting from the combination of Chinese importunity and military conflict was largely his own, since Coolidge manifested slight interest and no leadership in Far Eastern matters. He encountered no small difficulty in formulating it, since John Van Antwerp MacMurray, the American Minister, was ill disposed toward China's aspirations and inclined to side with such powers as favored more drastic treatment; moreover, with the boldness of an expert instructing a tyro, he often undertook to push his views, on occasion drawing sharp rejoinders from Washington. Nelson Trusler Johnson, another Old China Hand who moved from the field into the Department, had greater rapport with Kellogg's generous tendencies and helped greatly in formulating and carrying out the Secretary's policy.

Violence erupted in the "Shanghai Incident" of May 30, 1925, when British troops fired on a Chinese mob invading the International Settlement. This raised the immediate problem of American cooperation in moves for suppressive action, which marched in parallel with preparations for the tariff conference, brought into relief by a Chinese demand (of June 24–25) for overhaul of "all the unequal treaties which had been concluded in the past." After momentary hesitation, Kellogg decided (on July 1) that the United States would consider modification of *both* tariff and extraterritorial restrictions, though Chinese pressure for the latter had not yet been spelled out in detail. He dragged his feet for some time in making joint (and somewhat severe) representations with Britain and the other interested powers, being much more willing than Britain to include extraterritoriality in the discussions and quite reluctant to join in the proposed British demand that restoration of order must precede *any* discussion of treaty revision.

These maneuvers occupied over a month, during which Kellogg became increasingly convinced that unless China received some concessions she would move unilaterally to throw off treaty restrictions. It was only on August 11 (French ratification of the Washington treaties had been deposited on the 5th) that Britain and the United States agreed on the text of a reply to the Chinese notes of June 24–25; here Kellogg won his point of including both tariff and extraterritoriality in the forthcoming talks. China seized the initiative before the other treaty powers could be brought into agreement, inviting all the powers concerned (on August 19) to a tariff conference to open on October 26, and serving notice of her expectation that "some arrangement will be made to remove the tariff restrictions hitherto imposed. . . ." Thus pushed, the powers agreed on a note of September 4, prior to which Kellogg told China (through an address to the American Bar Association on the 2d) that the United States was willing to consider comprehensive tariff revision, and also to talk about extraterritoriality. He warned, however, that China must earn remission of her burdens by establishing stability to match her emancipation; embarrassingly, he asked whether she possessed a government capable of meeting this challenge.

The hot Washington summer had incubated the essentials of policy: to treat China with consideration in both areas of her inequality, and to deal with her unilaterally if others failed to follow the example of American liberality. Kellogg, then, against the wishes of his Minister in the field, and going contrary to Anglo-Japanese desires for strong representations, had personally embarked the United States on a conciliatory path.

Meantime, preparations for the Tariff Conference to be held in Peking, and opening on October 26, 1925, were under way. Kellogg, believing that he reflected public and congressional attitudes, instructed the American delegation that the meeting might discuss "the entire subject of the conventional tariff, even proposals looking to ultimate tariff autonomy." He was willing, too, for it to become the vestibule to considering "other subjects" if the remaining conferees agreed to enlarging its scope. And to Strawn he expressed his private conviction that the United States would soon have to surrender both tariff and extraterritorial controls. The session thus opened on schedule and under good auspices as far as the United States was concerned. The local signs were less favorable, since Peking soon fell prey to hostilities which caused the hasty departure of three Chinese delegates whose faction had fallen behind in the fighting.

Skirmishing characterized the conference as well as its surroundings. China demanded removal of restrictions and recognition of tariff autonomy, promising in return to abolish "likin," a levy on goods moving through the interior and independent of port-of-entry duties; this had been important to the inland provinces, where its revenue would be surrendered only reluctantly. C. T. Wang, the Chinese spokesman, added proposals for specific tariff increases, to become effective three months after tariff autonomy had been recognized; his arguments failed to quiet American doubts as to his Government's ability to enforce abolition of likin. MacMurray offered a counter proposition, permitting China to levy a surtax of 2½ per cent and a levy of 5 per cent on luxury items. (This was a proposal made at the Washington Naval Conference, and will hereafter be referred to as the "Washington Conference surtaxes.") Matters presently moved into committee hands on the working level, and by March, 1926, factional strife had degenerated into full-scale civil war, confirming Strawn's judgment (expressed on December 9, 1925) that the central government no longer possessed authority.

The provisional government of Tuan Ch'i-jui fled Peking in mid-April, 1926, before Manchurian forces, which promptly occupied the capital; the American delegation continued to busy itself hopefully in preparing a scheme designed to become operative upon the return of political stability. With Chiang Kai-shek on the move northward in the summer, such a development was highly problematical; Ferdinand L. Mayer, an official American observer of Chiang's operations concluded (July 6) that it would be "years" before central authority emerged, and counseled abandonment of the "phantom regime" at Peking and assumption of relations with regional leaders. The American plan, formulated by mid-May, was designed to bolster a Chinese regime by making tariff revenue quickly available; it kindled little enthusiasm among the other delegations and led to deadlock, in the face of which Eugene Chen, Chiang's cocky Acting Minister of Foreign Affairs, warned from the south that Canton would regard resumption of the Tariff Conference as an attempt to intervene in Chinese affairs.

Under these circumstances MacMurray concluded in mid-August that China was moving toward atomization and reluctantly seconded Mayer's recommendation of a regional approach. Such unilateral action would of course involve abandoning American leadership in cooperation via the Tariff Conference, which Kellogg was for the moment unwilling to do; tariff matters hung on this uncertain note until November, 1926.

Discussion of extraterritoriality moved even more rapidly from unreality into phantasy. Attention has been called to Kellogg's willingness to explore the problem, and sufficient interest developed to secure agreement of twelve nations to attend a conference on the subject, scheduled to open on December 18, 1925. Military hostilities delayed the talks until January 12, 1926, and internal confusion necessitated postponement of an in-the-field examination of the operation of the Chinese legal system. China nevertheless urged that the Commission be given plenipotentiary powers, enabling it to pass beyond mere discussion and negotiate a treaty actually abolishing the capitulations. Field work began only in May, 1926, the Commission meantime occupying itself in Peking hearing evidence as to the stability of Chinese legal and judicial institutions, including examination of "beautifully printed laws" which had but slight relation to actual cases. A final report was signed on September 16, agreeing that the *status quo* could only be altered after submission of convincing evidence that the judiciary was free of political or military influence. China herself signed this humiliating recognition of the obvious, though refusing to accept all its strictures.

The Cantonese authorities, gaining confidence with growing strength, entered the tariff picture in September, 1926, announcing their intention to levy "consumption and production" taxes equivalent to those earlier proposed by Mac-Murray. Douglas Jenkins, Consul General at Canton, recommended acceptance of the burden, arguing that protests against such levies would be disregarded. Though MacMurray was on record as favoring deals with regional authorities, he shied off from this concrete proposal, urging that other leaders would follow Canton's example, to the ultimate peril of the Washington treaty structure. His suggestion of joint action to discourage the scheme was not accepted, and Canton placed it in operation on October 11, 1926.

The Department protested this action as illegal (November 5), impartially to both Canton and Peking; Chen vigorously denied the charge in a note patently designed to test whether the powers would present a united front against Cantonese aggressiveness. At this point MacMurray sought guidance from the Department, to be met by reiteration of willingness "to do everything it can to make clear that it is willing to meet the aspirations of China in regard to the tariff question." Confused internal conditions combined with growing Nationalist strength to persuade MacMurray (early in December, 1926) that the powers must grant China the Washington surtaxes without further ado. He persuaded Kellogg to join Britain in such action on condition that actual collection be handled through the Chinese Maritime Customs Service (operated by foreign nationals), to insure that the money went to whatever local authority controlled the ports of entry.

So far Kellogg had possessed a somewhat uneasy initiative on tariff matters, and his willingness to parley had set him off from other nations, unhappy at the thought of concessions to China. In September, 1926, the British asked his attitude toward resurrecting general tariff talks and secondly, his feeling about South China's rising strength. Still reluctant to espouse regionalism, his conventional reply (October 5) expressed continued desire to talk only with a "responsible" government and objection to negotiating with "individual provinces or groups of provinces." With an eye on her stagnant trade and, perhaps, on securing a diplomatic advantage, Britain proposed to the Diplomatic Body (composed of the chiefs of mission at Peking) on December 18 that China be granted, immediately and without strings, the Washington surtaxes; somewhat ambiguous verbiage further recognized the justice of China's claims to tariff autonomy without spelling out how it might be attained.

This espousal of China's pretensions became public property in what came to be called the "Christmas Memorandum." It took essentially the same position publicly that Kellogg had occupied privately some months earlier, but it stole the Secretary's thunder and piqued him considerably. He could only follow the British lead, however, and drafted a reply so sympathetic to China as to cause MacMurray to ask (December 30) to be called home for consultation on the sharp differences subsisting between himself and his chief; he felt that Kellogg's approach to the British *démarche* was "inadvisable," and would be viewed as "a competitive protestation of American sympathy for China," as well as a capitulation to Chinese pressure.

A Nationalist assault on Britain's concession at Hankow (January 3, 1927) overshadowed this difference between Secretary and Minister and piled added burdens on Kellogg's head, already whirling in complications emanating from Mexico, Nicaragua, and Tacna-Arica. His temper and health became so precarious that the President virtually ordered him out of Washington for a rest. The Hankow attack caused steps to be taken for evacuating Americans in case hostilities spread, as seemed not impossible, to the Shanghai area. Kellogg reminded MacMurray sharply (January 31) that use of American force in China would be confined to protecting life and property but not, as Britain was hinting, with MacMurray's approval, to defending the International Settlement at Shanghai. That the Secretary's attitude was closer to domestic opinion than MacMurray's is indicated by the introduction and passage (January 21) of Representative Stephen B. Porter's resolution requesting the President to negotiate revision of both tariff and extraterritorial restrictions to put China upon "a wholly equal and reciprocal basis." This was a bid for independent negotiation, and the only expressed limitation was that it should be conducted with a government qualified "to speak for the entire people of China."

Kellogg published his riposte to the British Christmas Memorandum on January 27. His bid was high, as it had to be: he was willing to negotiate independently of other powers on both tariff and extraterritoriality, and implied strongly that he would talk with a joint delegation if Peking and Canton could unite upon one. Though the bid was high, it had a somewhat familiar sound, differing from the Christmas Memorandum mainly in degree; both Britain and the United States were moving toward recognition of Chinese demands.

A spectacular Nationalist advance down the Yangtze Valley, culminating in the Nanking Incident, presently overshadowed both bids for Chinese favor. After capturing Shanghai on February 21, the Nationalist forces entered Nanking on the 24th and took over the city on March 25th, 1927. This time the Chinese attacked all foreigners impartially, instead of focusing on the British as at Hankow, and MacMurray dispatched urgent requests from Peking for transfer of troops to both Peking and Shanghai. He and his fellow diplomats began, too, to try to deal at a distance of several hundred miles with Nationalist violence and truculence in the Nanking-Shanghai sector. He was to find his own superiors as thorny a problem as the Chinese.

He united with his British and Japanese colleagues (on March 29) in proposing to present a sharp ultimatum (the gist of which he enclosed to Kellogg) directly to Chiang, presumably less Communist-dominated than Eugene Chen, making clear that forcible reprisals would follow failure to make amends for Nanking's excesses. Thoroughly alarmed, he insisted that unless united action were taken along the suggested lines China might fall under Russian domination and completely oust Western influence from the Orient.[*] While the Department delayed, the diplomats agreed (April 1) on a form of ultimatum which they believed essential, and presented it to their governments. Washington developed so many reservations as to discourage MacMurray. There must be no deadline for acceptance of the proposed ultimatum; the United States reserved the right to pass upon any sanctions which might be levied; and, presently, Kellogg let it be known (April 5) that the Department "completely dissents" from a British suggestion that all hands "accept in principle" a resort to sanctions in case China failed to give satisfaction, asserting that he would refuse even to discuss such a commitment.

This hesitancy filled MacMurray with anger and chagrin, since he had taken the earlier reservation to apply to the *nature*, and not the *fact*, of sanctions, and the new position left him in an intolerable position with his counterparts. The Secretary conveyed deep sympathy, reaffirmed the departmental position of April 5, and left MacMurray in squirming discomfiture. Kellogg thus found himself alone against the field since MacMurray agreed essentially with Anglo-Japa-

---

[*] It should be noted that while MacMurray was envisioning a Communist bugaboo, the Nationalists themselves were entering a period of soul-searching reorientation which led to a purge of Communist elements from the Kuomintang.

nese desires for a stiffer policy; by April 6 he was telling the British Ambassador that his Government was entirely averse to sanctions. His caution seems to have stemmed from a belief that public opinion was opposed, and from a brief submitted by one of his legal staff pointing out that, though there were precedents for presidential application of sanctions, "such acts may lead to war."

With further military movements endangering the safety of Peking and Tientsin, MacMurray again tried to bring Kellogg to act, earning only another rebuff in his continuing efforts to secure joint action with Japan and Britain. Kellogg's aversion to sanctions gained support from reports that internal strains were rending the Kuomintang. Less than a month after the Nanking Incident it was learned that Chiang had broken with Communism and set up shop at Nanking, leaving the pro-Communist faction in possession of Hankow. This split suggested a wait-and-see policy to Kellogg, seldom given to hasty action, and he wrote on April 21, 1927, replying to MacMurray's request for joint and vigorous steps, that he was "opposed at this time to drastic punitive action. We must be patient with a country which is torn by revolutions and under the control of various military commanders." This note was not sent, but when MacMurray persisted, he philosophized pointedly (on April 25) that "Leadership inheres in moderation as well as forceful action, and . . . you should use your influence in behalf of moderate action."

The departmental influence, thus exercised on behalf of caution, probably prevented cooperative chastisement of the Nationalists, for on May 3 the British announced abandonment of the idea. Against this background of moderation

Chiang first defeated his radical enemies and then went into temporary retirement. Through months of fighting, the situation remained too fluid for negotiations to be profitable, and Kellogg found it easy to continue his temporizing policy.

Civil war and intraparty feuding failed to dampen Nationalist demands for tariff concessions, and the Nanking government set September 1, 1927, for assumption of tariff autonomy. But the day produced no more than token exactions and renewed efforts to negotiate. These in turn presented the Department with embarrassing jurisdictional questions, after the appearance in Washington (in September) of Frank Lee, bearing the formidable title of "Chief of the Political Department, Ministry of Foreign Affairs, Nationalist Government." He represented the more radical Nationalists, but was personally friendly with C. C. Wu, who spoke, from China, for the moderate group. Dr. Sao-ke Alfred Sze was still the authorized representative of Peking, and steps were taken in the autumn, apparently, initiated by Lee but acceptable to Sze, to merge the two missions into a delegation representative of all China; this, of course, was what Kellogg had been insisting upon since January 27. At Strawn's suggestion, he instructed MacMurray (home for the consultations postponed by the Nanking Incident) to draw up a draft of treaty revision, which, in MacMurray's version of October 21, 1927, was confined to the tariff and designed to be negotiated with a group representing all Chinese factions.

Lee and Sze urged Kellogg (on December 18) to accept a joint delegation to negotiate on the basis of the Secretary's proposal of January 27. This roused MacMurray's ire by reintroducing the question of extraterritoriality, which he had carefully excluded; moreover, it would move the discussions from the field, where they had been conducted for two years, to Washington. Chiang returned to power early in 1928, liquidated the Peking regime in June, and sent Wu to Washington for treaty talks. MacMurray (now returned to China) moved matters a long step forward by negotiating (on March 29–30, 1928) a settlement of the Nanking Incident in which Huang Fu (Chiang's Minister of Foreign Affairs) indicated "profound regret" and, though insisting that Communists were responsible, assumed the onus and promised compensation for American loss of life and property.

Sze, presently bereft of a government but still the accredited Chinese representative, joined Lee in pushing Wu's claims, and in late May, 1928, he was received informally and accorded the privilege of conducting "conversations," as distinguished from negotiations. During the remainder of the month the Department moved gradually into a state of *de facto* recognition of the Nationalist regime and of willingness to consider tariff matters *in China,* as Wu wished, rather than in Washington. MacMurray was by this time resigned to tariff discussions, though he believed that no Chinese undertakings on extraterritoriality could be depended upon. Moving as always, faster than MacMurray, Kellogg instructed him (June 23) to begin conversations on tariff revision, on the basis of early abandonment of current restrictions. Kellogg not only went faster, but farther: having settled the tariff, MacMurray might also discuss extraterritoriality. Kellogg made it clear, moreover (in another dispatch), that the United States would negotiate on the tariff "either with or without" the other powers.

The Nationalists increased the pressure in July, 1928, proclaiming (on the 7th) all unequal treaties void on expiration and demanding negotiation of new agreements; they formally requested appointment of American plenipotentiaries for this purpose. Before this reached him, Kellogg sent MacMurray a draft statement designed to bring the Nationalists, who for all their bold talk had shown no desire to parley with MacMurray, to the council table. This he proposed to release to the press shortly unless the Minister could persuade him to the contrary. MacMurray stubbornly opposed initiation of tariff discussions and urged avoidance of any overt move, approaching insubordination in his hostlity to Kellogg's suggestion.

In insisting that MacMurray inform C. T. Wang (now Chiang's Minister of Foreign Affairs) of American willingness to move, Kellogg emphasized "the rising demand in the press that the United States recognize the Nationalist Government and proceed with negotiations." As MacMurray, thus coerced, reluctantly prepared to approach Wang for tariff negotiations in China, Kellogg took fright lest Nationalist urgency move the talks to Washington and broaden them to include extraterritoriality, from which he began for the first time to recoil. To forestall these undesirable developments he drafted an announcement (on July 20, for release on the 25th) offering to negotiate a tariff settlement *in China,* without mention of extraterritoriality, which, he told MacMurray, he now wished to postpone until the tariff question was settled.

The fortuitous presence in Peking of T. V. Soong, Nationalist Minister of Finance, enabled MacMurray to short-circuit Wang's aloofness, to cut red tape, and to bring matters to a speedy conclusion. Knowing that MacMurray was in a position to negotiate, Soong inquired whether the matter could not be handled prior to his scheduled departure on the 26th. Since Chiang himself was also in Peking, he opined that their joint influence would insure acceptance in Nanking. Kellogg agreed and matters marched rapidly; on the 25th the Soong-MacMurray Agreement granted China "complete national tariff autonomy" on essentially most-favored-nation terms, to which last Wang had apparently objected, but which Soong readily accepted.

This speedy action did violence to several diplomatic proprieties. It abandoned, almost without notice, any pretense of cooperation with the other powers, since the complete treaty text was released at midnight, July 26, following thus closely on the heels of Kellogg's notice of July 24, 6 P.M., to twelve interested powers that his government was ready to *begin* discussions. Neither Soong nor MacMurray, moreover, had received the "full powers" entitling them to conduct formal discussions. The agreement's effectiveness matched the informality of its establishment. China put it into operation on February 1, 1929, and three days later Wang abandoned his initial hesitancy and accepted a full most-favored-nation interpretation; the Senate acted favorably on the 11th and ratifications were exchanged on the 20th. Tariff initiative had returned to the United States, and it remained only for the other nations to fall in line, as they presently did. Washington thus contributed decisively to Chinese attainment of one important national objective.

Kellogg's China policy was now complete. His steady good

will toward that strife-torn land had been evident throughout, though implementation of his good intentions was somewhat erratic and often complicated by friction with Mac-Murray. This career diplomat's first-hand observation of China's weaknesses and uncertainties made him, quite understandably, less willing to assume the risks involved in adjusting, on her own terms, to the dynamic changes occurring within her borders. Kellogg permitted other and to him decisive factors to bring him to a more favorable attitude. His real desire to be helpful fitted neatly into his almost pathological sensitivity to a domestic public opinion which he judged well disposed toward the Chinese cause. In the broader area, his aversion to MacMurray's push for stronger measures toward China tended to alienate the United States from the traditional attitude of united and vigorous opposition to the Nationalists' somewhat obstreperous progress toward national status and international recognition. MacMurray, subjected to repeated frustrations, doubtless felt himself most poorly rewarded for his earnest but unsuccessful efforts to prevent Nationalist China from realizing her objectives.

Kellogg did no little backing and filling on extraterritoriality, and it remained an unsettled problem throughout his tenure. At first willing to consider it, he became squeamish on the subject, returning to it just at the end of the tariff negotiations. His note of June 15, 1928, opening the final stages of the tariff story, expressed a desire for gradual relinquishment, under careful interim safeguards. Five days later he began to hedge, omitting mention of the matter from the draft of a proposed statement to the Nationalists. Wang had no intention of abandoning it, however; the ink was hardly dry on the tariff treaty before he announced Wu's appointment as plenipotentiary delegate and in a note to MacMurray indicated his hope for early negotiations to settle "all questions which are in need of immediate solution." * Without consulting the Department, MacMurray on his own foreclosed discussion of extraterritoriality by blandly assuming that Wang's remark referred solely to the tariff discussions, which, as he correctly but disingenuously pointed out, were already completed. Kellogg criticized him for not consulting his superiors on the note, in the same breath admitting (July 30) that further negotiation was not on his current agenda.

Kellogg's attitude had softened a bit by autumn and he permitted members of the Department to engage in conversations. Wu and Stanley K. Hornbeck opened this phase of affairs on October 30, 1928. Hornbeck caviled at Wu's proposal to cancel the capitulations as of January 1, 1930, arguing that it seemed founded on the misapprehension that the United States would act unilaterally, as it had done on the tariff. Several days of talk convinced him that some concessions would become necessary, despite China's unreadiness.

* The reader may well wonder at the position of the various Chinese agents in Washington; so did the Department and the men themselves. By the time covered in this paragraph, Wu had received Nationalist appointment; Sze was still in Washington and Wu would shortly inform the Department (in September) that he (Sze) was still Minister of China, though he had refused Nationalist appointment to the post. Frank Lee, moreover, was still present and involved in affairs. The three seem to have cooperated amicably and reasonably effectively.

314

On November 21 Kellogg informed seven nations of the talks and solicited their judgment in the premises, but the replies did not encourage a joint approach. China had meantime divested several minor powers of their extraterritorial privileges, and had told Japan that her treaty had expired; the end of the Kellogg incumbency found China still pushing for abolition but recognizing that Britain, France, and the United States retained their status undiminished. Here Kellogg's good will, operating in an area much more delicate than the tariff, one in which lives rather than dollars were at stake, took less vigorous positions and made less headway.

Stimson was hardly settled in office when he received Wang's note of April 27, 1929 (delivered on May 2), addressed to several governments and expressing hope of early removal of the capitulations. He sought MacMurray's advice, giving the Minister another opportunity to press for a united front among the powers and his conviction of China's unreadiness for liberation. As on other occasions the diplomats on the scene agreed upon a proposed identic reply, designed to avoid categorical refusal and to minimize injury to Chinese feelings. Hornbeck's memo generally supported the MacMurray/Diplomatic Body approach. Somewhat later the British advocated similar but not identical replies, in deference to Chinese sensibilities. The feeling presently developed that domestic agitators, rather than real hope or conviction, had inspired Chinese demands; under such circumstances deliberation in replying to the note seemed in order.

By early summer, however, it began to appear that influen-

REPUBLICAN FOREIGN POLICY

tial Chinese were seriously concerned; MacMurray reported (June 10) a conversation in which Wang Ch'ung-hui, Minister of Justice, hinted that China might bring on a crisis by January 1, 1930. Wang repeated this publicly on June 28 while passing through New York on the way to Europe. Since he was no fly-by-night, but a statesman who had done much, over two decades, to improve the Chinese judiciary, his words carried weight and convinced MacMurray of the vigor of Chinese intentions. Thus pressed, Stimson again sought advice (June 25), this time asking MacMurray to assess the consequences of immediate abandonment. The reply (July 5) again advocated joint action with France, Great Britain, and Japan to offset the Chinese hope of winning from divided powers, the technique which had succeeded in the tariff area.

If MacMurray had hoped to find Stimson more sympathetic than Kellogg, he was due for further frustration. The Secretary virtually accused him of fomenting an anti-Chinese movement and abandoning the policy of independent action hitherto successful in dealing with China. Like Kellogg, he too deferred to a public opinion which he believed favored an independent rather than a cooperative approach; he suspected, moreover, that China had already passed the point where cooperation could succeed.

The formal American reply to C. T. Wang's note of April 27, 1929, delayed until August 12, moved no whit beyond the position of the long-extinct Commission on Extraterritoriality. Its carefully guarded language expressed willingness to "participate in negotiations which would have as their object the devising of a method for the gradual relinquishment of extraterritorial rights either as to designated territorial areas or as to particular kinds of jurisdiction, or as to both. . . ." China derived little satisfaction from the other nations' replies, but after due deliberation returned to the attack, asking on September 5 for immediate discussion on terms which ignored the gradual approach posited in the American note.

Further delay ensued, and the American reply, forthcoming only on November 1, again stressed gradualism. Stimson and MacMurray devoted the interim to exchanges reminiscent of the Kellogg-MacMurray correspondence and perpetuating the split between Department and field men characterizing the tariff story. They added little to the substance of difference, but consumed considerable energy on each side. By inference Stimson accused MacMurray of subserviency to Sir Miles Lampson, the British Minister to China, a charge which MacMurray denied vigorously. Stimson also pointed out, quite pertinently, that a united front had never survived the supposed convenience of a particular nation. On his side MacMurray supported the Diplomatic Body's belief that the Chinese, after maneuvering the powers into negotiating, would consider nothing short of complete abolition of extraterritoriality, thus shifting the onus of possible failure from their own shoulders. Somewhere along the line Stimson concluded that the negotiations, to which he had committed himself, should take place in Washington; discussion, he further concluded, was the only way to postpone unilateral denunciation of the treaties to the detriment of foreign interests thus deprived of interim safeguards.

317

A general stocktaking accompanied this lull. The diplomats in China split over a British instruction which reached the field on November 8, proposing to attack the problem by jurisdictional categories rather than geographical areas, involving restoration of Chinese autonomy successively in civil, criminal, and personal status matters, all to be accompanied by establishment of courts staffed in part by foreign judges. France generally followed the British lead. The Dutch shared MacMurray's preference for an area approach, as, somewhat less enthusiastically, did Japan. All hands wished foreign judges to sit in the courts of the principal cities. Both categorical and geographical approaches reflected the feeling of the field men that China had yet to produce either paper or practical guarantees of individual security in the face of capricious or weak officialdom; back of this was the specter of Kuomintang downfall and recurrence to earlier chaos. The general tendency in the field was to bow as slowly as possible to the ultimately inevitable abolition by resorting to some sort of gradualism, upon the details of which agreement was lacking.

A Chinese mandate of December 28, 1929, repeated the earlier threat of abolition on January 1, 1930; orders to prepare specific plans, issued the same day and thus close to the proclaimed deadline, made it plain, however, that China was not likely to move precipitately. Thus she saved face by continuing to threaten, and postponed the possibly undesirable consequences of unilateral abolition. Nineteen-thirty passed without overt action and furnished time for Western stock-taking and the development of an Anglo-American *rapprochement*. Nelson T. Johnson succeeded MacMurray as

318

American Minister in February and shortly began working with Lampson to harmonize existing differences. This proceeded amicably, and similar but not identical proposals went forward to China in the autumn (the American draft was presented on October 28). The Chinese reply (of December 7) took a forward tone, insisting upon speedy and complete repeal; this was followed shortly by a demand for final action prior to March 1, 1931.

This belligerence drew a mild reply, reiterating the importance of negotiation, Johnson presently reported that the current pressure probably stemmed from the Chinese authorities' need to display some sign of international vigor prior to the National Peoples' Convention of May, 1931. He judged that unless the powers agreed on representations, and were prepared for long discussions, the present was not a good time to negotiate. Presently the Department considered whether to continue the practical cooperation with Britain which had characterized 1930, as compared with following an independent course. The first involved the risk of unilateral Chinese action, as well as delay due to the British necessity of concerting policy with the Dominions, and a tentative decision was taken to move unilaterally, through Johnson at Nanking. China placed roadblocks in the way of this plan and nothing positive had occurred when the National Peoples' Convention opened. It promptly (May 13, 1931) proclaimed the end of all unequal treaties.

This bluster had no influence on continuing Chinese conversations with both Britain and the United States, and these studiously ignored the manifesto, a fairly clear indication that the Convention was speaking for domestic rather than foreign consumption. On September 18, 1931, the Department authorized Johnson to proceed to Nanking for discussions with C. T. Wang. The reader will readily connect this date with Manchurian developments, to be described in the following chapter. These developments effectively postponed any real consideration of extraterritoriality, causing it to be swallowed up in the Far Eastern confusion continuing to World War II. Not until 1942 did the question receive real attention, and the Roosevelt Administration's final abolition of the capitulations in 1943 emerged as a political maneuver rather than a recognition of Chinese merit.

The Republican years saw China realize one of her great objectives and fail in the other, a record by and large reflecting the realities of the situation. Domestic chaos, long preventing establishment of central authority, made surrender of established privileges a real threat to foreign lives and property. Kellogg's persistent good will aided China in attaining the half-loaf of tariff autonomy, his breach of the united front in 1928 being more successful, if less significant, than the British move in 1926. Neither Britain nor the United States took such a forthright stand on extraterritoriality, and Japanese aggression in 1931 disrupted what appeared to be developing into a parallel approach to gradual abolition. Kellogg's policy accurately mirrored his own attitudes, which were compounded of a well intentioned but somewhat vaguely grounded desire to aid China along the road to nationhood and a firm belief that domestic opinion, of which, during his entire incumbency, he was hyperconscious, favored such a course. Stimson made no constructive contribution, but continued to manifest willingness to continue exploring Chinese demands. It seems fair to conclude that Republican policy had moved, by 1931, as far toward realization of China's goals as the realities of Chinese affairs could justify; China's position, however precarious, had improved appreciably between 1921 and 1931, and to this improvement Hughes and Kellogg had made solid contributions, from which Stimson, if not moving foward, had made no retreat. Attention, finally, may be called to the almost total lack of presidential participation in the preceding story; policy was made, and implemented, without appreciable leadership from 1600 Pennsylvania Avenue.

X

The Far East:
Manchuria, 1929–1933

Half a world lay between Washington and Manchuria. Few Americans had economic interests in this remote area; few realized its importance in the East Asian power complex or glimpsed its potential significance in relation to the peace machinery so painstakingly elaborated since the War of 1914–1918. None dreamed that it would become a laboratory where the tensile strength of that machinery would fail under the strains imposed by Japanese pretensions to its land and resources. None could know that in the mid-thirties Benito Mussolini would emulate Japanese defiance, accelerating that long descent into international chaos which bred another war in 1939.

It was to be, also, a laboratory for Republican policy makers, presenting again the necessity to choose whether to proceed from inevitable involvement to full commitment to international cooperation—a choice resolved, as always during the Republican years, by refusal to take the ultimate step. In this episode Hoover and Stimson would cooperate and clash, as in other aspects of their mutual endeavors, and here Stimson would perform his most important task as Secretary of State, in conformity with a pattern established as early as 1915, and in a losing cause. And here, finally, the United States would share with the League and with its leading components the blame for the first and crucial failure to interpose available economic and/or military obstacles in the path of willful aggression—a failure which made no small contribution to a decade and a half of mounting hatred and of war and to postwar decades of bitterness and frustration.

China first forced Manchuria on American attention in 1929, as the Hoover-Stimson Administration, still riding the Big Bull Market, seemed to be settling in for a peaceful and profitable summer. Both Russia and Japan had long held treaty-based rights in this seat of rival imperialisms still claimed by China. Now the Nationalist regime emphasized the Chinese angle of the triangular relationship in a move embodying at once its aggressive nationalism and its anti-Soviet leanings. Barely master in his own house, Chiang Kai-shek sought to extend his influence north of the Great Wall. As has been noted above, he had purged the Kuomintang of Communists in 1927. In the following year the death of the "Old Marshal" Chang Tso-lin brought to power in Manchuria his son, Chang Hsüeh-liang. The Young Marshal's preference for the Nationalist point of view stepped up Chinese military potential as Chinese nationalism waxed vigorous. Simultaneously Russia, hitherto largely unconcerned with this far hinterland, began to manifest interest.

The specific clash of aggressions occurred over the Chinese Eastern Railway, an important artery along which northern Manchurian agricultural produce moved south. Though the facility was presumably owned jointly, Russia had gained complete control by 1929. On July 10 Nationalist troops seized the road, following earlier skirmishing. Presently the two nations severed diplomatic relations, raising the possibility of real hostilities.

This was much more exciting, and potentially more dangerous, than the leisurely sparring over disarmament which had recently occupied the cables. Both Russia and China had signed the Kellogg-Briand Pact, but it would only become fully effective in the United States after ceremonies scheduled for July 24. Overt hostilities in the Far East would advertise such an occasion poorly, and would endanger the vital principles of the Pact itself; the whole situation gave Stimson cause for anxiety, especially in view of its obvious connection with current Chinese efforts to abolish extraterritoriality. Some inconclusive attention had already been devoted to the matter, apparently at the instance of Hoover, who wished to strengthen the Pact and had proposed to Secretary Kellogg an added article providing that when a violation occurred the remaining signatories would sever relations with the peace breaker, set up an investigative commission, and refuse to recognize any territorial fruits of aggression. Though Kellogg had disapproved of this approach to nonrecognition, Stimson agreed with Hoover that the Pact needed tightening. Thus both general considerations and Manchurian developments helped to move the Pact upstage and brought Stimson to consider action which might blunt the dragon's teeth—hopefully, before July 24.

His efforts were somewhat handicapped by lack of formal diplomatic contact with Russia. Undeterred, he applied indirect pressure through other Foreign Offices, and July 24 passed peacefully. His next gambit, opened the following day, was less successful. He summoned the Ambassadors of Japan, Great Britain, Germany, France, and Italy and in an *aide-mémoire* proposed that a six-power commission approach the Manchurian problem in terms of the now operative Peace Pact. He found himself unpopular on two counts: first, he had neglected the amenities by failing to forewarn any of his hearers; again, it appeared to them, probably correctly, that he was proposing to endow the Pact with qualities beyond its framers' intentions. Katsuji Debuchi subsequently asked point-blank whether, in case a recommendation were made by such a body, and rejected, Stimson proposed to carry matters further—i.e., to use force. He moved painfully from this position, ending his first approach to the problem, and Japan, which wanted no outside meddling in an area she had marked as her own preserve, could relax and observe further Sino-Soviet maneuvers.

These, somewhat delayed, furnished the occasion for Stimson's second unsuccessful approach. Russian troops, invading Manchuria in mid-November, 1929, encountered no more than token resistance, and in a few days Castle, who had never been more than lukewarm toward the Pact, recorded that Russian antics were making it "look like 30 cents." Stimson instructed the American representatives in Britain, France, Germany, Italy, and Japan (November 26) to inform the respective Foreign Offices of his Government's conviction that Russian and Chinese standing among the nations would depend in considerable measure on the extent to which, in the current crisis, they carried out their obligations under the Pact. If the reactions were favorable, he proposed to send this admonition to the Far Eastern protagonists. Only Italy, least directly involved, agreed unequivocally.

Still undeterred, Stimson stoutly asserted, as John Hay had done in somewhat similar circumstances in 1900, that, since all hands agreed with him "in principle," he would address the parties directly. This he did, sending his hortatory "statement" invoking the Pact to Russia via France (on December 2), due to lack of immediate contact, and to China directly. Thirty-seven of fifty-five signers followed his example, but the results were negligible. China denied violation of the Pact, but indicated willingness to negotiate. Russia suggested that the Kellogg-Briand powers might well mind their own business, as the parties to the argument were doing, who by that time were well on the way toward signing the Protocol of Khabarovsk (December 22), establishing a truce on the basis of the *status quo*. She also turned loose the controlled wrath of one of her most vitriolic orators, Maxim Litvinov, who made an inflammatory speech (on December 4) in Moscow accusing the United States of interfering on China's behalf in a quarrel which the latter had precipitated in contravention of Russian treaty rights, and of trying to underwrite American economic interest in Manchuria.

This, one of Stimson's early essays in diplomacy, gained him no kudos. His effort to promote the Kellogg-Briand Pact into a consultative agreement was laudable but without real foundation, either in the facts surrounding its origin or in the temper of 1929. He gained no friends by making his opening move without prior notice. He afforded Russia a gratuitous opportunity to heap contempt on capitalist imperialism, and helped China not at all. He apparently did not realize that the danger of war was nil, and wrote later unduly magnifying the deterrent effect of his activity; Russia was too busy at home to want a war, and China too weak to support one. This first test of the Pact showed it powerless against threatened but unlikely hostilities; the second Manchurian test in 1931–1932 would show it equally ineffective against real aggression.

Manchuria was still half a world away in 1931, but new and sharper urgencies had been added since Stimson had first turned his attention to it in 1929. Three decades of imperialistic rivalry had obscured China's juridical sovereignty over its many acres and vast resources. Japan and Russia had first fought over it and then shared in exploiting it. Japan, particularly, had busily acquired bought-and-paid-for rights which resulted in a capital investment of over a billion yen and engaged the operations of over a thousand Japanese companies. Manchurian raw materials, moreover, were believed essential to Japan's industrial economy. It was, too, an outlet for Japanese manufactures, though few of Japan's surplus people found their way thither. Any challenge to these varied entrenchments would threaten not only Japan's economy but her psyche.

Plural threats, from Russia and from China, emerged in parallel. The Sino-Russian imbroglio of 1929 had concerned Japan seriously but briefly, since the settlement at Khabarovsk seemed to move this rivalry into the wings. Presently, however, a resurgent Russian activity in Manchuria raised the specter of a Communist push into the Far East and a recurrence of old rivalries. China, too, continued the aggressive nationalism which had triggered the 1929 eruption. Still barely master south of the Great Wall, Chiang gazed northward, and the stronger support of Chang Hsüeh-liang after 1928 threatened Japan's happy hunting ground in Manchuria. Vigorous anti-Japanese boycotts followed a series of military skirmishes in the summer of 1931. As the year wore on, therefore, the tripartite rivalries in Manchuria seemed to some in Japan to have assumed a sort of now-or-never status, demanding forthright action to fend off a dire threat to Japan's position.

Internal affairs in Japan also contributed decisively to the outbreak of hostilities. For decades military and civilian forces had contended for control of the Japanese policy-making machinery. Ostensibly a Western-type democracy, there were enough loopholes in the constitutional paraphernalia to permit activists among military and naval leadership to challenge, from time to time, the civilian control of affairs, producing an oscillatory effect in Japanese governmental practice. Such a challenge, by military leaders, had apparently contributed to the assassination of Chang Tso-lin in 1928. The civil authorities successfully rode out this storm, which had blown up in the Kwantung Army in Manchuria. Presently the Navy, greatly incensed at alleged civilian surrender of Japanese interests at the London Naval Conference, had charged the civilian arm with exceeding its authority; the controversies attendant upon those accusations contributed to the attempted assassination of Prime Minister Yuko Hamaguchi on November 13, 1930. Again, the civilian authority had maintained its primacy.

These were but two instances among many in which the armed services had suffered in power and in prestige at the hands of their own government, to say nothing of the myriad insults and injuries administered by the Chinese. During the summer of 1931, indeed, activist officers of the Kwantung Army had convinced themselves that only positive military steps could secure the national legal position against growing Chinese intransigence. Thus the international rivalries of the early 1930's transpired against a background of Japanese infighting in which military and naval elements repeatedly sought to dominate the civilian arm. So far, indeed, had certain elements of Manchurian field forces progressed with their plans that it can be said with some confidence that the Mukden Incident provided an excuse, rather than a reason, for developments which would probably have occurred anyway, though doubtless in a somewhat different framework.

Much ink has been spilled over the question of what actually happened during the evening of September 18, 1931. The standard story, as it was repeated for years, was to the effect that Japanese troops guarding the right of way some three miles north of Mukden were startled by an explosion and observed Chinese soldiers hastening from the scene.

330

These fired upon the pursuing Japanese, who returned the compliment, touching off the long succession of events leading to the Japanese occupation of Manchuria. Certain problems, however, presented themselves. If, as the Japanese claimed, the explosion ripped apart thirty-one inches of track, at a point where two rails joined, how was it possible for the southbound express from Changchun to cross the gap at full speed and reach Mukden on time, and intact? Why, again, were representatives of foreign governments, investigating on the scene within a few days, shown rail fragments, allegedly from the explosion site, which were of different origin from those still located where the blast supposedly occurred?

These questions puzzled students for some time, and the obvious discrepancies caused the Lytton Commission, investigating on behalf of the League of Nations, to step gingerly, admitting only that there was an explosion, but carefully avoiding assignment of its exact location. The Chinese, on their side, claimed that the Japanese had carefully staged the whole affair to give an excuse for the drastic action which ensued. Matters remained in the area of claim and counterclaim until testimony put into the records of the Tokyo War Crimes Trials of 1946–1948 supported the Chinese contention. On the basis of this evidence Professor Ferrell has unequivocally branded the episode "a complete fabrication of the Japanese army . . . the Kwantung Army's manufactured incident."

The "manufactured incident" induced widespread repercussions. Engineered, as it was, by a small clique in the Kwantung Army, it surprised most Japanese in Manchuria. It caused consternation in Tokyo, where Foreign Minister Kijuro Shidehara had been attempting, he hoped successfully, to assert civilian supremacy within the Japanese Government. The extremist elements had, in fact, been ordered to exercise self-restraint; the bearer of the instruction had arrived in Mukden in time to deliver them, but allowed himself to be diverted overnight. The morrow was too late, and the way lay open for the long series of steps by which inadequate Chinese resistance was overcome, Manchuria was overrun, and the puppet state of Manchukuo was established. China, by the same token, faced the first all-out assault on her attempts to regain possession of her patrimony. Neither Chiang's bombastic claims nor Chang's army could cope with the fanatically efficient Japanese military machine, and China's dream of national recrudescence faded miserably into the reality of Japanese success.

Reasoned calculation could hardly have given the Kwantung Army hotheads a more auspicious moment for their adventure, since all the prospective custodians of the peace were deeply concerned with matters closer to home. These centered mainly on the all-pervasive Depression. In Europe, center of the League of Nations aspects of the peace machinery, the Hoover Moratorium was in midcareer and Pierre Laval was preparing for a trip to Washington to discuss the war-debt problem, which still impended despite the Moratorium's reprieve. Three days after Mukden Britain went off the gold standard, creating preoccupations for herself and for other nations faced with the same situation or its imminent prospect; on Mukden Day itself Ambassador Dawes had reported near-panic in Holland, Switzerland, and Germany.

The United States was in no better case. Here, where the Open Door had long been an article of faith, if not always of works, and where the Kellogg-Briand Pact was still a prized possession, Herbert Hoover was on the long toboggan-slide which would bring him, at the end of his Administration, to a low point in presidential prestige; meantime, he was desperately preoccupied with domestic affairs. Within forty-eight hours of Mukden the stock-market averages sank to a low not reached since 1924; none knew whether they had touched bottom. A national deficit of $2 billion faced this stickler for balanced budgets. And ten millions, more or less, were unemployed. Small wonder, then, that there was no great urge in Washington to become involved in a controversy so far removed in space and immediate interest from problems of such consuming importance.

The problem as Hoover, Stimson, and their advisers faced it, was how far would, or could, the United States go, either singly or in cooperation with other components of the peace machinery, to cope with this threat to its effectiveness. Though the United States had been drawing closer to the League (see p. 66 ff.), formal participation in a first-rate controversy was something else again. On the other hand, more might be expected from one of the chief protagonists of the Peace Pact. Most of all, perhaps, it might be hoped that the incident could be kept localized or, failing this, that the parties might themselves work out their own salvation. Looking back, it is not hard to sympathize with Stimson's initial adoption of this wishful thinking. His Diary in the early days shows clearly his desire to keep the decks clear in the hope that Shidehara might himself solve the problem. By September 23, however, he was telling Katsuji Debuchi, the Japanese Ambassador, that "they must settle it mighty quick," though on the preceding day he had assured Debuchi that Shidehara would be left alone in his attempts to reestablish civilian supremacy.

Manchuria was not only half-a-world away from the United States, but from the League of Nations, formal custodian of the peace-keeping machinery. Actual exercise of this machinery in political crises had been limited to relatively minor strains between Turkey and Iraq (1924–1926) and Greece and Bulgaria (1925). Though owning pretensions to worldwide influence, its operations were primarily geared to Europe rather than the far places, and it had been expected that Europe, and some aftermath of Versailles, would furnish the scene and the origin of any major threat. Economic matters preoccupied Britain at the time of Mukden, as already noted. France, in somewhat better economic case, was entering one of those frequent periods of malaise which afflict the French body politic, one of her repeated government upheavals being in the making. Neither of the principal League figures, then, was anxious to pick up an issue which might remain both distant and minor; small wonder that, despite China's insistence that the area of hostilities was broadening rapidly, an aura of seemingly deliberate procrastination invested League circles until well into October. There is some indication, too, that Anglo-French predispositions lay toward Japan and away from China. At any rate, early action was confined to admonitory notes urging the parties to conduct themselves properly—under the circumstances practically equivalent to a *carte blanche* to Japan.

On September 23, the day Stimson had told Debuchi that Japan must act quickly, he was setting up a series of policy alternatives of his own. He would oppose a proposed on-the-spot examination by a neutral commission, but would support the League in urging direct Sino-Japanese negotiations; if outside action should become necessary, he would favor a joint submission of the problem to League of Nations machinery; and, if none of these sufficed, he would consider action under the Nine-Power or the Kellogg-Briand Pact. In essence, this amounted to a policy of action parellel with but independent of the League, and set the stage for his reaction, on the 24th, to a message from Geneva asking whether his Government would participate in a joint commission of investigation. After consultation with the President, they agreed upon a cautious approach, Stimson fearing lest the League use American participation as a club to bludgeon Japan. Identic notes dispatched on the same day to the Asiatic adversaries embodied the policy of independent but concerted action.

The first week of the crisis, therefore, shows the Secretary manifesting a caution commensurate with the realities, leading Castle to comment that this time he was not going off half-cocked, in pleasant contrast with 1929. As September turned into October, Stimson's thoughts turned toward Laval's visit, preparations for the general Disarmament Conference, and an injunction to Dana Munro, returning to his post in Haiti and "expecting trouble with his niggers," that "the only thing to do is to swat them in case they try to inch up on us any more."

October was another month, however. On the 5th Stimson politely sidestepped Sir Eric Drummond's invitation to join a neutral investigation, a refusal designed to prevent the League from "dumping that baby into my lap." By the 9th he was becoming really perturbed by news that Japan had bombed Chinchow (far removed from the scene of the incident) on the 8th, and spent the best part of an hour briefing the Cabinet on the problem; he was concerned, too, that Hoover, up to his ears in Depression matters, was unaware of either the facts or the possibilities latent in the situation. When finally (on the 10th) he found Hoover with a free mind and free time, the two agreed promptly to avoid custody of the Manchurian infant. Thus, for the time being, President and Secretary were agreed (departmental subordinates shared their judgment) that the United States should wait for and support League initiative so long as Geneva's action did not draw the United States into active steps. Such a policy reflected the realities of America's meager economic interest in Manchuria, of domestic public opinion, and of American power potential in the Far East; it gave no joy to China, anxious for support in ousting her unwelcome tenants, and convinced, correctly as events would show, that American aloofness contributed to Japanese aggression and discouraged League action. Stimson's critics have castigated his alleged supineness in these September and October days as contributing to League abandonment of the plan for an on-the-spot investigation. There is, however, no conclusive evidence that his reluctance was decisive in Anglo-French inaction. Nor is there any certainty that a joint investigation would have deterred Japan. The strongest verdict that can be returned, therefore, is perhaps one of contributory negligence—with mitigating circumstances in the form of a weak navy and an almost total lack of domestic pressure for a stronger policy.

The bombing of Chinchow, in southern Manchuria far from the area of original hostilities, convinced all concerned that something serious was afoot. At the Hoover-Stimson conference on October 10, the President suggested that "our men in Switzerland" be authorized to sit with the League Council when it considered Manchuria. An invitation was sought and obtained, despite Japanese objections, and on October 17 Prentiss Gilbert, Consul at Geneva, became the first American to sit at the Council table. He participated in the discussion leading to a decision to draw the attention of China and Japan to their solemn promises under the Peace Pact, and to notify all subscribers to the Pact of the Council action. The solemnity and significance of Gilbert's presence on October 17 were largely lost in a seriocomic aftermath involving his attendance at subsequent Council deliberations, some of which were secret and thus suspect in some American quarters. Long consideration, including transatlantic telephone talks, finally authorized his continued participation in open sessions, even to the extent of sitting at "the damned table," instead of ranging himself along the wall, as Stimson at one point had decreed; all this, however, on condition that he speak no word.

The next League action was a resolution of October 24 again exhorting the parties to compose their differences at first hand and demanding that Japan withdraw from her newly occupied territories prior to November 16, date of the next session of the Council. The proposal of a deadline was the first positive League action in the premises. Besides arousing Japanese hostility, such a near-ultimatum raised doubts in Washington, since it threatened to interfere with a direct Sino-Japanese settlement. Some days of deliberation produced a formula which vigorously urged Japanese withdrawal but omitted the deadline. This protest, delivered in Tokyo on November 5, found United States action lagging well behind the League, both in time and substance. It was designed to forward Stimson's hopes for a local settlement and was framed, too, in the light of rising Japanese resentment at American interference with the realization of her legitimate hemispheric ambitions; a minor flurry had been stirred, also, by publication of an American cryptographer's claim that he had broken the code used in communication with the Japanese delegation to the Washington Conference of a decade earlier.

Stimson elaborated his policy of maintaining "a position of freedom" at a lengthy Cabinet briefing and in a personal conference with the President on the 6th. Both Cabinet and President approved. Reports from Tokyo that Shidehara was losing control prompted Stimson to see the President on the 7th, when Hoover expressed opposition to action such as an "embargo or an attempt to put on economic pressure . . . on the ground that it was a step which would be provocative and lead to war," though he believed that voluntary limitation of trade would eventually subject Japan to appreciable pressure. Here he was reiterating a fear of possible sanctions which he had expressed to the Secretary as early as October 17, and which would become the main theme of presidential thinking. So strong was his feeling that he expressed himself (on November 7) as ready, in case of need, to recall the American Ambassador and announce "that we would not under any event go to war and that that was contrary to our present policy and contrary to the views of the world," an attitude which induced Stimson at a later date to pencil mutliple exclamation marks in the margin of his Diary. At the time, however, he concurred with the presidential belief that a blockade would lead to war.

Within forty-eight hours Hoover had second thoughts about withdrawing the Ambassador and leaned toward the belief "that if the treaty [a possible Sino-Japanese settlement] is made under military pressure he [Hoover; the statement is Stimson's] will not recognize it or avow it." This is an interesting forecast of the nonrecognition policy which had apparently already been discussed in the Department and been discounted, at least by Hornbeck, on the ground that William Jennings Bryan's adoption of a similar approach in 1915 had been ineffective. Stimson himself was already beginning to believe that nonrecognition, if universally avowed, might prove a powerful weapon. This, Stimson's first diary mention of nonrecognition, seems to indicate that, as between President and Secretary, the former had first brought up the matter, with the latter's general concurrence in such a technique.

As November 16, approached it was evident that the League Council had overreached itself in giving Japan a deadline for withdrawal; continued Manchurian hostilities

REPUBLICAN FOREIGN POLICY

threatened Geneva's prestige and faced the United States with the problem of a proper posture of cooperation. The day came and went, with Japan defiant, the Council perturbed, and the United States unrepresented at its deliberations. Hoover, yielding to Stimson's pressure, had authorized Charles G. Dawes to transfer his flamboyant personality from London, where he had been greatly preoccupied with the current monetary crisis, to Paris, where he concerned himself actively, but somewhat less than knowledgeably, with the Manchurian problem, taking a stance at the Hotel Ritz and ostentatiously avoiding formal contact with the Council. Here his frenetic interviews wth all and sundry failed to halt the developing deadlock in that body, but helped to minimize the frictions inevitably attendant upon such a session.

Events in Europe and in the Far East alike embarrassed the Council. Japan occupied the strategic town of Tsitsihar on November 19, three days after expiration of the ultimatum, and an assault on Chinchow seemed in the making. Two days earlier (on the 17th) Tsuneo Matsudaira had proposed to the British Government that the League sponsor a commission of inquiry. Sir Eric Drummond, representing the League, and Sir John Simon, representing Great Britain, formalized the proposal on November 22. China swallowed this bitter pill with a wry face, since it left Japan in possession of her spoils pending the commission's report and a final Sino-Japanese settlement which, with current military ascendancy in Tokyo, could hardly be favorable to China. General pressure secured her unwilling acquiescence, and on December 10, after complicated negotiations, a formal vote established

340

the commission whose inquiry and report would take title from its chairman, the Earl of Lytton. It will be noted that the United States approved the action and permitted General Frank Ross McCoy to serve as a member; this of course reversed Stimson's earlier opposition to an on-the-spot investigation, and seems a strong indication that he was losing hope of a direct settlement. From the broader standpoint, resort to a commission immensely strengthened the Japanese position in the controverted area.

At this point brief consideration should be given to the American attitude toward the possible application of economic sanctions through an embargo on trade with Japan, as permitted under the League Covenant. Considerable thought was given to the matter, and there was some favorable sentiment. Presidential influence, however, while occasionally wavering, ultimately tilted the balance toward sole reliance on moral force and thus helped to move official thinking toward the less vigorous (and less dangerous) nonrecognition doctrine. An earlier paragraph has noted Hoover's fears, expressed to Stimson on October 17, lest an embargo involve the United States in sanctions. Shortly afterward Hoover told the Cabinet unequivocally that he would not participate in "sanctions either economic or military, for those are the roads to war." His reiterated opposition on November 7 ruled out an embargo completely. About the time of the Japanese occupation of Tsitsihar, some League sentiment developed in favor of economic sanctions and feelers as to the American attitude went out on the 19th.

After conferring with the President, Stimson telephoned Dawes that "if they did put on an embargo, we would not allow our fleet to do anything to oppose it or to interfere with them in their attempts." This was the strongest statement made by any responsible American.

On the 27th, in light of news that Japanese forces were advancing on Chinchow, Stimson asked the President to examine the arguments in favor of an embargo, but they were not sufficiently cogent to persuade Hoover to consider such drastic action. On December 6, while Stimson was toying with a nonrecognition statement, a conference including Castle, Hornbeck, Klots, and Rogers discussed the question of "economic measures," after which Stimson waited upon Hoover, whom he found less adamant than previously, on condition that the matter be first explored with the signatories of the Nine-Power Pact. The likelihood of an embargo faded, of course, with the action of December 10 establishing an investigatory commission. Stimson's own attitude toward sanctions was somewhat ambiguous; he repeatedly raised the question with the President, reiterating the favorable arguments. His own advisers, however, were divided, Klots and Rogers generally favoring action, with Castle and Hornbeck advocating caution.

The decision, of course, was Hoover's, and with only one moment of vacillation (on December 6) he stood unwaveringly in opposition. Therefore, if adverse judgment is to be rendered on American inactivity in what would later be recognized as one of history's crucial and decisive moments, the onus must be placed on this distracted and depression-ridden man. Stimson's Diary bears repeated witness to the President's intense preoccupation with domestic affairs and to the difficulty with which the Secretary gained access to his chief's ear for consideration of foreign-policy problems. Those who, like the writer of this account, experienced these days of disaster will sympathize with his preoccupation. Any American obtuseness as to the caliber of the crisis must, moreover, be shared at least equally with London and Paris and, consequently, with Geneva, where there was no greater zest for sanctions than in Washington. The whole question of sanctions remains, therefore, academic, even as the collective failure to deal effectively with the crisis remains one of the tragedies of the age.

With sanctions ruled out, with Japanese aggression proceeding against ineffective opposition, and with the investigatory commission indefinitely postponing any ultimate settlement, attention turned to a consideration of other means of expressing American disapproval and in the hope of applying some sort of brake to the Japanese juggernaut. The result was the note of January 7, 1932, announcing nonrecognition unilaterally to the Far East, to the League, and to the world. Numerous factors conduced to its promulgation. On December 11 the government of Reijiro Wakatsuki fell, carrying with it Shidehara's moderate policy, on which Stimson had been counting to produce a local settlement. The new government of Tsuyoshi Inukai soon clarified its course. Within a fortnight the Chinese army above Chinchow retreated before new onslaughts which evidenced the Japanese intention (the cabinet decision was taken on December 17) to occupy all of Manchuria. The new aggression proved the insincerity of Japanese promises to halt operations pending the Lytton Commission's report, and the advance on Chinchow pushed ahead the deadline which Stimson had set for himself, he having decided to "lambaste them" if they reached this point. The city fell on January 2, 1932. Japan soon stood poised at the Great Wall waiting a favorable moment to invade Jehol, and Stimson went into action, realizing that all previous techniques had now failed.

The nonrecognition doctrine, on which would rest one of Stimson's chief claims to fame, was announced under the influence of high feeling, in a sincere effort to halt aggression. Its ineffectiveness in one of the great turning points of history has been likened to a pebble which failed to halt a rushing stream; Stimson himself in later years admitted that his resort to the inkpot was "wholly inadequate." In light of the climate of the time, the complete opposition of the President to sanctions—the only method by which Japan could have been halted—and the attitude of the League of Nations, it is difficult to think of a viable alternative.

In the framework of his built-in limitations, Stimson acted vigorously. The very day of Chinchow's fall he alerted Claudel to what he had in mind and, finding himself sleepless on the following morning (a Sunday), he drafted a longhand note to China and Japan, "based largely upon the [Bryan] note of 1915." * This he presented to several of his associates

---

* This was Bryan's riposte of May 11 (drafted by Robert Lansing) to the Twenty-One Demands levied by Japan against China. It was a gesture designed to protect temporarily the principle of the Open Door until the arrival of a more convenient season. Quite ineffective, it was the only protest raised at the time of China's behalf.

344

during the evening and reworked into another draft on the 4th before taking it to the White House, where Hoover approved it. Two more days were spent in refining the phraseology, and the notes went to China and Japan on January 7; the Secretary called in the representatives of the other Nine-Power Pact signatories and informed them of the action taken by the United States on its own initiative. The notes informed both parties that the United States

> cannot admit the legality of any situation *de facto* nor does it intend to recognize any treaty or agreement entered into between those governments . . . which may impair the treaty rights of the United States or its citizens in China, including those which relate to the sovereignty, the independence, or the territorial and administrative integrity of the Republic of China, or to the international policy relative to China commonly known as the open-door policy; and that it does not intend to recognize any situation, treaty, or agreement which may be brought about by means contrary to the covenants and obligations of the Pact of Paris of August 27, 1928. . . .

At some time prior to delivery he read a draft to the British and French Ambassadors, but did not solicit their cooperation; having decided upon unilateral action, an advance on any position yet publicly assumed, he proceeded without further ado. Nor, seemingly, was he greatly perturbed at the time when informed that Sir John Simon's view of things was "somewhat different" from his own. His Diary condoned the noncommittal British official statement of January 9, declining to pick up the American initiative, in the light of British troubles over the currency and with India, as a "cautious attempt to get the benefit of our stand without running any risk." By the time he was penning, with McGeorge Bundy, his *On Active Service in Peace and War* (1948), however, he had developed some feeling of resentment, finding the Foreign Office statement "a plain rebuff . . . even more astonishing in what it did not say than in what it did." It is not improbable that this choler was something of an afterthought, perhaps born of a Foreign Office press release which irritated him at the time.

Before proceeding with the story of events, a word should be said concerning the "authorship" of what will doubtless continue to be called the "Stimson Nonrecognition Doctrine." Few great American pronouncements can claim such unique authorship as Lincoln's Gettysburg Address. More often, particularly in the field of foreign relations, they are joint products, as in the case of the Washington/Hamilton collaboration on the Farewell Address and the Monroe/ Adams contributions to the Monroe Doctrine. Briefly, the situation seems to stand as follows: Textually, the notes stem from Stimson's personal drafting in the first instance, plus considerable reworking by departmental professionals. Ideologically, as already suggested, and as admitted frankly by Stimson, the doctrine which they carried goes back to the Bryan note of 1915. As far as the record goes, Hoover suggested the notion of using the nonrecognition approach in a conversation with Stimson on November 9; Stimson's Diary is unequivocal on this point. It seems likely to the writer that the matter had been discussed in the Department prior to Hoover's suggestion, though here the evidence is less forthright. Stimson records that on the 9th he had carried Hoover's suggestion to Castle, Klots, and Hornbeck and that "Hornbeck had advanced the rather common idea in the Department that this remedy didn't amount to anything because we had tried it in 1915."

The President evidently became piqued at the publicity accorded Stimson on account of a move which he himself had suggested, and in his *Memoirs* developed an argument designed to suggest his own primacy in the affair. Professor Elting E. Morison adduces somewhat tentative evidence connecting James Grafton Rogers with making the original proposal. There is no doubt that it was a composite performance, and there is doubtless sufficient credit for all contributors. Professor Armin Rappaport has concluded that, since Chinchow set Stimson on the path leading to the enunciation of the policy, which would otherwise have gone unborn, the term "Stimson Doctrine" should stand; this seems a reasonable disposition of the case.

The Stimson *démarche* had few constructive results. It did, indeed, put the United States on record, in terms of the Bryan caveat of 1915; it went further in calling world attention to the jeopardy threatening the Kellogg-Briand Pact. It also left Stimson a leader without followers. He can perhaps be fairly criticized for making no real effort to enlist British, French, or League cooperation in a move which had little chance of success as a solo performance. On the other hand, these powers had hitherto done nothing more drastic than to support the evasive tactic of the Lytton Commission, and there was slight likelihood that their temper had changed sufficiently to support even so mild a move as Stimson's essentially negative objection to Japan's imperial march. In addition to putting the United States on record, the notes focused Japanese resentment on Washington, and left the United States, alone, to consider further measures or to admit defeat. For Japan's reply of January 16, hardly cloaking derisive repudiation in the verbiage of diplomacy, left no doubt that his play had failed.

If words were not enough, deeds soon followed. Within the month Japan bombed the Chapei district of Shanghai (January 28, 1932), determined to end a stubborn Chinese boycott. This threatened to carry the war beyond the Great Wall into China proper. Here foreign economic interests, as distinct from those of Japan, were greater; here, too, was the land to which the Open Door principle had been first applied, and where missionary and other ties were stronger and more numerous. Stimson learned of the impending attack on the 25th. Wrenching his attention from preparations for the Disarmament Conference, which he had reluctantly agreed to attend as titular head of the American delegation if no one else would accept the appointment, he plunged vigorously into action.

This time he sought British cooperation from the start. With Hoover's approval, he called in Sir Ronald Lindsay and asked, via an *aide mémoire,* the British reaction to the twin suggestions of (a) a notice pointing out the large Anglo-American interests in Shanghai and asserting that existing circumstances furnished no excuse for landing Japanese troops in the International Settlement; and (b) sending fleet contingents under both flags to the Shanghai area. Presenting his ideas to the Cabinet on the 26th, he found Secretary of War Patrick J. Hurley advocating even stronger measures. The Navy, however, was less belligerent, the Fleet Commander reporting that, aside from the flagship, his vessels were overage and manned by crews too small and too poorly trained to make the move a wise one—an interesting side commentary on one road to the "disarmament" which had elecited so much negotiation during the Republican years.

The Shanghai incident moved the conflict into a new dimension, and early signs seemed somewhat more propitious. Chinese resistance stiffened as compared with the relatively weak opposition previously offered. Domestic public opinion was aroused, somewhat in proportion to the greater American fiscal and moral involvement in China proper. The bombing of Chapei brought a prompt British demand (on the 29th) that the International Settlement be kept free of hostilities. The whole situation evidently encouraged Stimson to hope that an international "Thou Shalt Not" might be issued to Japan, but he was destined to disappointment. The Chapei bombings, the prompt British protest, and reaction to press reports on the publication (on the 28th) of the correspondence with Japan over Manchuria nerved him to hope for a stronger line, perhaps to the point of menacing Japan. At any rate, he urged the members of the Cabinet (on the 29th) to refrain from any statements indicating "that we were not going to use any weapon that we might have, whether it be the fleet or the boycott." And on receipt of a copy of the British protest he promptly called for the drafting of a note to Japan backing the British action. This budding plan of cooperation with the British, however, was doomed from both sides of the Atlantic.

Hoover, as usual, was in no mood for threats, though on January 30 he sounded Britain on the idea of a joint appeal to the Japanese Emperor by himself and the British monarch. MacDonald pleaded constitutional difficulties in the way of such a sovereign-to-sovereign approach, but offered himself to repeat to the Japanese Prime Minister anything the President might say to the Emperor. Mushrooming military activity, in the form of an attack on Nanking on February 1, 1932, formed an obbligato to the next Hoover maneuver, formulated on February 1 and announced the following day, proposing a joint tender of good offices urging the parties to halt the fighting and negotiate their differences directly in the presence of neutral observers. China accepted and Japan, predictably, refused (on the 4th). The next gambit, again involving joint Anglo-American representations, proposed an invocation of the Nine-Power Pact. By February 9 Stimson was working on a draft of such a move, which was suggested to London on the 11th, proposing joint testimony to continued adherence to the Pact, the seventh article of which, it would be contended, entitled the signatories to take formal cognizance of such matters as were transpiring in China.

Days of discussion (February 11–16) with Sir John Simon ensued. Much of the dialogue was by transatlantic telephone, still a poor medium for the transmission of nuances of temper and of meaning and a poor vehicle for Stimson's cautious approaches and Simon's often equivocal replies. Though the two reached a close approximation on mechanics and details, it seems apparent that Stimson was willing to go further, and anxious to go faster, in testing Japanese intentions than Simon wished, or could have induced the British Cabinet, to go. There is some evidence to indicate that at this point Stimson was willing to take a calculated risk of war with Japan; some evidence, too, that Simon was willing to assist him in invoking the Nine-Power Pact. Even had these two possibilities coalesced, however, there would have remained Hoover's oft-expressed and adamant opposition to anything which might lead to war, and the highly problematical question of Simon's ability to carry his Cabinet colleagues along such a venturesome road.

The British Cabinet terminated the hectic exchanges on the 17th with a decision to decline Stimson's proposals for joint representations under the Nine-Power Pact, and the Secretary found himself frustrated once more. British recalcitrance, from Stimson's point of view, was this time palpable on the record, and he was accordingly disturbed. He could take but little comfort from the news that the League Council had adopted (on the 16th) a protest including the nonrecognition doctrine of January 7, which was inserted at the behest of the British Foreign Office. By the 18th he was confiding to his Diary that recent developments were "beginning to shake me up and get me back to a little bit nearer my old view that we haven't yet reached the stage where we can dispense with police force. . . ." And, after a hectic day of discussion had produced a decision not to proceed without British support, he asked the Navy (on the 20th) what Pacific forces were available. Hoover stifled any belligerence which this might have betokened in "quite a lively interview" in which he reiterated his opposition to an embargo. Thus estopped from any potentially aggressive action, the Secretary turned again to the inkpot, producing in due course the Borah Letter of February 24.

Like the proposed Anglo-American cooperation under the Nine-Power Pact, this was another attempt, in default of any stronger weapon, to focus the weight of world opinion upon Japan. It reflected, as had all previous moves, the narrow area of maneuver open to the United States, the President's firm hostility to measures smacking of force, and the hard facts of American naval inferiority in case of a Pacific show-down. It represents a third approach by the persistent Secretary who, having made no headway with an independent gambit or with a joint Anglo-American appeal, sought yet again to reach Japan directly. This was, indeed, the only avenue open to him; he was too realistically aware of executive and senatorial opposition to take up with the idea, current at the time, of stimulating the Assembly of the League of Nations to take action under Article xvi of the Covenant. And so he tried again, but by indirection, using a device popularized by Theodore Roosevelt—a letter to an individual but designed for general consumption. This, his next-to-last effort, would have no greater results than the others, but would carry a note of menace foreign to previous formulations.

His Assistant Secretary, James Grafton Rogers, suggested, on a morning canter through Rock Creek Park (on the 21st) that Stimson "might write a letter to somebody on the subject" which had been occupying so much of his recent attention. He promptly decided on Borah as his target, spent much time in drafting the letter on the 22d and 23d, assisted by Rogers, Klots, and Hornbeck, secured Hoover's approval of the document and Borah's consent to the move, and dispatched the letter on the 24th. In it he castigated and threatened without calling names. Taking as his text the seamless character of the fabric created by the Washington Conference treaties, he pointed out that if a party to the complex violated one of its parts, such as the Open Door guarantee, he could hardly expect to remain covered by the rest—a sharp reminder that Japanese failure to observe the Nine-Power Pact would justify American reconsideration of the nonfortification provisions of the Five-Power Pact. This passage sounded a note of deep alarm in Japan, reinforced by announcement on the same day that the Senate Committee on Naval Affairs had approved new construction to the tune of $1 billion.

Threats to rearm and refortify were not, of course, the Secretary's only object. His own exegesis of his motives remains the classic statement: He would encourage beleaguered China; he would enlighten his own citizens on the policy of their government; he would cut a pattern on which the forthcoming Assembly of the League might model its action; he would remind those British Tories who had brought to naught his recent proposal for joint action that the Open Door and the Nine-Power Pact had a British as well as an American flavor. And finally and particularly, he would remind Japan of the interdependence of the Washington Conference agreements. In this he succeeded; he succeeded too, as had Americans on earlier occasions, in leaving himself the sole obstacle to Japanese ambition.

The obstacle was moral and psychological rather than

physical. The puppet state of Manchukuo had already (on February 18, 1932) declared its independence of China. On March 9 it was placed under the putative rule of Henry Pu-Yi, the deposed remnant of the Manchu line, who had lived most of the preceding decade as a Japanese protégé; three days later a new state was declared in existence. The Borah Letter itself had to fight for space with two other arresting stories—the Lindbergh kidnapping and the suicide of the Swedish match king and international plunger, Ivar Krueger. Its net effect, therefore, was practically nil, though it may have exerted some influence on the passage by the League Assembly of a resolution (on March 11) rubberstamping the Nonrecognition Doctrine of January 7. This action, though interpreted as League support of the American position, was actually a maneuver designed to forestall possible invocation of the sanctions in Article XVI of the Covenant. This had been greatly desired by the smaller nations but opposed by Britain and France, which had prevented action in the Council, which they controlled. The small fry had the votes and were pressing for action in the Assembly; Sir John Simon proposed, and the Assembly accepted, nonrecognition as a substitute for the sanctions of Article XVI. Again Stimson hoped that Britain was about to see the light.

He promptly put her Government on notice, in a conversation with Lindsay on February 25, that the Borah Letter had been addressed in part to those Tories who, he believed, had stifled Britain's better sentiments. It was now, he said in effect, the League's move, and no further American action could be expected until the League had condemned Japan. He took hope in early April when reports from Geneva predicted the League adoption of nonrecognition mentioned just above, interpreting the Assembly action of March 11, hopefully, as a possible sign of increasing British firmness. Any self-satisfaction he may have felt on Far Eastern matters, however, was rudely shaken when the House of Representatives on April 4 passed a bill freeing the Philippines following an eight-year transition period. This Stimson labeled "a terrific blow to our position in the Far East, the most irresponsible act of Government that I think I have ever come in contact with." This act of "mad lunatics" occurred just as the Secretary was making ready to go to Europe to lend his influence, if not his presence, to the League's Disarmament Conference.

Stimson made occasion to inform Simon of his disappointment with the Tories, and told Ramsay MacDonald of his fruitless February negotiations with Simon, of which the Prime Minister disclaimed knowledge. He discovered to his sorrow, however, that neither France nor Britain was minded to move beyond the position of March 11, and that they were prepared to suppress any such untoward tendencies in the Assembly. Actions taken at home during his absence, moreover, minimized any chances he might have had of stiffening European spines. Undersecretary Castle made two speeches in early May reiterating official opposition to the use of boycotts against Japan and standing firmly upon nonrecognition as the limit of the American attitude. This use of Stimson's second-in-command to hinder Stimson from taking any advanced position could hardly make for good relations between the Secretary, his chief, and his subordinate. Castle, moreover, had turned the knife in the wound by publicly referring to nonrecognition as the "Hoover Doctrine." Hoover, in fact, was now trying to maximize his own share in the January pronouncement in view of his forthcoming race for reelection, and Secretary of War Hurley had already waited on Stimson (on March 12) with a request that the Secretary acknowledge the President's share in the *démarche*. Stimson had responded, a bit stiffly, that the Borah Letter contained a statement to the desired effect; he neglected to add that it had been inserted at Hoover's express, if somewhat embarrassed, request.

None of these discouragements prevented the Secretary's making a fourth and final effort designed to repair the damage done by Castle's speeches and to erect an alternative roadblock against Japanese aggression as a substitute for the boycott threat which Hoover and Castle had destroyed. His plan involved several aspects. One was to send Joseph C. Grew as Ambassador to Japan in place of W. Cameron Forbes, who for some time had not commanded his confidence. Another was to propose, with the support of Secretary of the Navy Charles Francis Adams, that the President leave in the Pacific a naval contingent, sent thither for war games, instead of returning it to Atlantic waters. Hoover acquiesced in this, though not without mention of the extra expense involved in the gesture. A third, and most important, grew out of questions which had been asked of Stimson during his spring trip to Europe, and which had been incubating in his mind for some time; it began to come to focus in mid-July

356

when he was in extended and acrimonious disagreement with the President on the explosive war-debt issue, being pressed on American attention as a result of the Lausanne Conference.

Europeans had inquired in the spring what posture his government would assume in case of a war between League forces and a nation which the League had branded as an aggressor. It had been pointedly suggested that neutrality in such a conflict would, by opening American sources of supply to the offender, render League efforts at punishment difficult or impossible. It was Stimson's idea to make a public statement applying the principles of the Kellogg-Briand Pact to the above circumstances. By July 14 he had determined to write out a speech on the American role in the development of the Pact, present it to the President, and "tell him I am going to make it unless he forbids me." The proposal grew in his mind into a plan of possible action in the light of the forthcoming report of the Lytton Commission. By July 20 he was considering an analysis of the Pact "and the importance of the concerted action of the nations under it . . . ," an eventuality hardly contemplated by the careful framers of that document. He would then go on to the "action" to be taken under the Nine-Power Pact in case the Lytton Commission made a "good" (i.e., condemnatory) report on Japan's role as midwife to Manchukuo. He would then keep the record clear for posterity by "some invocation, some direct invocation . . ." of the Nine-Power Pact, and by a step-by-step ventilation of Japanese actions in the premises. At this point in his thinking he took the precaution of trying out

357

his ideas on Borah, who, in a moment of postprandial relaxa-tion, agreed that "we could not possibly sacrifice the peace treaties to any friendship with Japan."

It remained to explore the presidential reaction to this long step forward. There could not have been a worse time for exploring. Hoover was greatly occupied with the Depres-sion, angry about the "gentlemen's agreement" emerging from the Lausanne Conference to the effect that a European reparations settlement would be conditioned upon American adjustment of war debts, perturbed over further Japanese military advances, and looking at everything through the dis-torting prism of its influence on the coming election. For days, therefore, Stimson was unable to discuss his proposal to rally Europe around the Kellogg Pact for a showdown with Japan. This he proposed as a parallel action to any which the League might take. When finally, on July 27, the President had had an opportunity to examine the draft, he took exception, not to the proposed use of the Kellogg Pact, but to Stimson's mention of the League (which he had done only to point out the impossibility that the parallel ap-proaches would clash) as likely to stir up the Hearst press. He objected, too, to an attempt to move Britain to a defense of the peace treaties, again, in Stimson's view, with one eye on the Lord of San Simeon and the electoral vote of Califor-nia. Despite his strictures, Hoover dubbed it "a magnificent speech," though he obviously insisted upon soft-pedaling the League allusion, which Stimson softened into a comment that "consultation" would inevitably follow "the proper de-velopment of the Kellogg Treaty."

The Council on Foreign Relations provided an occasion for delivery of the address on August 8. This first full-dress public pronouncement in eighteen months was one of Stimson's best. In it he took a strong stand against Japan's blatant violations of the Kellogg Pact; he also proposed to use the Pact to range the United States alongside any overt steps the League might take in the premises. Professor Armin Rappaport, in a telling analysis, has pointed out that in thus sidling toward the League Stimson was aiming a death-dealing blow at the traditional policy of neutrality—a policy which had never weathered a first-class storm, and which had stood as one of the great obstacles to Anglo-American understanding.

The reactions were predictable. China was pleased but not excited, since no specific plan of action was set forth. Isolationist and internationalist press organs in the United States blamed or praised, according to their predilections. Britons took heart at the prospect, however mild, that American neutrality might pass into history. Japan, again, placed the United States in the van of her tormentors.

If the reactions were predictable, the results were negligible. Hoover's acceptance speech of August 11 admitted the commitment to consultation, but denied any obligation to support peace by force. He went further by narrowing the nonrecognition doctrine to a simple denial of American recognition of *title to territory* gained contrary to the Kellogg Pact, whereas Stimson's definition had been broader, extending to "any situation, treaty, or agreement" established in violation of the Pact. Since Japan was busily erecting Manchukuo into an "independent" state (the recognition process

359

was completed by mid-September), she needed no "title to territory" and, had she been suffering qualms of conscience over her recent performance, Hoover's gloss on nonrecognition would have afforded her absolution. This action, taken without waiting for the Lytton Commission's report, drained Stimson of initiative, and he turned to worrying lest the Navy be in a poor position to offset a possible attack stemming from the hostility which his address had aroused in Japan.

When the Commission finally reported (on October 2), blaming both sides but chiefly Japan, the League faced a *fait accompli*. Stimson, reading a preliminary digest to the Cabinet on September 27, found President and colleagues "so deeply immersed in domestic politics and the harassment of bad news that is coming from every side" as to have little concern with such far-off matters. Nor was Stimson himself eager to renew the fray. He followed the counsel of his advisers against initiating any further action, and let it be known that, the problem being one within League membership, that agency should formulate and submit a policy which the United States would then consider. Japan's request for a six-week period in which to study the report and prepare a reply carried into the lame-duck period in which no Administration moves far in foreign policy. Stimson's last accomplishment, at his first conference with the President-elect, was to secure Roosevelt's approval (announced on January 17, 1933) of Republican handling of Manchurian affairs. Again, as so often earlier, Stimson contributed to Japanese ill will by dashing any hopes that this power may have cherished that the new President would be more complaisant than the old.

•

The policy of the United States toward Manchuria presents a prime example of the inutility of words without willingness to resort to deeds, the necessity, if success is to be achieved, of contriving a viable relationship between ends and means. Few of the episodes examined above have produced more words; none, certainly, produced fewer deeds. Again, as has been seen in other episodes, the end may be adjudged highly laudable, but unless the means are made available, the end disapppears into defeat. Still again, using terms oft-repeated here, unless involvement be accompanied by commitment, accomplishment is likely to be minimal.

Manchuria offers, too, a fascinating study in conflicting personalities. Hoover, the Quaker, the opponent of war or of any sanctions that might lead to war, the chief executive harried by a host of domestic pressures, wavered only momentarily and never significantly, from his position. Since he was in command, it was his will that prevailed. Stimson's repeated and resourceful maneuvers around this almost monolithic stand earn him high marks for persistence, if not for success. How far he himself would have been willing to go, given presidential cooperation, may be guessed but cannot be proved. Neither is an answer to the question important, since it is highly unlikely that united executive intent would have prevailed to carry an activist policy against the weight of public and congressional inertia. American activism, moreover, would in all probability have been matched by a corresponding, if not greater inertia in London, Paris, and Geneva.

Moving from the realm of what might have been, an observer is struck by Stimson's persistence, in the face of multiple obstacles, in trying to bring Japan to book. After his initial period of aloofness, for which he has been severely if perhaps unjustly criticized, with lawyerlike tenacity he failed in four successive attempts to pillory Japan. His first gambit, the Nonrecognition Doctrine, was a unilateral and traditional cry of alarm at violation of the Open Door. Learning wisdom, perhaps, from this unsuccessful solo essay, he next sought to enlist Britain in a cooperative approach under the Nine-Power Pact. Definitely rebuffed here, he indulged in unilateral threat in the Borah Letter. A final approach, also unilateral, but hopefully looking to cooperation, was an attempt to endow the Kellogg-Briand Pact with unsuspected sinews.

In all of these he failed. Domestic public opinion did not support him. The President suspected his tactics and frustrated him repeatedly. His Undersecretary undercut him (by order, of course) at a critical point. Sir John Simon talked much but did nothing, reflecting, perhaps, the Anglo-French view that a strong Japan was a desirable Asiatic counterweight to Russian Communism. The League, dominated by France and Britain, took no effective action.

One may well ask, however, whether Stimson failed, or whether a whole generation and a whole approach to peace had failed in face of a single, determined onslaught. The magnitude of the ensuing disaster multiplied the degree of the failure. The successful Japanese adventure furnished a happy example to those apt pupils, Adolf Hitler and Benito Mussolini, and Japan herself fed upon her own precedent

362

within the decade. At this distance in time, Stimson should perhaps be commended for his repeated efforts. In his own day, his failure reflected the tragic unwillingness of all concerned to pay the necessary price for peace.

In Conclusion

In penning this final section of the present work, the writer concludes his second tour of the years 1921–1933. The first passage, spent as a young teacher, a graduate student, and again as a teacher, took him successively into the South, the Midwest, and the East, in all of which, it must be confessed, his observation of the events here chronicled was as superficial as those of most of his associates. His second traverse, completed in these pages, has covered well over a decade spent in close study of all or part of the period under review —first among the prime sources in preparing a volume on Secretary Kellogg and more recently among the works of his fellow investigators who have plowed similar materials for the remaining years. These prime sources and their secondary by-products have, it is to be hoped, added a perspective reflected in the preceding pages and here reduced to brief concluding observations.

First, let it be suggested again that a period or an age, for that matter, must be subjected to more than a backward glance over the shoulder of a later observer whose eye has been sharpened by subsequent developments to detect short-comings which became evident only with the passage of time. The observer must, if he is to be fair, push himself back and try to see his period of study from behind, noting the circumstances from which events and men took their cues. He must, too, approach contemporary reality as closely as possible through the words of the men of the day as written by themselves and about each other. He must deliver his judgments, after these excursions, not only with the wisdom of hindsight, but in terms of what went before and what accompanied the events which he describes.

Having attempted these gymnastics of space and time, what shall be said of Republican conduct of foreign policy? To the writer it seems to represent a normal stage in national development, conditioned both by what had gone before and by contemporary events. Given the experience of the War of 1914–1918 and the ensuing partisan antagonisms, it was hardly to be expected that Republican leadership would transcend the obviously adverse verdict on Woodrow Wilson and all his works and welcome association with the League which bore his stamp. Nor, given the contemporary climate, were tariff and immigration laws surprising, respectively reflecting as they did historic policy and prewar trends. Nor, again, was insistence upon payment of war debts and an ostrich-like refusal to connect these obligations with reparations an entirely unnatural phenomenon. All these reflect the parochial attitude of a nation newly embarked upon a career as a creditor and a world power, dealing with nations, forces, and a world organization all of which were more or less suspect or untried. He would have been bold indeed, Republican, Democrat, or demigod, who opened American doors, forgave legally contracted obligations, and linked arms with "the League at Geneva," as Mr. Kellogg persisted in denominating that agency to the end of his term. The United States thus entered, under somewhat modest Republican leadership, a world of which she had hitherto been hardly aware.

This entry was made, be it remembered, under extremely difficult auspices. The cycle of postwar depression, recovery, boom, and depression reached heights, and depths, the like of which few could remember and none could remedy, subjecting the leadership to such strains as would, it might seem, leave only the crumbs of energy for foreign affairs. Small wonder, then, that adjustment to a new world was partial, and tardy.

It seems to the writer, moreover, that Republican leadership did achieve a considerable degree of adjustment to this new world. The preceding chapters have made it abundantly clear that the word "isolationism," as applied to the Republican years, is a misnomer, except possibly in the narrow sense of refusal to join the League of Nations. The word "involvement" has found its way repeatedly into the narrative; to the extent that involvement characterized Republican policy, to that extent isolationism must be minimized. There is no need to call the roll of involvement in detail — disarmament, Latin America, the Far East, Kellogg-Briand, even the

League itself in the Manchurian episode, all witness American willingness to associate, to participate, and even occasionally to lead in international activities.

Republican leadership, however, never carried involvement to the extent of international political commitment to the use of economic or military force. Consultation was accepted in the Four-Power Pact, but there was no force to preserve the political and naval equilibrium to which it contributed; at London Stimson, under Hoover's direction, shied off from even a mild consultative approach; American names were lent to the Dawes and Young attempts to settle the reparations tangle, but there was no governmental authority to aid in their implementation; the Kellogg-Briand Pact enlisted a world's promises, but no single sanction, in its support; transition and amelioration marked Latin-American policy, particularly in Hoover's day, but reliance remained placed on unilateral action rather than the commitment to nonintervention which Latin America was more and more vociferously demanding as the period closed; and Hoover firmly limited American participation in the Manchurian episode to measures short of force.

All this should not be taken as condemnation of the leadership alone. It is axiomatic that foreign policy in a democracy conforms in the long run to the popular will, and at no time (with the possible exception of the World Court), so far as the evidence goes, could Republican leadership have taken the United States into positions stronger than those here described. Nor was international leadership in better case, as neither France nor Britain, when the ultimate issue arose in Manchuria, was willing to take the only steps which might

368

have halted Japanese aggression; here the United States was no more than a shareholder in disaster.

The foregoing paragraphs, however, should not be taken as an effort to exculpate Republican leadership completely, and it is also necessary to stand off and view the period in a longer perspective. Granted that a newly powerful nation needs time to acquaint itself with the responsibilities of power; granted that considerable adjustments to the new position were achieved; and granted that leadership was lacking in other lands as well. The fact remains that the men in charge of foreign policy of 1921–1933 were reluctant to put matters to the test; they refused repeatedly to equate involvement with commitment, or to balance desired ends with essential means.

To this extent it can be seen, looking back upon them, that they were no more than good journeymen, lacking the attributes of greatness. Having said this, one may sorrow, briefly and retrospectively, that the times produced men of no greater caliber and may conclude finally that, their limitations being what they were, it is hardly strange that the policy they developed was somewhat less than a spectacular success.

Bibliographical Essay

The present work rests mainly upon that of others, being intended principally as a survey and synthesis of existing secondary materials. As such, like the brook, it can rise no higher than its sources. If it attains their level, the writer will be content, and at the outset would acknowledge generally the contributions of his predecessors which have made possible his own. The grist of monographs and special studies had grown in recent years as governmental and personal records became available, until it seemed that the time was ripe for an overall look at foreign relations during the Republican years —hence this essay at the task.

There has been one deviation from dependence upon secondary materials, in that some use has been made of the papers of the three Secretaries of State. The writer examined

371

this material carefully in doing his monograph on Secretary Kellogg, the findings of which are included in the present volume. To balance the scales in part, the pertinent Beerits Memoranda in the Charles Evans Hughes Papers (in the Division of Manuscripts, The Library of Congress) have been used and incorporated, with identifying comment, in the narrative. Since these were written under Hughes's supervision, and base not only upon the Papers themselves but upon research in governmental and other materials, they furnish a useful and authoritative short cut into the mass of the Hughes material. In a somewhat similar manner, the accounts of Henry L. Stimson's incumbency have been supplemented by a full reading of his Diary (in the Library of Yale University).

The language of the text makes clear when quotations are taken from these primary sources. Where the writer has borrowed source quotations from the monographs, these have been checked back, wherever possible, to the originals. Finally, quotations from the monographs themselves have been acknowledged, though not by page references, in the text itself. It is hoped that these devices, plus some annotations in the chapter bibliographies, will be sufficient to enable the reader to refer successfully to the specialized accounts without the burdensome paraphernalia of footnoting.

The informed reader will note at once that the following bibliography does not include every volume dealing with the subject. It does list every title which the writer has actually used in constructing his narrative, and is confined to such titles. By keeping in mind this correspondence between narrative and sources, the reader will be able to note what the writer has used, and to check the author's list against the full bibliography.

A word as to mechanics. The Essay opens with a listing of overall accounts dealing with the entire period or major portions of it from general as well as diplomatic angles. Second is a grouping of accounts dealing with all or part of the period from the particular standpoint of diplomacy. Then, under each chapter in a single alphabet, are listed the works from which it has been written. Bibliographical data and any comment on a title will be made at its first chapter citation; thereafter it will simply be listed.

GENERAL ACCOUNTS

Adams, Samuel Hopkins, *Incredible Era: The Life and Times of Warren Gamaliel Harding* (Boston, 1939).

Allen, Frederick Lewis, *The Big Change: America Transforms Itself, 1900–1950* (New York, 1952).

———, *Only Yesterday: An Informal History of the Nineteen-Twenties* (New York, 1931).

———, *Since Yesterday: The Nineteen-Thirties in America, September 3, 1929–September 3, 1939* (New York, 1940).

Dulles, Foster Rhea, *Twentieth Century America* (Boston, 1945).

Faulkner, Harold Underwood, *From Versailles to the New Deal: A Chronicle of the Harding-Coolidge-Hoover Era* (New Haven, 1951; a volume in the Chronicles of America series).

Hicks, John D., *Republican Ascendancy, 1921–1933* (New York, 1961; a volume in the New American Nation series).

Hofstadter, Richard, *The Age of Reform; From Bryan to F.D.R.* (New York, 1956).

Leuchtenberg, William E., *The Perils of Prosperity, 1914–1932* (Chicago, 1958; a volume in the Chicago History of American Civilization).

Mitchell, Broadus, *Depression Decade: New Era through New Deal,*

1929–1941 (New York, 1955; a volume in the Economic History of the United States series).

Moos, Malcolm, *The Republicans: A History of Their Party* (New York, 1956).

Schlesinger, Arthur M., Jr., *The Age of Roosevelt: The Crisis of the Old Order* (Boston, 1957).

Schriftgiesser, Karl, *This Was Normalcy: An Account of Party Politics during Twelve Republican Years, 1920–1933* (Boston, 1948).

Soule, George Henry, *Prosperity Decade: From War to Depression, 1917–1929* (New York, 1947; a volume in the Economic History of the United States series).

Sullivan, Mark, *Our Times: The United States, 1900–1925* (6 vols., New York, 1926–1935; Vol. vi, *The Twenties*).

Wecter, Dixon, *The Age of the Great Depression, 1929–1941* (New York, 1948).

ACCOUNTS EMPHASIZING FOREIGN AFFAIRS and covering all or a part of the period under consideration.

Adler, Selig, *The Uncertain Giant, 1921–1941: American Foreign Policy between the Wars* (New York, 1965).

Dulles, Foster Rhea, *America's Rise to World Power, 1898–1954* (New York, 1955; a volume in the New American Nation Series).

Ellis, L. Ethan, *Frank B. Kellogg and American Foreign Relations, 1925–1929* (New Brunswick, 1961).

Ferrell, Robert H., *American Diplomacy in the Great Depression: Hoover-Stimson Foreign Policy, 1929–1933* (New Haven, 1957).

———, *Frank B. Kellogg/Henry L. Stimson* (New York, 1963; Vol. xi of *The American Secretaries of State and Their Diplomacy*, Robert H. Ferrell, ed.).

Graebner, Norman A. (ed.), *An Uncertain Tradition: American Secretaries of State in the Twentieth Century* (New York, 1961).

Nevins, Allan, *The United States in a Chaotic World: A Chronicle of International Affairs, 1918–1933* (New Haven, 1950; a volume in the Chronicles of America series).

Perkins, Dexter, *Charles Evans Hughes and American Democratic Statesmanship* (Boston, 1956).

Bibliographical Essay

CHAPTER I: SIGNS AND PORTENTS

Adams, Samuel Hopkins, *Incredible Era: The Life and Times of War-ren Gamaliel Harding* (Boston, 1939). A racy account by a per-cipient contemporary journalist.

Allen, Frederick Lewis, *The Big Change: America Transforms Itself, 1900–1950* (New York, 1952); *Only Yesterday: An Informal History of the Nineteen-Twenties* (New York, 1931); and *Since Yesterday: The Nineteen-Thirties in America, September 3, 1929–September 3, 1939* (New York, 1940). In these three accounts the late editor of *The Atlantic Monthly* takes a sharp retrospective look at the foibles and the mores of his own day.

Angoff, Charles, *H. L. Mencken: A Portrait from Memory* (New York, 1956). A long-time associate pens a portrait full of keen insights, showing the seamy as well as the brighter side of the Sage of Baltimore.

Bagby, Wesley M., *The Road to Normalcy: The Presidential Cam-paign and Election of 1920* (Baltimore, 1962). A careful account of the upheaval which ushered in the Republican years.

Bohn, Frank, "The Ku Klux Klan Interpreted," *The American Journal of Sociology*, 30 (1925), 385–407. A contemporary sociological analysis of this frightening phenomenon.

Dulles, Foster Rhea, *Twentieth Century America* (Boston, 1945). All scholars and students of American history owe a debt of gratitude to Professor Dulles for his volumes of painstaking summary and analysis of many phases and periods of American history, dealing with both domestic and foreign aspects of the national scene.

Faulkner, Harold Underwood, *From Versailles to the New Deal: A Chronicle of the Harding-Coolidge-Hoover Era* (New Haven, 1951).

Greene, Laurence, *The Era of Wonderful Nonsense: A Casebook of the Twenties* (Indianapolis, 1939).

Griswold, A. Whitney, *The Far Eastern Policy of the United States* (New York, 1938). For years the standard work on Far Eastern policy, this must still be consulted by any serious student of the area. Griswold is critical of Henry L. Stimson's policy in Man-churia, asserting that the Secretary went too far in the premises.

Hicks, John D., *Republican Ascendancy, 1921–1933* (New York, 1961). The standard overall account of the period, it puts all students in its debt for straightforward narrative and intelligent perspective.

375

Hicks, John D. and Theodore Saloutos, *Agricultural Discontent in the Middle West, 1900–1939* (Madison, 1951).

Higham, John, *Strangers in the Land* (New Brunswick, 1955). The standard study of Nativism, this volume sheds considerable light on the immigration problem of the postwar years.

Hofstadter, Richard, *The Age of Reform: From Bryan to F.D.R.* (New York, 1956).

Johnson, Walter, *1600 Pennsylvania Avenue: Presidents and the People* (Boston, 1960).

Kuznets, S., *Economic Change: Selected Essays in Business Cycles, National Income, and Economic Growth* (New York, 1953).

Leuchtenberg, William E., *The Perils of Prosperity, 1914–1932* (Chicago, 1958). An excellent companion volume to Hicks, above, for gaining an overview of the period under consideration.

Manchester, William R., *Disturber of the Peace: The Life of H. L. Mencken* (New York, 1951).

Merz, Charles, *Dry Decade* (Garden City, 1930).

Mills, Frederick C., *Economic Tendencies in the United States: Aspects of Pre-War and Post-War Tendencies* (New York, 1932).

Mitchell, Broadus, *Depression Decade: New Era Through New Deal, 1929–1941* (New York, 1955). The standard account.

Moos, Malcolm, *The Republicans: A History of Their Party* (New York, 1956).

Murray, Robert K., *Red Scare: A Study in National Hysteria, 1919–1920* (Minneapolis, 1955).

Nevins, Allan, *The United States in a Chaotic World: A Chronicle of International Affairs, 1918–1933* (New Haven, 1950). Professor Nevins was the first to essay an account of the period dealt with in the present volume. Based on printed sources, it displays the author's usual facility of narrative and keen insights.

Paul, Rodman W., *The Abrogation of the Gentlemen's Agreement* (Cambridge, 1936).

Schlesinger, Arthur M., Jr., *The Age of Roosevelt: The Crisis of the Old Order, 1919–1933* (Boston, 1957).

Schriftgiesser, Karl, *The Gentleman from Massachusetts: Henry Cabot Lodge* (New York, 1942).

Schumpeter, Joseph, *Business Cycles: A Theoretical, Historical, and Statistical Analysis of the Capitalist Process* (2 vols., New York, 1939).

376

Soule, George, *Prosperity Decade: From War to Depression, 1917–1929* (New York, 1947).

Sullivan, Mark, *Our Times: The United States, 1900–1925* (6 vols., New York, 1926–1935). Vol. vi, *The Twenties,* shows this veteran reporter at his gossipy and reflective best.

Wecter, Dixon, *The Age of the Great Depression, 1929–1941* (New York, 1948).

White, William Allen, *Masks in a Pageant* (New York, 1930). White knew most of the leading men of his time, and had strong views, which sometimes changed, on all of them.

CHAPTER II: O TEMPORA, O HOMINES

Adams, Samuel Hopkins, *Incredible Era: The Life and Times of Warren Gamaliel Harding.*

Adler, Selig, *The Isolationist Impulse: Its Twentieth-Century Reaction* (New York, 1957).

———, *The Uncertain Giant, 1921–1941: American Foreign Policy between the Wars* (New York, 1965). The best single account of the interwar years.

Allen, Frederick Lewis, *Only Yesterday: An Informal History of the Nineteen-Twenties.*

Bailey, Thomas A., *Woodrow Wilson and the Great Betrayal* (New York, 1945). An able account of the Senate fight on the Versailles Treaty and the election of 1920.

Current, Richard N., *Secretary Stimson: A Study in Statecraft* (New Brunswick, 1954). A pioneer study, characterized by sharply critical judgments of Stimson.

Dulles, Foster Rhea, *America's Rise to World Power, 1898–1954* (New York, 1955).

———, *Twentieth Century America.*

Ellis, L. Ethan, *Frank B. Kellogg and American Foreign Relations, 1925–1929* (New Brunswick, 1961).

Essary, J. Frederick, *Covering Washington: Government Reflected to the Public in the Press, 1822–1916* (Boston, 1927).

Faulkner, Harold Underwood, *From Versailles to the New Deal: A Chronicle of the Harding-Coolidge-Hoover Era.*

Ferrell, Robert H., *American Diplomacy in the Great Depression:*

Hoover-Stimson Foreign Policy, 1929–1933 (New Haven, 1957). The standard, and very able, account of the Hoover-Stimson period.

———, *Frank B. Kellogg/Henry L. Stimson* (New York, 1963). In this, the first volume of an extension of the well-known series edited by Professor Samuel Flagg Bemis, Professor Ferrell has ably condensed, as well as added new material, to the stories told in his own volume and that of the present writer, listed under this chapter.

Fifield, Russell H., "Secretary Hughes and the Shantung Question," *The Pacific Historical Review*, 23 (1954), 373–385.

Fuess, Claude M., *Calvin Coolidge: The Man from Vermont* (Boston, 1940). One of the standard biographies of Coolidge, this is written with a somewhat kinder judgment than William Allen White's studies.

———, "Calvin Coolidge—Twenty Years After," *Proceedings of the American Antiquarian Society*, 63, Part 2 (1953), 351–369.

Gilbert, Clinton Wallace, *The Mirrors of Washington* (New York, 1921).

Glad, Betty, *Charles Evans Hughes and the Illusions of Innocence: A Study in American Diplomacy* (Urbana, 1966). This important study of Hughes's twentieth-century diplomacy in the light of his nineteenth-century background places greater emphasis on personal and national shortcomings than upon successes.

Graebner, Norman A. (ed.), *An Uncertain Tradition: American Secretaries of State in the Twentieth Century* (New York, 1961). This volume contains brief sketches of each Secretary of State, combining factual information with interpretation.

Hicks, John D., *Republican Ascendancy, 1921–1933*.

Leuchtenberg, William E., *The Perils of Prosperity, 1914–1932*.

Johnson, Claudius O., *Borah of Idaho* (New York, 1936). The pioneer study, it is favorable to Borah. It should be compared with the works of McKenna and Vinson.

Johnson, Walter, *1600 Pennsylvania Avenue: Presidents and the People*.

Leighton, Isabel (ed.), *The Aspirin Age, 1919–1941* (New York, 1949). A collection of sketches, of uneven caliber. Those on Aimee Semple McPherson (by Carey McWilliams) and Warren G. Harding (by Samuel Hopkins Adams) are useful.

Lincoln, G. A., "Military and Strategic Aspects of American Foreign

Policy," in Alfred H. Kelly (ed.), *American Foreign Policy and American Democracy* (Detroit, 1954), 21–40.

Lodge, Henry Cabot, "Foreign Relations of the United States, 1921–1924," *Foreign Affairs*, 2 (1924), 525–529.

Lubell, Samuel, *The Future of American Politics* (New York, 1952).

McCoy, Donald R., *Calvin Coolidge: The Quiet President* (New York, 1967). A new and full-scale account which still leaves Coolidge a minor figure in the diplomacy of his administration.

McKenna, Marian C., *Borah* (Ann Arbor, 1961). The most recent full-dress study.

Morison, Elting E., *Turmoil and Tradition: A Study of the Life and Times of Henry L. Stimson* (Boston, 1960). A magisterial treatment.

Nevins, Allan, *The United States in a Chaotic World: A Chronicle of International Affairs, 1918–1933.*

Pearson, Drew, and Constantine Brown, *The American Diplomatic Game* (Garden City, 1935). Though marked by the stigmata of contemporary journalism, this title and the one next following provide the scholar and the student with a great deal of information, which must be taken into account until proven less than accurate, as sometimes happens.

Pearson, Drew, and Robert S. Allen, *Washington Merry-Go-Round* (New York, 1931). A lively, shrewd, and often accurate account of early developments under the Rogers Act of 1924.

Perkins, Dexter, "American Foreign Policy and Its Critics," in Alfred H. Kelly (ed.), *American Foreign Policy and American Democracy*, 63–88. Here the veteran Professor Perkins tilts against the "realistic" school of critics of American foreign policy.

———, *Charles Evans Hughes and American Democratic Statesmanship* (Boston, 1956). A somewhat generous assessment of Hughes's incumbency, which might be read in conjunction with the sketch in the Glad and Graebner volumes mentioned above.

———, "The Department of State and American Public Opinion," in Gordon Craig and Felix Gilbert (eds.), *The Diplomats, 1919–1939* (Princeton, 1953). An essay emphasizing the influence of public opinion as a factor in the formulation of foreign policy.

Schlesinger, Arthur M., Jr., *The Age of Roosevelt: The Crisis of the Old Order, 1919–1933.*

Schriftgiesser, Karl, *This Was Normalcy: An Account of Party Politics during Twelve Republican Years, 1920–1932* (Boston, 1948). An account of the Republicans, from a vigorously Democratic standpoint.

Simonds, Frank, *American Foreign Policy in the Post-War Years* (Baltimore, 1935). An early attempt at overall analysis, from a highly critical approach.

Sinclair, Andrew, *The Available Man: The Life behind the Masks of Warren Gamaliel Harding* (New York, 1965). Gives minimal attention to foreign relations.

Stimson, Henry L. and McGeorge Bundy, *On Active Service in Peace and War* (New York, 1948). This third-person study, in which Stimson was an active collaborator, is essentially a memoir. It should be checked against the Hoover memoirs for some evidence on their variant points of view, and against his Diary and the works of scholars in the interest of obtaining a complete picture.

Tugwell, Rexford Guy, *Mr. Hoover's Economic Policy* (New York, 1932). A tract for the times.

Vinson, John Chalmers, *William E. Borah and the Outlawry of War* (Athens, 1957). An able portrayal of the Idahoan's not inconsiderable role in the negotiation of the Kellogg-Briand Pact.

Williams, William Appleman, "The Legend of Isolationism in the 1920's," *Science and Society*, 18 (1954), 1–20. With his customary vigor, Professor Williams attacks the notion of isolationism in the period. To some who at the time considered themselves isolationists, his arguments might have seemed extreme.

White, William Allen, *Masks in a Pageant*. . .   . .   .

——, *A Puritan in Babylon: The Story of Calvin Coolidge* (New York, 1938). In this, his second study of Coolidge, he moderates some of his earlier judgments. Compare with Fuess's study and with that of McCoy, above.

Wilson, Hugh R., *Diplomat Between Wars* (New York, 1941). The observations of a veteran of the Foreign Service, who looks with wry philosophy on the events in which he participated.

CHAPTER III: EUROPE: IN OR OUT?

Adler, Selig, *The Isolationist Impulse*.
——, *The Uncertain Giant*.
Bailey, Thomas A., *Woodrow Wilson and the Great Betrayal*.
Berdahl, Clarence A., "Relations of the United States with the Assembly

of the League of Nations," *The American Political Science Review*, 26 (1932), 497–526.

Browder, Robert Paul, *The Origins of Soviet-American Diplomacy* (Princeton, 1953). The latest and best-balanced account.

Dulles, Foster Rhea, *The Road to Teheran* (Princeton, 1944).

Fleming, Denna Frank, *The United States and the World Court* (Garden City, 1945). This volume and the one noted just below, by a long-time and ardent advocate of American co-operation in world affairs, remain the best accounts in their respective areas.

————, *The United States and World Organization, 1920–1933* (New York, 1938).

Grew, Joseph C. (Walter Johnson, ed.), *Turbulent Era: A Diplomatic Record of Forty Years, 1904–1945* (2 vols., Boston, 1952). Combining personal records and editorial comment, these volumes picture developments of the period from the standpoint of a professional diplomat and shrewd observer, who was at various times in and out of Washington.

Howland, Charles P., *American Foreign Relations, 1928* (New Haven, 1928). This, the initial volume of what has become an annual publication now sponsored by the Council on Foreign Relations under the title *The United States in World Affairs*, deals, as does its immediate successors, with long-time trends and underlying principles as well as with current developments, thus furnishing a fitting introduction to what has become one of the most useful aids of the student of foreign relations.

Jessup, Philip C., *International Security, the American Role in Collective Action for Peace* (New York, 1935).

Leopold, Richard W., *Elihu Root and the Conservative Tradition* (Boston, 1954).

Morison, Elting E., *Turmoil and Tradition: A Study of the Life and Times of Henry L. Stimson.*

Nevins, Allan, *The United States in a Chaotic World: A Chronicle of International Affairs, 1918–1933.*

Vinson, John Chalmers, *William E. Borah and the Outlawry of War.*

Williams, William Appleman, *American-Russian Relations, 1781–1947* (New York, 1952).

CHAPTER IV: DISARMAMENT: THE WASHINGTON CONFERENCE

Battistini, Lawrence H., *The United States and Asia* (New York, 1955). Interprets the Conference as "a brilliant American success" in its political arrangements.

Brebner, J. Bartlet, "Canada, the Anglo-Japanese Alliance, and the Washington Conference," *The Political Science Quarterly*, 50 (1935), 45–58. A pioneer study, emphasizing the influence of Canada in the Imperial Conference of 1921.

Buell, Raymond Leslie, *The Washington Conference* (New York, 1922). An almost contemporary study, which is still useful for an understanding of day-to-day events. Its sharply critical tone, which the author subsequently modified somewhat, had considerable influence on early assessments of the Conference.

Clinard, O. J., *Japan's Influence on American Naval Power, 1897–1917* (Berkeley, 1947). Dedicated to the thesis that the Naval Program of 1916 was directed against Japan.

Dulles, Foster Rhea, *Forty Years of American-Japanese Relations* (New York, 1937).

Galbraith, John S., "The Imperial Conference of 1921 and the Washington Conference," *The Canadian Historical Review*, 29 (1948), 143–152. A further study of the influence of Imperial affairs on the calling of the Conference.

Greene, Fred, "The Military View of American National Policy, 1904–1941," *The American Historical Review*, 66 (1961), 354–377.

Griswold, A. Whitney, *The Far Eastern Policy of the United States.*

Hicks, John D., *Republican Ascendancy, 1921–1933.*

Ichihashi, Yamato, *The Washington Conference and After* (Stanford, 1928). An adroitly pro-Japanese account, by the secretary to the senior Japanese delegate.

Jessup, Philip C., *Elihu Root* (2 vols., New York, 1938). The fullest account of Root's participation in the Conference.

Johnson, Claudius O., *Borah of Idaho.*

Knox, Dudley W., *The Eclipse of American Sea Power* (New York, 1922). Knox said what most Navy men felt, that the Conference had dealt a smashing blow at the American position in the world.

Leopold, Richard W., *Elihu Root and the Conservative Tradition.*

May, Ernest R., "The Development of Political-Military Consultation in the United States," *The Political Science Quarterly*, 70 (1955), 161–180.

Moore, Frederick, *America's Naval Challenge* (New York, 1929). An anti-Navy tract and defense of the Conference settlements.

Morton, Louis, "War Plan ORANGE: Evolution of a Strategy," *World Politics*, 11 (1959), 221–250.

O'Connor, Raymond G., *Perilous Equilibrium: The United States and the London Naval Conference of 1930* (Lawrence, 1962). See comment on this title under Chapter V.

Osgood, Robert, *Ideals and Self-Interest in American Foreign Relations* (Chicago, 1953). A pioneer volume in the school of writing which has criticized American foreign policy for its moralistic/idealistic shortcomings. For a critique of this approach, see Professor Perkins' article listed under Chapter II.

Perkins, Dexter, *Charles Evans Hughes and American Democratic Statesmanship.*

Pusey, Merlo J., *Charles Evans Hughes* (2 vols., New York, 1951). An authorized biography, based on the Hughes Papers, which also makes use of a number of other important source collections. It tends to view the Conference in a somewhat rosy light.

Rappaport, Armin, *The Navy League of the United States* (Detroit, 1962).

Sprout, Harold and Margaret, *Toward a New Order of Sea Power: American Naval Policy and the World Scene, 1918–1922* (Princeton, 1943). A very able study.

Sullivan, Mark, *The Great Adventure at Washington: The Story of the Conference* (Garden City, 1922). All subsequent accounts take color from this careful reportage.

Tate, Merze, *The United States and Armaments* (Cambridge, 1948). A pioneering study, and still the best overall account of the disarmament experiments of the Republican years.

Tuleja, Thaddeus, *Statesmen and Admirals: Quest for a Far Eastern Naval Policy* (New York, 1963). Useful mostly for the Hoover period in the present volume, the account continues down to Pearl Harbor.

Vinson, John Chalmers, *The Parchment Peace: The United States Senate and the Washington Conference* (Athens, 1955). A meticulous and thoroughgoing study.

———, *William E. Borah and the Outlawry of War.*

Wheeler, Gerald E., *Prelude to Pearl Harbor: The United States Navy and the Far East, 1921–1931* (Columbia, 1963). Adds greatly to knowledge of naval thinking and its influence (or lack of it) on foreign policy.

Young, Eugene J., *Powerful America: Our Place in a Rearming World* (New York, 1936).

CHAPTER V: DISARMAMENT: GENEVA, LONDON, LEAGUE OF NATIONS

Allen, H. C., *Great Britain and the United States: A History of Anglo-American Relations, 1783–1952* (London, 1954).

Davis, George T., *A Navy Second to None* (New York, 1940). An account of the fight for complete parity.

Dawes, Charles G., *Journal as Ambassador to Great Britain* (New York, 1939).

Dulles, Allen W., "The Threat of Anglo-American Naval Rivalry," *Foreign Affairs*, 7 (1929), 173–182.

Ellis, L. Ethan, *Frank B. Kellogg and American Foreign Relations, 1925–1929.*

Ferrell, Robert H., *American Diplomacy in the Great Depression: Hoover-Stimson Foreign Policy, 1929–1933.*

———, *Frank B. Kellogg/Henry L. Stimson.*

Fleming, Denna Frank, *The United States and World Organization, 1920–1933.*

Hicks, John D., *Republican Ascendancy, 1921–1933.*

Hoover, Herbert Clark, *The Memoirs of Herbert Hoover* (3 vols., New York, 1951–1952; Vol. II, *The Cabinet and the Presidency, 1920–1933.*

Hoover, Herbert Clark and Hugh Gibson, *Problems of Lasting Peace* (New York, 1942).

Howard, Sir Esme William, *Theatre of Life* (2 vols., Boston, 1935–1936).

Howland, Charles P., *American Foreign Relations, 1931* (New Haven, 1931).

Lippmann, Walter, *The United States in World Affairs: An Account of American Foreign Relations, 1932* (New York, 1933).

Moore, Frederick, *America's Naval Challenge.*

Morison, Elting E., *Turmoil and Tradition: A Study of the Life and Times of Henry L. Stimson.*

Morton, Louis, "War Plan ORANGE: Evolution of a Strategy."

O'Connor, Raymond G., *Perilous Equilibrium: The United States and the London Naval Conference of 1930* (Lawrence, 1962). Through extensive use of Navy records, Professor O'Connor gives a new awareness of interdepartmental relationships and a fuller picture of naval opinion on disarmament in the 1920's.

————, "The 'Yardstick' and Naval Disarmament in the 1920's," *The Mississippi Valley Historical Review*, 45 (1958), 441–463.

Pearson, Drew and Robert S. Allen, *Washington Merry-Go-Round*.

Pearson, Drew and Constantine Brown, *The American Diplomatic Game*.

Perkins, Dexter, *America's Quest for Peace* (Bloomington, 1962).

Rappaport, Armin, *The Navy League of the United States*.

Stimson, Henry L. and McGeorge Bundy, *On Active Service in Peace and War*.

Tate, Merze, *The United States and Armaments*.

Tuleja, Thaddeus, *Statesmen and Admirals: Quest for a Far Eastern Naval Policy*.

Wheeler, Gerald E., *Prelude to Pearl Harbor: The United States Navy and the Far East, 1921–1931*.

Wheeler-Bennett, John Wheeler, *The Pipe Dream of Peace: The Story of the Collapse of Disarmament* (New York, 1935).

Williams, Benjamin H., *The United States and Armaments* (New York, 1929).

Wilson, Hugh R., *Diplomat Between Wars*.

CHAPTER VI: EUROPEAN MISCELLANY: WAR DEBTS, REPARATIONS, KELLOGG-BRIAND

Allen, H. C., *Great Britain and the United States: A History of Anglo-American Relations, 1783–1952*.

Bennett, Edward W., *Germany and the Diplomacy of the Financial Crisis, 1931* (Cambridge, 1962).

Chamberlin, Waldo, "Origins of the Kellogg-Briand Pact," *The Historian*, 15 (1952). An attempt, through interviews and the use of personal papers, to place Professor James T. Shotwell in the story of the Peace Pact's origin.

Current, Richard N., *Secretary Stimson: A Study in Statecraft*.

Ellis, L. Ethan, *Frank B. Kellogg and American Foreign Relations, 1925–1929*.

Ferrell, Robert H., *American Diplomacy in the Great Depression: Hoover-Stimson Foreign Policy, 1929–1933*.

————, *Frank B. Kellogg/Henry L. Stimson*.

————, *Peace in Their Time: The Origins of the Kellogg-Briand Pact* (New Haven, 1952). The definitive account.

Fleming, Denna Frank, *The United States and World Organization, 1920–1933.*

Fuess, Claude M., *Calvin Coolidge: The Man from Vermont.*

Hicks, John D., *Republican Ascendancy, 1921–1933.*

Hoover, Herbert Clark and Hugh Gibson, *The Problems of Lasting Peace.*

Howland, Charles P., *Survey of American Foreign Relations, 1930* (New Haven, 1930).

Johnson, Claudius O., *Borah of Idaho.*

Lippmann, Walter, *The United States in World Affairs: An Account of American Foreign Relations, 1932.*

Lochner, Louis P., *Hoover and Germany* (New York, 1960).

McKenna, Marian C., *Borah.*

Morison, Elting E., *Turmoil and Tradition: A Study of the Life and Times of Henry L. Stimson.*

Moulton, Harold J. and Leo Pasvolsky, *War Debts and World Prosperity* (New York, 1926).

————, *World War Debt Settlement* (New York, 1932). These two titles remain the standard works.

Perkins, Dexter, *Charles Evans Hughes and American Democratic Statesmanship.*

————, "The Department of State and American Public Opinion."

Simonds, Frank, *American Foreign Policy in the Post-War Years.*

Stimson, Henry L. and McGeorge Bundy, *On Active Service in Peace and War.*

Stoner, John E., *S. O. Levinson and the Pact of Paris* (Chicago, 1943). The story of an ardent advocate of the outlawry of war, who spent much time and energy in prodding Senator Borah to interest himself in the cause.

Vinson, John Chalmers, *William E. Borah and the Outlawry of War.*

CHAPTER VII: LATIN AMERICA: MEXICO AND NICARAGUA

Bemis, Samuel Flagg, *The Latin American Policy of the United States* (New York, 1943). Professor Bemis is kinder to the Colossus of the North than most of his compatriots.

Cline, Howard F., *The United States and Mexico* (Cambridge, 1953). The standard account.

Cox, Isaac Joslin, *Nicaragua and the United States, 1909–1927* (Boston, 1927; World Peace Foundation Pamphlets, vol. 10, no. 7).

Current, Richard N., *Secretary Stimson: A Study in Statecraft.*

DeConde, Alexander, *Herbert Hoover's Latin-American Policy* (Stanford, 1951). A careful study, successfully pushing some aspects of the Good Neighbor Policy back into the Republican years.

Denny, Harold N., *Dollars for Bullets: The Story of American Rule in Nicaragua* (New York, 1929). A journalistic account which runs remarkably close to the documents.

Dulles, Foster Rhea, *Twentieth Century America.*

Ellis, L. Ethan, "Dwight Morrow and the Church-State Controversy in Mexico," *The Hispanic American Historical Review*, 38 (1958), 482–505.

———, *Frank B. Kellogg and American Foreign Relations, 1925–1929.*

Ferrell, Robert H., *American Diplomacy in the Great Depression: Hoover-Stimson Foreign Policy, 1929–1933.*

———, *Frank B. Kellogg/Henry L. Stimson.*

Hicks, John D., *Republican Ascendancy, 1921–1933.*

Howland, Charles P., *American Foreign Relations, 1931.*

Morison, Elting E., *Turmoil and Tradition: A Study of the Life and Times of Henry L. Stimson.*

Munro, Dana G., *The United States and the Caribbean Area* (Boston, 1934).

Nicolson, Harold, *Dwight W. Morrow* (New York, 1935). The standard biography of an amateur diplomat, by a professional.

Perkins, Dexter, *Charles Evans Hughes and American Democratic Statesmanship.*

Ross, S. R., "Dwight Morrow and the Mexican Revolution," *The Hispanic American Historical Review*, 38 (1958), 506–528.

Stimson, Henry L., *American Policy in Nicaragua* (New York, 1927). The proconsul's account of his mission.

Stimson, Henry L. and McGeorge Bundy, *On Active Service in Peace and War.*

Tannenbaum, Frank, *Mexico: The Struggle for Peace and Bread* (New York, 1950).

387

CHAPTER VIII: LATIN AMERICAN MISCELLANY: INTERVENTION, RECOGNITION, BOUNDARY CONTROVERSIES

Balch, Emily Greene, *Occupied Haiti* (New York, 1927).

Bemis, Samuel Flagg, *The Latin American Policy of the United States.*

DeConde, Alexander, *Herbert Hoover's Latin-American Policy.*

Ellis, L. Ethan, *Frank B. Kellogg and American Foreign Relations, 1925–1929.*

Ferrell, Robert H., *American Diplomacy in the Great Depression: Hoover-Stimson Foreign Policy, 1929–1933.*

———, *Frank B. Kellogg/Henry L. Stimson.*

———, "Repudiation of a Repudiation," *The Journal of American History,* 51 (1965), 669–673.

Hicks, John D., *Republican Ascendancy, 1921–1933.*

Knight, Melvin M., *The Americans in Santo Domingo* (New York, 1928). Sharply critical of occupation policy.

Lippman, Walter, *The United States in World Affairs: An Account of American Foreign Relations, 1932.*

Millspaugh, Arthur Chester, *Haiti under American Control* (Boston, 1931).

Montague, Ludwell Lee, *Haiti and the United States, 1714–1938* (Durham, 1940). The standard account.

Nevins, Allan, *The United States in a Chaotic World: A Chronicle of International Affairs, 1918–1933.*

Pearson, Drew and Constantine Brown, *The American Diplomatic Game.*

Perkins, Dexter, *Charles Evans Hughes and American Democratic Statesmanship.*

Stimson, Henry L. and McGeorge Bundy, *On Active Service in Peace and War.*

Welles, Sumner, *Naboth's Vineyard: The Dominican Republic, 1844–1924* (2 vols., New York, 1928). The classical account, by one who was personally involved during the occupation.

Wood, Bryce, *The Making of the Good Neighbor Policy* (New York, 1961).

CHAPTER IX: THE FAR EAST: CHINA

Borg, Dorothy, *American Policy and the Chinese Revolution, 1925–1928* (New York, 1947). A pioneering study.

388

Ellis, L. Ethan, *Frank B. Kellogg and American Foreign Relations, 1925–1929.*

Ferrell, Robert H., *American Diplomacy in the Great Depression: Hoover-Stimson Foreign Policy, 1929–1933.*

————, *Frank B. Kellogg/Henry L. Stimson.*

Fishel, Wesley R., *The End of Extraterritoriality in China* (Berkeley, 1952). The best overall account.

Griswold, A. Whitney, *The Far Eastern Policy of the United States.*

CHAPTER X: THE FAR EAST: MANCHURIA, 1929–1933

Allen, H. C., *Great Britain and the United States: A History of Anglo-American Relations, 1783–1952.*

Bassett, R., *Democracy and Foreign Policy: A Case History, The Sino-Japanese Dispute, 1931–1933* (London, 1952). A defense of British policy, both in the premises and *vis-à-vis* the United States.

Clyde, Paul H., "The Diplomacy of 'Playing No Favorites': Secretary Stimson and Manchuria, 1931," *The Mississippi Valley Historical Review*, 35 (1948), 187–202.

Current, Richard N., "Consequences of the Kellogg Pact," in Anderson, Geo. L. (ed.), *Issues and Conflicts: Studies in Twentieth Century American Diplomacy* (Lawrence, 1959), 210–229.

————, *Secretary Stimson: A Study in Statecraft.*

————, "The Stimson Doctrine and the Hoover Doctrine," *The American Historical Review*, 59 (1954), 513–542.

Dulles, Foster Rhea, *China and America: The Story of Their Relations since 1784* (Princeton, 1946).

————, *Forty Years of American-Japanese Relations* (New York, 1937).

Ferrell, Robert H., *American Diplomacy in the Great Depression: Hoover-Stimson Foreign Policy, 1929–1933.*

————, *Frank B. Kellogg/Henry L. Stimson.*

————, "The Mukden Incident," *The Journal of Modern History*, 27 (1955), 66–72.

Griswold, A. Whitney, *The Far Eastern Policy of the United States.*

Hoover, Herbert Clark, *The Memoirs of Herbert Hoover*, Vol. II, *The Cabinet and the Presidency.*

Maxon, Yale C., *Control of Japanese Foreign Policy: A Study of Civil-Military Rivalry, 1930–1945* (Berkeley, 1957). An important study in the displacement of civilian leadership in Japan in the 1930's.

Morison, Elting E., *Turmoil and Tradition: A Study of the Life and Times of Henry L. Stimson.*

Nevins, Allan, *The United States in a Chaotic World: A Chronicle of International Affairs, 1918–1933.*

Pearson, Drew and Robert S. Allen, *Washington Merry-Go-Round.*

Rappaport, Armin, *Henry L. Stimson and Japan, 1931–1933* (Chicago, 1963). The latest and best account, attempting to answer the question why the United States and Great Britain did nothing to halt Japan in 1931–1933.

Smith, Sara R., *The Manchurian Crisis, 1931–1932: A Tragedy in International Relations* (New York, 1948). Written before many of the important sources were available, this is a sharply critical account of Stimson's policy.

Stimson, Henry L., *The Far Eastern Crisis* (New York, 1936). Stimson's apologia, written close to the event, it should be compared carefully with the following title, written in longer perspective.

Stimson, Henry L. and McGeorge Bundy, *On Active Service in Peace and War.*

Tompkins, Pauline, *American-Russian Relations in the Far East* (New York, 1949).

Vinson, John Chalmers, *William E. Borah and the Outlawry of War.*

Wallace, Benjamin B., "How the United States 'Led the League' in 1931," *The American Political Science Review,* 39 (1945), 101–116. Sharply critical of American actions.

Williams, William Appleman, *American-Russian Relations, 1781–1947.*

Index

League of Nations (*continued*)
visory Commission on Traffic in
Opium, 65; Advisory Commission
on the Traffic in Women and Children, 65; Disarmament Conference, 80; and Manchuria, 67, 342,
335–337, 340–341, 351, 353, 357,
359–360, 362; Preparatory Commission on the Disarmament Conference, 80; Wilson and, 63, 65;
and World Court Statute, 74–75

Lee, Frank, 309, 314 n.

Lee of Fareham, Lord, 93–94

Legislature, influence on foreign affairs, 13–24

Leticia, 279, 286, 287–288

Levinson, Salmon O., 215–216, 222

Liberia, 193

Liberty bonds, 23, 193

"Likin," 300

Lincoln, Abraham, 346

Lincoln, G.A., quoted, 33

Lindbergh, Charles A., 218

Lindsay, Sir Ronald, 348, 354

Litvinov, Maxim, 77, 327

Lloyd George, David, 93–94, 96, 98

Loans, U.S. to Germany, 201, 204,
209–210

Locarno Agreements (1925), 140,
173, 222, 225

Lodge, Henry Cabot, 3, 12, 18, 32,
35, 53, 69, 71; and Washington
Conference, 100, 102, 111, 130

Logan, Col. James A., 66

London Economic Conference
(1933), 214

London Naval Conference (1930),
52, 55, 149–165, 169, 173–174,
176, 178, 180–182, 277, 330, 368;
Briand and, 166, 173–174; cruiser
rivalry at, 169, 177–179; France
and, 164, 168, 171, 173, 175–177;
Gibson and, 154, 156, 170; Great
Britain and, 159, 163, 166–167,

169, 171, 174, 177; Hoover and,
153, 155, 158, 160–161, 164, 168–
169, 175, 177; Italy and, 164, 168,
172, 174, 176, 179; Japan and, 163,
168, 170, 177; MacDonald and,
156, 158, 160–161, 166–167, 169,
172, 174–176; Reed-Matsudaira
"compromise," 178; Stimson and,
154, 158, 162, 166, 168–169, 173–
176; Tardieu and, 166–167, 169,
172–173, 178

Long, Walter, 87

Loochoo Islands, 124

Lubell, Samuel, quoted, 32

Lusitania, 88

Lytton, Earl of, 341

Lytton Commission, 331, 341, 344,
347, 357, 360

McBride, Captain Lewis, 247

McCormick, Medill, 271

McCoy, General Frank Ross, 341

McCumber, Porter J., 21

MacDonald, Ishbel, 161–162

MacDonald, J. Ramsay, 154, 156,
158, 160–161, 166–167, 169, 171–
172, 174–175, 207, 210, 350, 355

MacMurray, J. V. A., 17, 57, 95–96,
128, 298, 301, 303–306, 309–313,
315–318

McNary-Haugen Bills, 21

McNeill, Ronald John (Lord Cushendun), 151

McPherson, Aimee Semple, 6, 7

Madero, Francisco I., 234

Maginot Line, 185

Mah Jongg, 6

Malacca, Straits of, 123

Manchukuo, 354, 357, 359

Manchuria, 54, 85, 100, 129, 287,
296–297, 320, 323–363, 368;
Borah Letter, 352, 354; France
and, 336, 347, 354, 362; Great